TASK ANALYSIS FOR
HUMAN–COMPUTER INTERACTION

ELLIS HORWOOD BOOKS IN INFORMATION TECHNOLOGY

General Editors: Dr JOHN M. M. PINKERTON, Information Technology Consultant, J & H Pinkerton Associates, Esher, Surrey , and formerly Manager of Strategic Requirements, International Computers Limited: and V. A. J. MALLER, VM Associates; Visiting Professor in Computer Studies, Loughborough University of Technology; formerly of Thorn EMI Information Technology Ltd.
Consulting Editor: PATRICK HOLLIGAN, Department of Computer Studies, Loughborough University of Technology

M. Barrett & A. C. Beerel	EXPERT SYSTEMS IN BUSINESS: A Practical Approach
M. Becker, R. Haberfellner & G. Liebetrau	ELECTRONIC DATA PROCESSING IN PRACTICE: A Handbook for Users
A. C. Beerel	EXPERT SYSTEMS: Strategic Implications and Applications
K. Bennett	SOFTWARE ENGINEERING ENVIRONMENTS: Research and Practice
A. C. Bradley	OPTICAL STORAGE FOR COMPUTERS: Technology and Applications
P. Brereton	SOFTWARE ENGINEERING ENVIRONMENTS
R. Bright	SMART CARDS: Principles, Practice and Applications
D. Clarke & U. Magnusson-Murray	PRACTICAL MACHINE TRANSLATION
V. Claus & A. Schwill	DICTIONARY OF INFORMATION TECHNOLOGY
D. Cleal & N. O. Heaton	KNOWLEDGE-BASED SYSTEMS: Implications for Human–Computer Interfaces
I. Craig	THE CASSANDRA ARCHITECTURE: Distributed Control in a Blackboard System
T. Daler, *et al.*	SECURITY OF INFORMATION AND DATA
D. Diaper	KNOWLEDGE ELICITATION: Principles, Techniques and Applications
D. Diaper	TASK ANALYSIS FOR HUMAN–COMPUTER INTERACTION
G. I. Doukidis, F. Land & G. Miller	KNOWLEDGE-BASED MANAGEMENT SUPPORT SYSTEMS
P. Duffin	KNOWLEDGE-BASED SYSTEMS: Applications in Administrative Government
C. Ellis	EXPERT KNOWLEDGE AND EXPLANATION: The Knowledge–Language Interface
J. Einbu	A PROGRAM ARCHITECTURE FOR IMPROVED MAINTAINABILITY IN SOFTWARE ENGINEERING
A. Fourcin, G. Harland, L.W. Barry & V. Hazan	SPEECH INPUT AND OUTPUT ASSESSMENT: Multilingual Methods and Standards
M. Greenwell	KNOWLEDGE ENGINEERING FOR EXPERT SYSTEMS
F. R. Hickman *et al.*	ANALYSIS FOR KNOWLEDGE-BASED SYSTEMS: A Practical Guide to the KADS Methodology
P. Hills & J. Beaumont	INFORMATION SYSTEMS: Management Implications for the Human–Computer Interface
E. Hollnagel	THE RELIABILITY OF EXPERT SYSTEMS
K. Koskimies & J. Paakki	AUTOMATING LANGUAGE IMPLEMENTATION
J. Kriz	KNOWLEDGE-BASED EXPERT SYSTEMS IN INDUSTRY
M. McTear & T. Anderson	UNDERSTANDING KNOWLEDGE ENGINEERING
W. Meyer & H. Walters	EXPERT SYSTEMS IN FACTORY MANAGEMENT: Knowledge-based CIM
U. Pankoke-Babatz	COMPUTER-BASED GROUP COMMUNICATION: The AMIGO Activity Model
J. M. M. Pinkerton	ADVANCED INFORMATION TECHNOLOGY
S. Pollitt	INFORMATION STORAGE AND RETRIEVAL SYSTEMS: Origin, Development and Applications
S. Ravden & G. Johnson	EVALUATING USABILITY OF HUMAN–COMPUTER INTERFACES: A Practical Method
P. E. Slatter	BUILDING EXPERT SYSTEMS: Cognitive Emulation
H. T. Smith, J. Onions & S. Benford	DISTRIBUTED GROUP COMMUNICATION: The AMIGO Information Model
H. M. Sneed	SOFTWARE ENGINEERING MANAGEMENT
M. Stein	BUILDING EXPERT SYSTEMS MODEMS FOR DATA TRANSMISSION
R. Stutely	ADVANCED DESKTOP PUBLISHING: A Practical Guide to Ventura Version 2 and the Professional Extension
J. A. Waterworth	MULTI-MEDIA INTERACTION WITH COMPUTERS
J. A. Waterworth & M. Talbot	SPEECH AND LANGUAGE-BASED COMMUNICATION WITH MACHINES:Towards the Conversational Computer
R. J. Whiddett	THE IMPLEMENTATION OF SMALL COMPUTER SYSTEMS

TASK ANALYSIS FOR HUMAN–COMPUTER INTERACTION

Editor:

DAN DIAPER Ph.D.
Department of Computer Science
University of Liverpool

ELLIS HORWOOD LIMITED
Publishers · Chichester

Halsted Press: a division of
JOHN WILEY & SONS
New York · Chichester · Brisbane · Toronto

First published in 1989 by
ELLIS HORWOOD LIMITED
Market Cross House, Cooper Street,
Chichester, West Sussex, PO19 1EB, England
The publisher's colophon is reproduced from James Gillison's drawing of the ancient Market Cross, Chichester.

Distributors:

Australia and New Zealand:
JACARANDA WILEY LIMITED
GPO Box 859, Brisbane, Queensland 4001, Australia

Canada:
JOHN WILEY & SONS CANADA LIMITED
22 Worcester Road, Rexdale, Ontario, Canada

Europe and Africa:
JOHN WILEY & SONS LIMITED
Baffins Lane, Chichester, West Sussex, England

North and South America and the rest of the world:
Halsted Press: a division of
JOHN WILEY & SONS
605 Third Avenue, New York, NY 10158, USA

South-East Asia
JOHN WILEY & SONS (SEA) PTE LIMITED
37 Jalan Pemimpin # 05–04
Block B, Union Industrial Building, Singapore 2057

Indian Subcontinent
WILEY EASTERN LIMITED
4835/24 Ansari Road
Daryaganj, New Delhi 110002, India

© **1989 D. Diaper/Ellis Horwood Limited**

British Library Cataloguing in Publication Data
Task analysis for human–computer interaction. —
(Ellis Horwood books in information technology)
1. Man. Interactions with computer systems. Ergonomic aspects
I. Diaper, D. (Dan)
004'.01'9

Library of Congress Card No. 89–19851

ISBN 0–7458–0721–6 (Ellis Horwood Limited)
ISBN 0–470–21606–9 (Halsted Press)

Typeset in Times by Ellis Horwood Limited
Printed in Great Britain by Hartnolls, Bodmin

Table of contents

Preface

The final sentences in this book claim that task analysis is potentially the most powerful method in the field of Human–Computer Interaction (HCI) either for evaluating systems or for producing requirement specifications. Task analysis is not new; indeed, it has a long history stretching back to near the turn of the century. However, it is not a method that is universally, or for that matter even commonly, used. Since the early 1970s a number of different task analysis methods have been developed that claim to be able to describe the cognitive aspects of tasks, as well as the traditional perceptual–motor aspects that task analysis has for decades been able to capture adequately. The impetus for these developments arose directly from the advances in computer technology and the gradually increasing concern about HCI issues. The number of real experts in task analysis is small and, unusually, most of them are in the United Kingdom. Furthermore, the majority of them are in academia, rather than in commerce or industry.

Descriptions of the last two decades of development in task analysis have been published in a variety of journal articles, conference proceedings and book chapters. Consequently, anyone new to the field will have a considerable job merely tracking down these diverse references. The original purpose of this book was to collect into a single volume descriptions of some of the major task analysis methods and thus to provide a single reference source for the beginner at task analysis. The book does not claim to be exhaustive with respect to the range of task analysis methods, but its contents are probably adequate for its purpose.

The anonymous, publisher's reviewer of the original, brief chapter outlines said of the proposal:

> The subject is fairly controversial, and the different points of view
> are likely to be reflected in the chapters of this book. As there is no
> published book on the subject there should be many new angles.

His, or her, comment was prophetic, particularly with respect to the diversity of points of view offered by the expert authors of the different chapters. As the editor, and someone who has been using task analysis since the early 1980s, I have tried to encourage such diversity and not to impose my own views on the other authors. Thus the books does not start with a straightforward definition of task analysis, and I am less confident of offering one now than when I commenced this project over a year ago. However, my own definitions of what is meant by a task, and by task analysis, are provided in Chapter 7. The reader is cautioned, however, that there is not an agreed terminology or set of definitions used in task analysis or in this book. Similarly, the range and importance of the theoretical issues associated with task analysis are not agreed. For example, while, unusually, all the chapters address some aspects of the relationship between the description of tasks and people's psychological representation of tasks, this is not an issue which the reader will find satisfactorily resolved in any of the chapters.

It is also clear that all the methods described in this book are still under development and, unfortunately, this book is not a simple tutorial on the methods. That such a book, even restricted to one method, would be desirable is undoubtedly true, but this one is not it. Part of the problem lies with the unfinished development of the methods. Another factor is that the very richness of task analysis makes it difficult to describe methods in a context-free manner. For example, I tried hard in Chapter 4 to provide an adequate description, and a worked example, of TAKD so that it could be used by novices, although I am suspicious of my success. Thus the same publisher's reviewer was correct in stating 'The book will not be a text book, for which the subject is not yet ready'. However, as the only book available that is devoted to the subject, I believe that it does provide a useful and convenient source for those new to task analysis. Of course, it is also intended for those familiar with task analysis who need to keep up to date with its current developments. Apart from practitioners who need to understand task analysis, I would also hope that many of, if not all, the chapters are suitable for advanced undergraduate and postgraduate students.

As the editor I have had considerable problems in deciding the order of the chapters. All the chapters, excluding Chapter 7, were the basis for a one day conference in May 1989, organized by the British Computer Society Human–Computer Interaction Specialist Group. For this conference I had arranged the presentations in a chronological order of development (i.e. starting with the oldest method). I have tried numerous more intellectually satisfactory organizations of the chapters and the one I finally selected turned out, to my surprise, to be the same chronological one that I had started with. Chapters 1 and 2, which are both about HTA, provide an introduction to what is a relatively simple, but effective, method. Chapter 3, on TAG, describes a method suitable for analysing the micro-architecture of human–computer interfaces. Chapter 4 provides a description of a method (TAKD) that can be used for the investigation of both micro level and global aspects of systems. Chapter 5 offers both a method (KAT) and a theoretical structure (TKS), which have been partly derived from TAKD, and which may be more suitable for investigations of the general properties of human–computer systems. In contrast, Chapter 6 describes a new method, ATOM, which is driven, in part, by the limitations imposed on the task analyst by current, non-academic system development environments.

Chapter 7 is different from the others and has now taken on the status of an appendix, although I had originally intended it as the first chapter. It deals with the methods and techniques of task observation, rather than with analysis. While it is still my opinion that the primary source of data for task analysis should be the systematic observation of people performing tasks, it became clear when editing the other chapters that my view is not fully shared by my colleagues. However, I would still recommend that it be read by those unfamiliar with observational studies, even if the data for a task analysis are to come principally, or wholly, from non-observational sources such as interviews. I recommend this because of the problems associated with such data sources with respect to task analysis and generally in HCI.

Dan Diaper
Department of Computer Science
University of Liverpool
June 1989

1

Analysis and training in information technology tasks

Andrew Shepherd
Loughborough University of Technology

1. INTRODUCTION

While computing systems can be improved by trying to design them to accommodate to characteristics of users, for example through dialogue style, screen layouts and pointing devices, attention must also be paid to improving people's skills in using systems. This can be done by addressing issues involving training, user manuals and appropriate management. The optimization of most applied situations usually entails addressing both the design of the task and developing and maintaining user skills. To do this we need an understanding of what the human user is required to do and how he or she processes information to achieve goals.

Trying to make sense of what people should do or what they actually do is the business of *task analysis*. There is no real consensus amongst practitioners concerning what task analysis is and this promotes considerable confusion. For some people it is concerned with gathering task information, for others it is about representing that information. Nor is there any real consensus about what is to be analysed. Some people feel that task analysis is about eliciting the actual behaviour of those people known to be competent at the task. Others are more concerned with focusing on what could, in principle, be achieved by a human being. Other approaches focus upon the goals that need to be achieved to meet system requirements, and then explore the ways in which the human operator may be limited in achieving these goals or the means by which they may be achieved.

There are many different approaches to examining human performance described under the banner of task analysis. These have been presented at regular intervals since the early 1950s (for reviews, see for example Miller, 1962, 1967; Duncan, 1972, 1974; Patrick, 1980; Wilson *et al.*, 1986; 1988). Recent attention to information technology tasks has prompted the view, in some quarters, that new approaches are necessary to capture the essential cognitive nature of tasks in this area. Certainly the nature of work has changed dramatically in the past 40 years, but whether existing approaches which purport to deal with cognitive tasks can be adapted to current usage, or whether a completely new approach is warranted, may be a matter of opinion. The main aim of the present chapter is to demonstrate that *Hierarchical Task Analysis* (HTA), developed by Annett and Duncan (1967) as a general form of task analysis, capable of dealing with cognitive as well as motor tasks, that embodies principles that are just as relevant to HCI tasks, especially with regard to aspects of training and supporting skill. Task analysts need a wide range of skills, including skills in eliciting information and designing solutions. In particular, they need to be clear about what they are trying to achieve and how their approach should be sensitive to the context in which the work is taking place.

Task analysis is useful to the extent that it helps us to improve the design or implementation of systems or, at least, to focus upon areas of poor human performance. Task analysis involves gathering information, representing it in an appropriate manner, and then utilizing this representation to establish the system improvements required or to communicate aspects of weakness to a client. While there is disagreement between authors about how these things are best done, there are two common points of focus — (i) the *task context and criterion* and (ii) the presentation of a *solution* to a client. Task analysis is about examining the context and criterion in order to establish a solution.

There are many ways in which an analyst moves from the context–criterion to the solution, ranging from intuition based on experience through to applying an explicit procedure which utilizes little analytical expertise, for example, by using a checklist or a set of design guidelines. Even people very familiar with an area of application are forced to use some sort of method of analysis to deal with unfamiliar problems, so that they may construe a novel situation in familiar terms. Between the intuitive approach and the more mechanical approaches are a number of methods which entail the need for some form of analytical skill for them to be executed effectively. Many of these methods are perfectly effective in the hands of an analyst who understands what he or she is doing. Some methods may be communicated to other would-be analysts more successfully than others. Some methods may sacrifice some flexibility in order to provide a more amenable tool for a less experienced analyst. Each of these routes from criterion to solution must follow a path which involves eliciting information from a real context, and organizing it in a fashion that leads to solutions being proffered. Many articles about task analysis deal with a part of this route, often the part concerned with representing the task in some fashion. However, the elicitation of information and the utilization of the final analysis is often left to the reader to sort out. We cannot really judge an approach to task analysis unless it is made clear how information is elicited and how the outcome may be used. However, this issue is addressed by most of the chapters in this book and is the central theme of Walsh (Chapter 6).

1.1   Hierarchical Task Analysis
In this chapter, I want to develop this theme with one popular approach to task analysis, namely HTA, proposed originally by Annett and Duncan

(1967) and more widely disseminated in Annett *et al.* (1971) and Duncan (1972, 1974). Shepherd (1985) reviews the basic ideas, showing further development. This is a very effective approach to task analysis, because it yields many practical benefits in complex occupational situations. HTA has not been generally acknowledged as being appropriate to HCI, because it is not seen as suited to the essential cognitive nature of HCI tasks. Fig. 1.1.

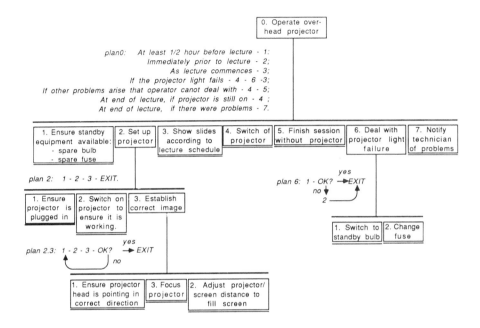

Fig. 1.1 — HTA of operating an overhead projector during the normal course of a lecture. This shows the basic layout of an HTA, including a hierarchical breakdown of operations (in boxes) and plans (in italics). Operations which the analyst has chosen not to take further are underlined.

illustrates the use of HTA for describing a reasonably straighforward and familiar task, that of 'operating an overhead projector'. A fuller explanation of the concepts entailed in this sort of task description follows shortly.

HTA was intended to be a general approach to task analysis and has, indeed, been applied to a wide range of contexts to develop a wide range of solutions. A field in which it has been successfully demonstrated is that of process control (Duncan, 1974; Shepherd and Duncan, 1980; Shepherd, 1986; Astley and Stammers, 1988). This field of application is noteworthy, because process control tasks entail a wide range of features, including *monitoring, invariant procedures* and a variety of *decision-making tasks,* such as fault diagnosis and compensation. Most tasks in most contexts can be understood in terms of elements that are represented in process control. A further point about process control is that it has always been an 'information technology' context, for the simple reason that control has to be remote, for reasons of safety and efficiency. This means that systems are controlled via control panels in accordance with relayed information (see Crossman, 1960). There has always been a problem of representing complex processes to operators by instrumentation. The choice, density and form of information displayed have always been in the hands of information designers. Admittedly, in earlier years, form and density of information were constrained by a different technology to that which constrains contemporary IT tasks, i.e. pneumatics rather than electronics, but the process industries were amongst the earliest to adopt computing technology in their control and display philosophies. Clearly, the pace of the information revolution has been dictated by developments and fashions in the commercial field, but many issues now emerging in, for example, flexible manufacturing processes and integrated management information systems have been observed previously in process contexts. The main point of my argument is that HTA has a good track record in demanding areas and deserves attention as a method for dealing with HCI tasks.

A major problem with published accounts of HTA (the same can be said for most other methods of task analysis) is that they have focused on only one part of the route, namely the manner in which tasks can be formally described. Consequently, readers gain little insight into how to apply the method. My aim in the present chapter is to provide some flavour of how task information is collected to furnish task descriptions and how these descriptions may then be used to provide practical solutions to problems. It is impossible to describe this route in terms of a series of simple guidelines to follow. It is necessary, therefore, to try to give some basic understanding of what is involved in the processes of analysis. Diaper (Chapter 4), for example, provides a detailed description and example of the subjective, context-sensitive approach that needs to be adopted in task analysis and a similar point is made, more or less strongly, in nearly all the other chapters in this book. In general, I doubt that simple procedures are appropriate for analysing any task other than those which are entirely straightforward or stereotyped.

The solutions I shall deal with later on are all concerned with aspects of training and supporting users. I do not wish to endorse the view that HTA is only suited to training applications or, on the other hand, to suggest that it is a panacea — my focus on training and supporting users and operators is because these are the areas where I have some experience. My general contention is that, with insight and imagination, the would-be analyst with a particular application in mind should be able to adapt HTA to develop a suitable approach to deal with new sorts of problems.

1.2   Outline of the chapter

The essence of dealing with a problem using HTA is to establish a task description according to a certain set of rules and principles. In section 2, therefore, I shall outline these general rules and principles.

In section 3, I shall try to convey some of the issues that should be considered when carrying out HTA. Practice and experience is the key to acquiring the necessary skills. However, people are often reluctant to start analysis because they have no feel for what they should be doing. Therefore, I shall describe some practical problems and ideas that have been found helpful in dealing with them. Once people gain the confidence to get started, they will soon find their own best ways of dealing with problems they encounter.

Section 4 will describe some actual examples of applications of HTA to different sorts of real HCI problems concerned with various aspects of skill. A major skill of HTA is to recognize how a new situation maps onto previously encountered situations — within any analysis, one encounters a number of elements which are similar to elements encountered before. This is one of the main ways experience can serve a task analyst. Therefore, apart from putting some practical flesh onto the bones of HTA, the ideas presented in section 4 serve to show how certain prototypical situations may be dealt with. The main applications that will be described include the following: (i) development of a user manual; (ii) analysis of a word-processing package to identify basic training versus point-of-need help; (iii) development of training and support for a computer-based clerical task; (iv) improvement of displays to support operability and learning; (v) the choice of a strategy to follow in a computer-controlled warehousing task.

2. HTA IDEAS AND CONCEPTS

The literature on task analysis introduces a number of concepts, including *goals, tasks, operations, plans, hierarchies, redescription, stopping rules.* These concepts are of prime importance for the reader needing to carry out HTA.

2.1   Goals

Meaningful activities, whether at work or recreation, entail human beings trying to attain *goals.* In occupational settings, goals are related to attaining desired states of systems under control or supervision, e.g. 'a clean floor', 'a safe and operable machine', 'a healthy and contented work force', 'an increased profit', 'a receptive client'. We can usually help people to carry out their activities more successfully, or to deal with actual problems they encounter, by focussing on the goals they must attain. HTA, along with other methods described in this book, examines what people need to do to attain their goals.

2.2   Tasks

An important distinction may be drawn between the goals people seek to attain and the manner in which they are permitted to attain them. For example, someone may want to get a hot meal on the table for a family of five. This goal may be attained in a number of ways, perhaps by 'cooking a fresh meal', 'warming up a previously cooked meal', or 'telephoning for a takeaway'. The method selected to attain the goal, in any instance, depends on factors such as competence (is the cook any good?), preference (what would we like to eat and do we enjoy cooking?), materials (can the ingredients be acquired easily?), facilities (does the cooker work?), resources available (has the electricity board cut us off yet?), and constraints (is there time?). All of these factors will influence the actual manner in which the goal is best attained. They may be seen as a set of *constraints, resources* and *preferences*. The problems encountered in providing the hot meal can only be identified by exploring the actual way in which the meal is to be provided.

We can easily see parallels in the world of work. For a simple example, we may consider a clerk who is required to 'produce multiple copies of a document'. A different task is entailed in using carbon paper, a photocopier, a pen and lots of paper, or specifying requirements to a printing firm. A line manager may be responsible for providing a colleague or a client with multiple copies of a document (i.e. the same goal) but may attain this goal by instructing a clerk.

I have used the word 'task' to refer to a rather broad set of things which influence the manner in which a goal may be achieved, including competence, preference, materials, facilities, resources and constraints. *Task* is a systems concept in that it is concerned with contextual constraints and facilities. Both Johnson (Chapter 5) and Diaper (Chapter 7) address the issue of the definition of the term 'task'.

2.3   Operations

Annett *et al.* also used the term 'operation'. They defined *operation* as 'any unit of behaviour, no matter how long or short its duration and no matter how simple or complex its structure, which can be defined in terms of its objective'. The difference between operations and goals is that operations are things that are actually done by people to achieve their goals. The word *operation,* defined in this way, differs from the way in which I have used the word task. While task is a systems concept, operation is seen as what the person actually does. Thus a *goal* which has to be attained by a person has an associated *task,* which offers facilities and constraints on how the goal might be attained, and an associated *operation* which refers to what is actually done in the set of circumstances constrained by the task.

Implicit in the behaviour entailed in an operation are (i) the capability of the person to carry out actions appropriate to attaining the specified goal, (ii) the capability to locate and encode information necessary for selecting appropriate actions, and (iii) the capability to locate and encode feedback (i.e. more information) which can show the person whether the goal has yet been attained or what else needs to be done to attain it. The action–information–feedback requirement is a first step in a behavioural analysis. A more ambitious cognitive analysis would focus on a particular operation and would therefore benefit from being carried out in the context of an HTA.

2.4   Hierarchies of goals and subgoals

HTA and the other methods of task analysis described in this book exploit the fact that goals can be described at various levels of detail, and that these may be described in terms of sets of subgoals. For example, to 'decorate a room', we may 'paper the walls', 'paint the woodwork' and 'lay a carpet'. Each of these activities may in turn be broken down, for example 'strip the walls', 'repair cracks in the plaster', 'seal the walls' and 'apply paper'.

A major aim of applied human factors work is to identify steps that can be taken to ensure that people are capable of carrying out operations to attain goals. We carry out task analysis to help us to identify what we can do to ensure competence at operations. When we state any goal we may ask 'is the operator capable of carrying out the operation to attain this goal or can we think of any acceptable measures to ensure this competence?'. If the answer is 'no' then we can exploit the hierarchical nature of goal descriptions discussed here and try to redescribe the goal in terms of its subgoals. This is a basic principle of HTA.

2.5   Plans and the organization of subgoals

Operational competency at all of a set of subgoals cannot logically imply operational competency at their common superordinate goal. We need to state the *conditions* which specify *when* each of these subgoals should be carried out. Knowing how to carry out each of the subgoals of 'decorating a room' without knowing when each of these things should be done could result in 'stripping the walls' after you have just 'put up the new paper' — a trite example, but the principle is very important. *When* to do things is as important as *what* to do.

Annett *et al.* suggest that a *plan* or *strategy* is used to describe how suboperations are organized to achieve an overall goal. It is apparent that we may confuse two separate things here. On the one hand we may consider a statement of conditions when each of a set of subordinate operations must be carried out to meet the system's goals — this treats a plan as a systems concept. On the other hand we may consider the plan to be some sort of unit of behaviour which enables a person to select and sequence activities in their repertoire. Annett *et al.* fail to distinguish between these two interpretations. Duncan (1974) clarified this, suggesting that *plans* should be considered to be units of description which specify the conditions under which each of the constituent subgoals needs to be carried out in order that the overall goal is attained successfully, that is a *system* rather than a *behavioural* concept. This is the sense in which plan is used in the present chapter.

Plans are not simply a logical nicety. They are of considerable practical importance in task analysis (Shepherd, 1985). First, plans contain or imply cues for action which the competent performer must necessarily observe. Second, since a plan which is stated thoroughly indicates the conditions when each of its suboperations should be carried out, the plan and the set of suboperations should *complement* each other — simply stated, the plan should contain reference to each of the subordinate operations listed and should not refer to any operations that are not listed. This point seems obvious, yet it has immense practial benefit in ensuring a thorough task analysis. Third, apparently complex activities can often be reduced to hierarchies of simpler activities through their representation by a hierarchy of plans. This point was illustrated by Shepherd and Duncan (1980). This case was concerned with working out how senior process operators controlling a complex of chemical plants balanced production and consumption of materials in order to optimize productivity and safety, when various perturbations occurred. In many respects, this was a complex management task. Plant managers stated that 15 different sorts of action could be taken; the problem was, how could the operators be trained to take appropriate decisions to select the correct combination of actions for particular circumstances? In terms of HTA, then, there were 15 operations, but what was their plan? Through HTA, the seemingly intractable plan governing 15 suboperations was analysed in terms of a hierarchy consisting of nine reasonably straighforward plans. A major benefit was that, through thoroughly stating this plan, it was realized that the original 15 suboperations had been confused with each other — operators were actually duplicating effort. Moreover, some important suboperations had been overlooked.

2.6   Stopping analysis

Redescribing goals into plans and suboperations can continue for a long time. This is time consuming and, therefore, should be avoided if possible. A useful feature of a hierarchical description is that we can stop where we feel it is justified. Sometimes operations need to be described in considerable detail; sometimes they can be described very briefly. The analyst may decide which *stopping rule* to ultilize for a particular task analysis. Similarly, Diaper (Chapter 7) addresses this issue with respect to the level of detail recorded during task observation.

Annett *et al.* proposed the $P \times C$ criterion to indicate when task analysis should cease. P refers to the *probability of inadequate performance* at the operation concerned and C refers to the *cost of inadequate performance*. Earlier, we considered the question 'is the operator capable of carrying out the operation to attain this goal or can we think of any acceptable measures to ensure this competence? This may now be rephrased as 'is the operator capable of carrying out the operation to attain this goal to the criterion implied by the $P \times C$ rule or can we think of any acceptable measures to ensure this competence?' Cost in this context is not simply a financial consideration but should include anything the system values, e.g. customer good will, a user's continued commitment to a piece of software, personal accident, lost files. Hence cost often cannot have a hard value attached to it. Likewise, estimating probability of inadequate performance is not feasible in the context of a complex task analysis, especially in a novel context. Therefore, $P \times C$ cannot be treated as a rigid formula suited to numerical analysis. However, it remains an effective basis for a stopping rule, since it prompts the analyst to consider both of these factors in deciding whether analysis need continue. Furthermore, the multiplicative nature of the rule is helpful (see Shepherd, 1985, for a fuller discussion) since, for example, it shows that, however likely a person is to make a mistake, it hardly matters if the consequences of inadequate performance are trivial.

The most important criticism of the P×C rule is that it is not appropriate to all situations. Annett and coworkers developed HTA in the context of training. In a training context the *P×C* rule is fine because we can stop anywhere where we have the means to ensure satisfactory performance. However, if we are carrying out task analysis for other purposes, this will not do. If we are looking to discover how people interact with a system, such as in the design of displays or the development of user manuals, we need to continue redescription until we are describing goals that can be achieved with *interfacing responses,* i.e. operations that will directly change the state of the system. In a computing application, interfacing responses include making 'keystrokes' and 'using pointing devices'. In process control situations, they include 'switching on pumps' or 'controlling valves' from the control panel or on plant. In an organizational–social situation, this will include 'communicating with people'. Our stopping rule in this context is that analysis continues until the stated subgoals may be attained by carrying out interfacing responses.

Another important reason why we might stop redescription is that we simply cannot work out how to redescribe an operation adequately in terms of suboperations and plans. There can be a number of reasons for this. A person new to HTA may not see how to organize a redescription, while a more familiar exponent may have no difficulty. Even experienced analysts may have never encountered a certain organization of task elements and be stuck. There are a number of things that can be done and section 3 offers some guidelines in this respect. A redescription might entail employing a different sort of data collection method or grouping suboperations in different ways. These guidelines, however, do not guarantee a solution and the analyst can remain puzzled. In these cases, help may be sought and, if this is forthcoming, another task 'prototype' may then be stored away into the analyst's repertoire for future occasions. Often, the analyst will continue to ruminate over a problem and days later a new option will emerge — this happens surprisingly frequently.

On some occasions, it must be emphasized that further redescription will be inappropriate since no explicit plan can confidently be stated. 'Changing gear' in a car is a good example. We know that we need to manipulate the accelerator pedal and the clutch, but the coordination of these two actions is very subtle; the cues to control the accelerator depend upon feedback from manipulations of the clutch which we must experience directly. We can talk about 'points of bite' on the clutch, but this is a rule of thumb that an instructor uses to help learner drivers to start to understand what is going on — it is left to learners to work out what this might mean in practice. They may be guided when to do these things, but only through relating a successful outcome from their actions to what they have done with their feet do they learn a set of appropriate cues. These cues, by their very nature, cannot be stated explicitly in plans. We assume that we all do the same psychological and physical things when we change gear in a car, but we have no real evidence for that. Psychomotor skills, such as controlling the foot pedals in the car, occur in HCI tasks, often with regard to pointing devices such as mice or tracker balls, for example. While it may be useful to explore the skills entailed in the control of such devices in order to optimize their design or to 'tune' them to a particular application, this is often unnecessary. A more common problem in HCI, concerning the difficulties of stating plans explicitly, occurs in decision-making tasks, usually entailed in system supervisory tasks, such as process control. In these situations the operator must infer causes of sytem states from available evidence and construct appropriate responses for dealing with them. For anticipated system disturbances, we may identify combinations of cues that link to a specific diagnosis; for unforeseen circumstances we cannot be explicit about what the operator should do on different occasions.

Where plans cannot be progressed because we cannot be explicit about when suboperations should be done, we may choose to *hypothesize* about psychological processes. A simple example is given in case 5 later in this chapter. In this case, two different memory strategies are considered to establish which is best as a basis for training. It is in this respect that an analyst might switch strategy and invoke a form of task analysis that could appropriately be described as *cognitive modelling*. I would argue strongly that these more hypothetical approaches of *cognitive task analysis* are best carried out within the context of an HTA, where their limits can be bounded by the more rational system analysis that HTA offers. The HTA will show where cognitive task analysis is necessary. Such *formal* speculation about cognitive processes is rarely necessary in most real tasks, although, of course, the analyst may be *speculating* about component psychological processes all of the time.

Sometimes, our difficulty in stating plans is a reflection on the *integrity* of the task and not on our competence as analysts. Sometimes, cues cannot be stated in plans because the system does not provide the user with any unambiguous cues. This very omission can be a major source of difficulty for the person using or controlling the system. The appropriate response here is to suggest what cues should be provided and to negotiate with management and engineers to ensure that these modifications are implemented. The cue can be incorporated into the plan and the HTA may progress. This can occur frequently in information techology tasks and, fortunately, the technology can often enable such modifications to be accommodated.

Stopping redescription is an important topic in a hierarchical approach to task analysis. It serves to ensure that redescription in various parts of the analysis is taken to an appropriate level of detail. It also reminds the analyst to continue to pay attention to the purpose for which the task analysis is being undertaken.

2.7 Representation of HTA

The discussion so far has been concerned with the various components of HTA and how they interact with each other. We shall soon consider descriptions of real tasks where it will be necessary to represent the task description in some form to record analysis and to communicate its results to interested parties. Forms of representation will be included in the next section. At this point I wish to emphasis that the form of representation chosen is independent of the main concepts of HTA. Sometimes *tables* will be used, whereas on other occasions *hierarchical diagrams,* such as that shown in Fig. 1.1, will be preferred. Each of these may relate goals and plans in the same manner. This point is stressed because people sometimes confuse the basic ideas of HTA with the manner in which an analysis is represented. People often assume that using diagrams rather than tables, for example, implies a different approach to task analysis. Furthermore, TAKD (Chapter 4), for example, explicitly exploits two different representations of the same information (a Task Descriptive Hierarchy (TDH) and a Knowledge Representation Grammar (KRG)) which are used at different stages within TAKD as they have a differing analytical convenience.

2.8   Summary of the basic ideas of task description

Task analysis is concerned with examining the context and criteria associated with goals in practical situations to identify how they are carried out or the problems associated with their execution. Through HTA, the analyst explores tasks by establishing a hierarchical task description which complies with a particular set of rules for description:

(1) The description is in the form of a hierarchy of *operations* and *plans* which describe the attainment of an overall *goal.*

(2) The overall goal has an attendant operation which needs to be carried out to achieve this goal, bearing in mind the task constraints.

(3) The overall operation is attained by carrying out a set of *subordinate* operations in accordance with a *plan* which specifies the conditions *when* each suboperation should be carried out.

(4) At each redescription, each suboperation is examined in turn to determine whether it needs to be further redescribed. If it does, then the operation becomes a candidate for further redescription as in point (3) above.

(5) The criterion for stopping analysis may vary between applications and contexts.

3.   CARRYING OUT TASK ANALYSIS

The previous section focused on the issue of task description, emphasizing that HTA is a process where the analyst works towards establishing an acceptable task description to guide the collection and organization of task information. Section 3 will now discuss some of the general practical issues that need to be considered when carrying out HTA, that is how the analyst should set about examining a task context in order to establish the task description. We shall start with an illustration of a simple analysis, then consider some of the features of plans that might be encountered, and then discuss some broader issues of data collection and handling sources of information. Finally, section 3.8 will describe how task analysis can be represented for the purpose of recording and communicating results to other people.

The type of material included in the following section is rarely included in articles on task analysis because it comprises advice and guidance, based solely on collected experience, rather than any logical or psychological description of method. However, I wish to emphasize that skill at HTA is concerned with applying effective methods to reach the various milestones embodied within the rules of description. How the analyst reaches each milestone varies from context to context and depends on the preferences of individual analysts. If this sounds vague it is because we are discussing *expertise* rather than simple procedures. Many people assume that HTA should be rendered down to a procedure (by doing HTA on it). To some extent this is possible, and Fig. 1.2 shows an algorithm outlining a tidy procedure. This works reasonably well on relatively simple tasks, but a much more flexible approach is required for most tasks. Just because the *product* of analysis looks tidy, that is, a hierarchical diagram or table, this does not mean that the *process* is necessarily straghtforward. This view is also explicitly supported by Carey *et al.*, Diaper and Johnson (Chapters 2, 4 and 6 respectively).

3.1   A simple example

Conveying the process of an HTA in print is extremely difficult. It is worth attempting, however, in order to convey that HTA rarely conforms to the tidy process of Fig. 1.2, and that it is a more active problem-solving process for the analyst.

For this example, I have chosen the operation of 'using a microwave cooker'. The analysis, although very short, is a real one which came about when a student, whom I had set a small assignment, came to me for some help. From our joint discussion I have pieced together the process followed to illustrate some common features. More complex examples of HTA can proceed in a similar fashion. This is not entirely surprising. The present example is small because it only extends to two redescriptions. HTAs become large because they entail more redescriptions. A more complex example is given in Shepherd and Duncan (1980).

Step 1: stating the overall goal and operation
It is first necessary to establish the overall goal and to state the operation to attain this goal. It is also important, in a real example, to clarify why the analysis is being undertaken — is it to ensure satisfactory performance at the task by whatever means, to write an operating procedure, or to examine the integrity of a display, for example? In our example we chose to consider establishing enough information to write a simple operating procedure for a new user. We started out with the overall operation 'cook a meal in the microwave cooker'.

Step 2: Redescription
Fig. 1.3(a) shows the first attempt at redescription. The student stated a set of five suboperations and a plan which governed when they should be carried out. She now needed to be sure that the redescription was adequate. It was adequate in the sense that it referred only to the five operations that had

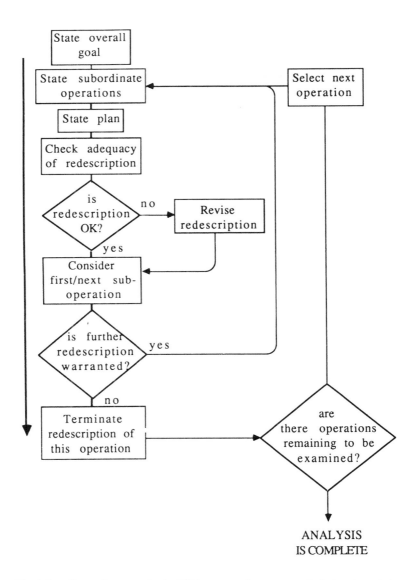

Fig. 1.2 — General strategy in the HTA process. In most practical situations, it is often inappropriate to follow this flow diagram too rigidly.

been stated, but there were some problems. First, she had indicated in operation 4 to 'remove the meal' but she had not said when the meal should be put into the oven. This ought to be included, partly for symmetry (not simply aesthetic; sometimes symmetry prompts the inclusion of important complementary actions), but also because it is necessary to state an operation so that we can state *when* this is done in the plan. Not being familar with microwave cooking myself, I genuinely did not know whether one had first to heat up the cooker before putting in the food, as with a conventional

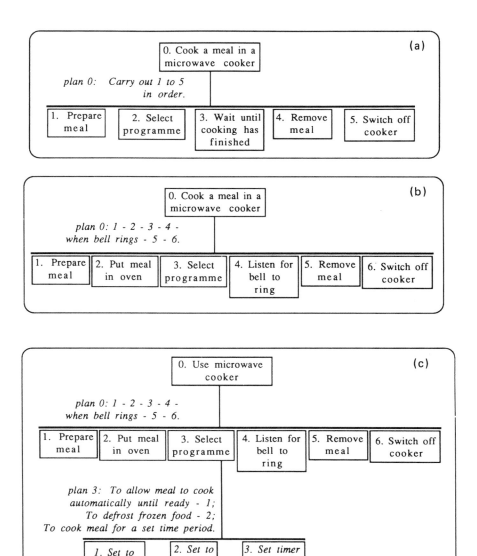

Fig. 1.3 — An illustration of the process of redescription: (a)–(c) show progress in the analysis of a simple task.

oven. So, the inclusion of operations or subgoals is necessary to ensure that they are included properly in plans and not necessarily because one suspects that there will be problems in their execution. A second possible problem is the way in which operation 3 has been dealt with. 'Wait until cooking finishes' is almost like saying 'do nothing', and it is not clear when the cooking will finish. A more satisfactory operation would be to 'listen for the finish bell'. This tells the user to pay attention and what to look for. It also means the plan should be revised to include the bell as the cue to do operation 4. Of course, people are busy and may not want to hang around, in which case it might be important to include further cues for operation 4, for example 'when the light has gone out'. So with these modifications, we have moved towards a more thorough description, as shown in Fig. 1.3(b). A clue to an inadequate HTA might be found in too many fixed procedure plans. While straightforward procedures, such as that in Fig. 1.3(a), are quite acceptable, and often feature heavily in HCI tasks, it is important to check carefully that the plan has not been oversimplified.

Step 3: Stopping redescription
It was now necessary to decide where analysis needed to be taken further and where it could be stopped. This entailed considering each of the six suboperations in turn. This is where the $P \times C$ rule might be applied if it was felt to be appropriate to the investigation. In the present analysis we were more interested in what knobs to press rather than assessing the user's competence. The student (who was the task 'expert') decided that 'select programme' needed to be taken further as there were some choices involved. The remaining five operations were all straightforward and further analysis was unnecessary: the actions were obvious as were the corresponding feedback conditions to tell the user that the operation had been carried out successfully. It is often useful to record formally the indices of successful execution of any operation so that it is quite clear what the user must look for.

Step 4: Further redescription
The student decided that 'select programme' should be broken down as 'select autosensor' (this is some sort of automatic timing device which ensures that cooking continues until the meal is ready), 'select defrost' and 'select cook' (which cooks according to a specified time). However, the analysis was now starting to appear inconsistent, since we were now looking at doing different things that, logically, could not be subsumed within the overall operation of *cooking* with the microwave cooker.

Step 5: Revising the analysis
To accommodate these observations, we needed to make some fundamental revisions to the analysis. Fig. 1.3(c) shows two changes. First, we had to revise the overall goal. Second, we needed to redescribe 'select programme' in terms of a choice plan with three options.

3.2   Observations on the processes of HTA
It is unlikely that another analyst tackling the same task using the same information would follow the same process. However, a logically similar hierarchy should result. Similarly, Diaper (Chapter 4) emphasizes the subjective nature of an analyst's decisions and discusses in detail the necessarily subjective nature of task observation in Chapter 7. As an analyst becomes more proficient at HTA and becomes familiar with how different sorts of task structure lend themselves to different sorts of occupational

goal, the analysis may proceed in a more systematic fashion from top to bottom. However, the analyst can never become complacent, since even very experienced analysts need to be flexible when dealing with unfamiliar situations, especially at the early stages of an analysis when one is trying to come to terms with the context and boundaries of the task. Chopping and changing is no bad thing and one quickly sorts out how the task can be organized. What must always be stressed is that ultimately one is trying to establish a description that obeys the rules of description of HTA.

3.3 Types of plan

A key feature in organizing a task hierarchy is the representation of appropriate plans. There are several different types of plan and they can be stated in many different ways. It is tempting simply to state difficult plans as merely reiterating a superordinate goal, that is by stating that the sub-operations must be carried out in order to attain the overall goal. For example, plan 0 in Fig. 1.3(a) could be stated as 'carry out suboperations 1 to 5 in order to cook a meal in a microwave cooker'. This logically completes the redescription, but it is not much use as a plan since we are no wiser about the cues for action and cannot be confident that the set of suboperations stated constitutes an exhaustive list. The most useful plans describe the conditions *when* suboperations must be attained. There are a vast number of different ways in which plans can be stated for different purposes, and some of these variants are illustrated in the examples of HTA given in this chapter.

Generally, there is little benefit in trying to categorize plans in HTA. There are many ways in which suboperations can be carried out to attain different goals and, for most practical purposes, we gain little by trying to standardize them. It is useful, however, to convey some of the ways in which plans might vary. Real plans often combine aspects of the following characteristics.

3.3.1 *Fixed sequences*

People are very familiar with fixed-sequence procedures. A fixed sequence is where a specified second operation is carried out when a first operation has been successfully attained. In terms of HTA, successful feedback to a first operation is the cue to carry out the second operation. This is a very common plan element in occupational settings, including computing applications. To save my text in Microsoft Word, for example, I have to click on my command line, click on 'transfer', click on 'save', then press the return key. Each of these is done in order when it is apparent that the previous operation in the sequence has been completed successfully.

3.3.2 *Cued actions*

When actions are cued, an appropriate operation from a set of possible operations is selected. This is a very common sort of plan element. It occurs very frequently in monitoring tasks, for example when a monitored signal becomes a cue for action. Cued actions can entail straightforward behaviours where the person merely has to link an action to a cue; for example, I have just been told to 'save' by my word processor, so I dutifully comply. Such cues are often time based, for example a diary appointment or an instruction to do everything at least once every 15 minutes. Another common form of cue is an instruction from, say, a supervisor — if the supervisor says start the pumps, you start the pumps. It is important to record this sort of instructional cue in a analysis, because it defines the manner in which authority and control are distributed throughout a team and, ultimately, who is responsible for invoking certain actions.

3.3.3   Contingent fixed sequence
The contingent fixed sequence is a combination of the fixed sequence and the cued action. In the contingent fixed sequence, following successful completion of a first goal (i.,e. confirmatory feedback), a second specified goal is carried out when a specified system condition develops. Plan elements such as this occur in tasks concerned with controlling large systems — a first operation may have caused a change to operating conditions which then cause system parameters to change. Process control situations provide obvious examples, especially when the system is being changed from one state to another as in, for example, start-up, e.g. a second action is carried out when a specified temperature is reached in a vessel. Just as with the choice plan element an important class of cues is the instruction from a manager, supervisor or other colleague. This is particularly important in complex systems where several people have to collaborate for a successful outcome. Often a person knows what to do next, but must wait for someone else with authority to say when it should be done. Authority is used here in a broad sense and not simply in the sense of managerial control. A sales manager may need to wait for the word from a production supervisor to say when fresh products will be available before clients can be told when they may expect them. Other examples can be given in hazardous environments, where one operator overseeing one crucial area may provide the cues for others to carry out operations to ensure that everything comes together at the right time. An important facet of genuine team-work is that individual team members supply specific cues for the plans of colleagues; effective team-work depends on how well instructions are transmitted and received.

3.3.4   Choices
Choices are logically similar to cued actions in that one of a set of subordinate operations is carried out according to prevailing conditions. However, the basis for choice is a decision or multiple discrimination that the operator has to make, e.g. in a fault diagnosis situation.

3.3.5   Cycles
In some tasks, operators have to repeat a sequence of operations until conditions arise when they must stop. A cycle is really a combination of fixed sequences and a cue to indicate when stopping is required. Sometimes the cue to stop is given by another person, e.g. a supervisor. This is typically the case in repetitive work situations. Sometimes the cue to stop is provided by a

test result. This is typical in situations where targets must be attained and action sequences must continue until this criterion is reached. Process control or maintenance tasks are typical examples.

3.3.6   Time sharing

Sometimes it is necessary for two (or more) operations to be carried out together. This has to be stated quite explicitly in the plan. Time-sharing elements are very common. Sometimes they may signal serious problems for the person carrying out the operation in terms of task loading and demands on attention, but this is not necessarily the case and the corresponding subgoals would need to be explored further.

3.3.7   Discretionary plans

The person is at liberty to do any one of a set of subordinate operations without constraint. This may seem a pretty stupid sort of plan, but it is a logical alternative and does sometimes occur in practice. It is good to look busy when the boss comes round, for example. In some situations, e.g. in the caring professions, it is important at least to be seen to be doing something in order to pay a patient or client some attention (i.e. a placebo effect).

3.3.8   Mixed plans

These plan elements have been outlined simply to show features of plans that might be encountered. Actual plans will be a mixture of these, as will be seen shortly, and there is often little practical benefit in trying to turn them into a specific type. Additionally, plans have a multiplicative effect in a hierarchy. If a choice plan, with two variants, controls plans which themselves have two variants, then their combination is a small hierarchy of plans which controls four variants. Thus, hierarchies of simple plans can account for very complex sequences of actions.

3.4   Some practical issues in data collection

The microwave cooking example illustrates how an HTA may be attained through a process of successively revising the description until it is satisfactory. I shall now consider, in sections 3.5–3.8, the problems of collecting and organizing information in a real application. Some writers on task analysis suggest a mechanical process of 'first collect data' then 'organize it'. This is almost certainly bad advice and results in a mass of unstructured information. Although HTA is primarily a prescription for describing tasks in terms of hierarchies of goals, operations and plans, it is also immensely valuable in organizing the search for relevant information, examining documentation, discussing with experts, observing job holders, issuing questionnaires. Both Johnson (Chapter 5) and Walsh (Chapter 6) describe a range of data sources and data collection methods and Diaper (Chapter 7) concentrates on the collection of observational data. Cordingley (1989) has provided an extensive review of non-observational data collection methods, such as interview techniques, in the context of knowledge elicitation for expert/knowledge-based systems, but these are generally equally appropriate in task analysis.

3.5   Getting started

3.5.1   Establishing the purpose of the analysis

The first stage in any analysis is to establish its purpose and the rules to be used for deciding where analysis should stop. If the purpose is to identify training needs, then analysis needs to progress no further than is necessary to prescribe training hypotheses (according to the $P \times C$ rule, or some variant thereof). If the purpose is to establish the extent to which a dialogue style is consistent, or to establish an operating procedure for inclusion in a manual for a new user, then analysis must progress until interfacing responses are being described. An analysis may be carried out to identify the extent to which a new task may be carried out by existing personnel. In this case it is worth trying to develop the analysis in terms of tasks that people already carry out where possible so that a match between jobs may be made. HTA can be varied in a number of useful ways to support a number of different applications. It is helpful to try to be as clear as possible about these at the outset, although it is not uncommon to realize that a completed analysis may be put to other uses with a small modification.

3.5.2   Stating the goal to be analysed

This is often less easy than one may imagine and, just as in the microwave cooking example, one may find oneself changing one's view regarding the precise goal to be analysed. The chosen goal may be too narrow. This can occur, for example, when one is examining a task that is carried out as part of a larger team effort — it is often necessary first to consider the broader role of the team in order to establish the precise boundaries of the main task of interest and how the operator should interact with other personnel in the system. Sometimes the chosen goal is too broad or too imprecise. Stating a first goal often entails examining the wider task context and its constraints. Similarly, Diaper (Chapter 4) emphasizes the importance of establishing, and then using, the purpose of performing a task analysis.

Considering computer applications such as word processors or spreadsheets, for example, can prove difficult since a useful task must first be defined. An obvious starting point might be 'use a word processor', but this may be insufficiently concrete as a starting point. It is helpful first to consider something more specific, for example 'write a letter'. Analysing this simpler goal is far easier than trying to encompass all the functions at once. When this restricted goal is understood, something more complex is considered such as 'write a report'. Additional broad goals can be accommodated to develop the scope of the analysis. An example of this approach to HTA will be given in section 4.

3.6   Sources of information

Information can be collected from a variety of sources. In order to ensure that the task analysis is reliable, it is useful to use different sources of information while developing and rechecking the task analysis. The analyst might start off talking to an operator or user, then check certain information from a document, and then re-examine the analysis with an engineer or supervisor.

3.6.1   Discussion with 'experts'

Analyzing complex tasks, especially those entailing considerable human skill, is usually best done in collaboration with a task expert. Anybody knowledgeable about a particular job or task might be described as an 'expert'. This includes an experienced job incumbent or a person who is responsible for the task such as a manager, supervisor or engineer. It is emphasized that this relationship with an expert is best seen as one of *collaboration*, rather than simply using the expert as a source of information. There are a number of reasons for this. First, it is a good strategy to get the direct commitment of someone actively involved in the system being examined and to let them 'own' the work — this is a standard consultancy ploy, effective when working inside an organization or from the outside as a consultant. Second, such a person becomes a doorway to the technicalities of the system under investigation — it is far more satisfactory to examine technical information, for example, through a person more familiar with the technology and culture of the system. Third, the closer working relationship that evolves when collaborating rather than observing enables richer facets of the system, its context and its culture to become apparent.

Experienced job incumbents can sometimes provide a practical account of what is done, including drawing attention to key points of skill. However, experienced people may be unable to describe their skills in words (Diaper (Chapter 7) discusses the psychology of this problem in detail). Alternatively, they may be reluctant to do so for fear of seeing their jobs devalued, or they may exaggerate their role. An analyst needs interviewing and counselling skills to work effectively with an expert.

The task(s) under scrutiny may not exist at present and may be still in the planning stage, such as for a new plant or office procedure. In this situation it is necessary to consult those responsible for designing and implementing the new system. It can be useful for such people to use HTA to specify their new requirements. HTA provides a useful tool for demonstrating the operability of systems and can point to areas which need redesign.

There are some practical points to observe when working with people to carry out HTA:

— It is useful to arrange a meeting away from the work environment to avoid interruptions, although it is also necessary to inspect the working environment from time to time.
— It is useful to reserve an initial period of at least a day, if possible, with an expert. This will enable significant progress to be achieved. Arrange

later sessions to go over key points and omissions, once you have started to tidy up the analysis.
— You will find that working with any new expert is a slow process to start with and you will have to discover the most effective way of working together.
— Explain to your expert the uses to which the completed analysis will be put. This is partly out of courtesy, but it can also help the expert to focus on the problem and bring to bear his or her own insights.
— Make clear to your expert that you are not expecting perfectly accurate information first time around; details need checking at a later stage. Otherwise, the expert will feel inhibited about making errors and this will slow up the analysis. It is better to push the analysis along at a reasonable rate and sort out various points of detail later.
— You will have to judge the extent to which it is feasible to involve your expert in the task analysis process. Some experts may rapidly learn the principles of HTA. This will speed up the process of task analysis and some experts may be able to complete some of the analysis themselves. In other situations experts might not have the time or inclination to understand the rules of task analysis and the analyst will be required to 'translate' information into the required form.
— When stating operations becomes difficult, it is important to remember that their purpose is to attain system goals — so ask, 'what is it that the person carrying out the task is trying to achieve?'.

3.6.2   Documentation
Useful documents may be available as sources of information. These include job descriptions, operating manuals, safety and emergency procedures, maintenance records, manufacturers' manuals, etc. Reference to such documents may be useful at early stages in the analysis to inform the analyst about the overall nature and breadth of tasks carried out. Later, as the detail of the task is becoming established, such documents serve to provide crucial information. The analyst will be directed to various parts of the documents in accordance with the emerging HTA. The use of experts in helping with the interpretation of documents is emphasized.

3.6.3   Observation and inspection
It may only be possible to make sense of some task elements if the analyst observes them being carried out. Analysis may also be aided by inspection of the devices or materials associated with the task. It is usually helpful to observe people at work at the task, in order to gain an impression of the kinds of pressures they are under and the kind of working environment in which they work. It is rarely a good idea to rely on observing performance as a prime source of task data, especially in tasks involving substantial decision making, since the operator's intentions and information-gathering strategies are seldom apparent. It is better to progress the task analysis by discussion with the expert or through examining existing documentation, and then to use observation and inspection to resolve specific issues. In such circum-

stances, the analyst should be free to use any data-collection technique that seems appropriate, including 'talk-through', 'verbal protocol analysis', video recording, 'activity sampling' and 'critical incident techniques'. It is worth stating that many writers refer to these various data-collection methods as task analysis techniques. Indeed they are, but they are not alternatives to HTA. They may be better regarded as specific data-collection methods that fit into the framework of broader approaches, such as HTA.

3.7   Stages of the analysis

Carrying out task analysis involves an iterative process of identifying goals, organizing them, breaking them into subgoals and checking the accuracy of the information. It is helpful to consider the following three stages of any analysis.

3.7.1   Starting redescription

Once a general goal has been stated (this may be subsequently revised), it is then subject to redescription.

— It is useful to try to break down the superordinate task into a handful of operations at the next level — between four and eight subtasks is a reasonable guideline. Make sure that these subtasks exhaustively cover the area of interest.
— Attempt to specify a plan for this first level of subtasks. Remember that the plan must state *when* each of the subtasks is to be performed. You may find that attempting to specify a plan will help to show where your analysis is inadequate. If there is a subtask not referred to in the plan, then either that subtask is unnecessary or the plan must be amended to include it.
— Always check that the subtasks and their associated plan are technically correct. If an 'expert' is being used it is worth asking whether performance of the subtasks with their plan by the job incumbent would be equivalent to the superordinate task. This is an effective cross-check which can be further improved by corroboration from different sources of information.

3.7.2   Progressing the analysis

When a redescription is judged to be satisfactory each subtask should be considered in turn to determine whether further redescription is justified. This is where you need to consider the stopping rule to decide whether existing performance can be carried out satisfactorily under the prevailing task conditions. Where further redescription is not justified, this should be clearly indicated and reasons for stopping should be noted. In this way, the whole task analysis can be tackled systematically.

— Stating plans can sometimes be difficult. Try to avoid stating plans which govern too many subtasks. A complex plan can often be simplified by finding whether its subtasks can be formed into subgroups. If this can be

done, then a complex plan can be replaced by a small hierarchy of simpler plans.
— You may find it difficult to resolve an issue. If you are working with an expert it might be helpful to have a rest or to continue with a different part of the analysis.
— If a problem emerges with a difficult choice plan, it is worth presenting the expert with sets of conditions and asking him or her to specify what further information would be sought and what action would be taken.

3.7.3 Finalizing the analysis
When issues concerning the content of the analysis have been sorted out, the analysis needs to be presented consistently.

— Prepare a clear representation of the task (see section 3.8).
— Present or 'talk through' the analysis with an expert who has not been intimately involved in the task analysis. Remember that you will have to explain how the task analysis is set out.
— It is a good idea.to use as many different sources of corroboration that you can to finalize your analysis. Inconsistencies and disagreements can be ironed out and your task analysis will be more reliable.
— It is not a good idea to leave someone to check out an HTA unaided. Most readers tend to skim over such documents looking for the presence of familiar words and rarely scrutinize the document as carefully as they should. People need assistance to guide them through the document to ensure that it is technically correct.
— It is also important to remember, and to remind your expert, that the representation of the HTA at this stage is not an operating manual, but a description of the relationship between task goals and conditions. The development of documentation will come later.

3.8 Representing the task analysis
I have stressed that tables and diagrams are not HTA, but merely a *representation* of HTA. They are nonetheless vital as a means of keeping a record of the issues identified in the analysis and as a means of communicating the work to others. Also, as we shall see in section 4, they can lead to the development of effective manuals. There are two main forms of representing an HTA, *hierarchical diagrams* and *tables*. Both have their uses. A further important issue is that of consistent numbering of the analysis.

With all of these issues concerned with representing an analysis, it should be appreciated that our prime concern is for *clarity, consistency* and *clerical convenience*. The options suggested are by no means the only ways of presenting this information. Indeed, any analyst should feel free to adopt any diagrammatic, tabular or numbering format he or she prefers, provided that it is internally consistent and rules for its interpretation are made clear to potential readers. The world might be a tidier place if we were to standardize such features, but I cannot really feel that standardization is very important in this context.

3.8.1 Hierarchical diagrams

Fig. 1.1 shows the hierarchical diagram of operating an overhead projector (from Shepherd, 1986). Diagrams are very useful as a means of conveying the structure of the hierarchy. The double underlining of boxes is used to emphasize that no further redescription is offered. Diagrams are limited if the analyst wishes to make copious design notes and comments.

3.8.2 Numbering the analysis

It is important to adopt a rational numbering system to keep track of the work. Any numbering system that works may be adopted. The system used in Fig. 1.1 has proven quite effective. The overall goal is numbered 0. its subgoals are numbered from 1 to whatever is necessary (7 in this case). The plan governing its subgoals is given the same number as its superordinate goal (in this case 'plan 0') and can then refer to the subgoals in terms of their numbers. Operation 2 is redescribed. Its subgoals are numbered from 1 to 3; its plan is labelled 'plan 2'. Its operation 3 is further redescribed; its subgoals are numbered 1, 2 and 3; and its plan is given the label 'plan 2.3'. People may find it clearer to write down a full number for each operation, rather than just a single digit, e.g. they may prefer 'switch to stand-by bulb' to be numbered 6.1. An objection to this is that numbers can become unwieldy if the analysis is taken to several levels. Another advantage of numbering operations with single digits is that it is easy to edit an analysis numbered in this way — modifying the numbers of higher level operations will not affect the numbering of lower level operations. I can say in defence of this numbering system described that I have found it to be very effective in a considerable number of applications. However, it is, after all, simply a clerical tool. It is most important that the analyst clearly states how the adopted numbering system works for each HTA recorded.

3.8.3 Tabular formats

Table 1.1 shows one way of representing an HTA in a table. The task is the overhead projector task, represented graphically in Fig. 1.1. The same numbering system is adopted. In this version, the left-hand column contains the absolute number of the goal or subgoal currently being described (e.g. 2.3 rather than just 3), that is the subordinate goal of the current redescription. The centre column contains the operations and plans that form the task analysis. The right-hand column contains any notes that are felt worth including. The 'notes' column provides one of the main benefits of the tabular format, since these can be allowed to extend as far as required. Diagrams are more easily assimilated by people, but tables are more thorough. It is often best to use both to record and communicate the analysis.

Annett *et al.*(1971) offered a different format, which was somewhat more difficult to follow and edit than the one presented here. Shepherd (1976) discusses the weakness in their original approach.

I have emphasized the criterion of clerical convenience and choice for these formats. Provided that a consistent format is offered that can be communi-

Table 1.1 — HTA in tabular form

Superordinate	Task analysis — operations–plans	Notes
0.	Operate overhead projector *Plan 0:* *At least 1/2 hr before lecture — 1;* *Immediately prior to lecture — 2;* *As lecture commences — 3;* *If the projector light fails — 4–6–5;* *If other problem occurs that you cannot deal with — 4–5;* *At end of lecture — 4 (if on — 7 (if problem)) — EXIT.* 1. Ensure stand-by equipment available — spare bulb — spare fuse// 2. Set up projector 3. Show slides according to lecture schedule// 4. Switch off projector// 5. Finish session without projector// 6. Deal with projector light failure 7. Notify technician of problems//	 Get replacements from the technician. This should never occur. Unfortunately it sometimes does. Be prepared! This is the only fault you should try to deal with yourself. Failure to do this may cause problems for colleagues or yourself later if equipment is unprepared.
2.	Set up projector *Plan 2: 1–2–3–EXIT.* 1. Ensure projector is plugged in// 2. Switch on projector to ensure it is working// 3. Establish correct image	
6.	Deal with projector light failure *Plan 6: Try 1. If that does not work, try 2 then EXIT:* *If 2 does not work you still exit since this contingency is dealt with in plan 0.* 1. Switch to standby bulb// 2. Change fuse//	
2.3	Establish correct image *Plan 2.3: 1–2–3 — If OK — EXIT: If not OK, start the cycle from 1 again.* 1. Ensure projector head is pointing in correct direction// 2. Focus projector// 3. Adjust projector–screen distance to fill screen//	A demonstration and a bit of common sense are all that are really necessary here.

This represents the same analysis as Fig. 1.1. Benefits of the tabular form are primarily that the analyst is not constrained by space in expressing operations, plans or notes concerning performance improvements.

cated and used easily by another person, there is no real basis for objection. For example, some of the computer-based outlining facilities and graphics packages available are extremely useful in preparing and editing HTA tables and diagrams. Within Microsoft Word, for example, there is an outlining facility, which allows the writer to enter one level of the analysis, and then to expand each of these as required. It enables automatic numbering and renumbering following any revision made. Notes may be entered as required. A style sheet may then be attached to the document to present the analysis in different columns and text styles as appropriate. Using the outlining tool means that subgoals are immediately redescribed, rather than completing a redescription then moving onto further breakdown as in Table 1.1. It is easy to get used to this alternative format and the outliner provides a very convenient way to enter and edit the analysis. Carey *et al.* (Chapter 2) similarly propose the use of such tools and Diaper (Chapter 4) and Johnson (Chapter 5) both suggest a need to develop software tools to support specific task analysis applications.

3.9   Section 3: Concluding remarks
In section 3 I have described a number of practical issues concerning conducting HTA. The emphasis has been on the need to work towards a target of a hierarchical description, rather than offering any convenient procedure. I am aware that this lack of rigid procedure is seen by some people as a major drawback to HTA. However, I seriously doubt whether any set of rigid procedures could cope with the variety of tasks and contexts that are encountered in real situations. Experience is soon gained such that analysis may proceed very effectively.

4.   APPLYING HTA AND SYNTHESIZING RESULTS

In this section I shall first justify why HTA leads to practical solutions in the following three main areas: providing support, usually in the form of documentation; training; and redesigning the work so that the task is trainable. I shall then illustrate applications of this approach in five cases of varying complexity that entail HCI.

4.1   Justification of HTA in task synthesis
4.1.1   The design of user documentation
User documentation, usually manuals or on-screen help facilities, is provided to help people to do things they would not otherwise be able to do. Confronted with a work-goal to attain, the capable user carries it out unaided, whereas the incapable user (as far as this goal is concerned) either guesses, which could lead to a mistake, or turns to a help facility. The help facility must enable the user to locate appropriate guidance, and then use it to direct a response to the set goal according to the prevailing task context.

Because of the form of description developed, HTA is ideally suited to helping to meet these requirements. The operational language used in the HTA conforms to the goals the user wishes to attain, enabling the user easily to locate required information. The straightforward expression is consistent with recommendations by, for example, Wright (1977), enabling the user to select an action to meet the specified instruction, provided that the appropriate action is within the user's repertoire. If the action is not available to the user, the help facility needs to provide a description in greater detail — the hierarchical form of HTA clearly lends itself to such further breakdown. The HTA, therefore, provides the *content* and *structure* of information which lends itself to presentation in a suitable form. Actual presentation can be made in a number of consistent ways. For example, the hierarchical features of the analysis can be preserved by moving to different pages for different levels of description. Alternatively, information could be contained on one page, by presenting more detailed descriptions in indented paragraphs or by exploiting different typefaces. HTA is ideally suited to presentation via hypertext systems.

4.1.2   Training design

There are three main links between HTA and training. First, where it is anticipated that the HTA is carried out solely for the purpose of developing a training programme, the analyst is able to stop redescription when a training solution is recognized. So, if an existing training course or method of instruction is available to enable people to be trained to a satisfactory standard, a great deal of unnecessary analysis can be avoided. Task taxonomies may be used by the analyst to help to identify useful training hypotheses.

Second, HTA enables concepts and procedures to be distinguished. As an analysis is carried out, non-procedural plans are encountered which highlight operational concepts that the user must possess in order to make choices. For example, to adopt a 'mail merge' facility in a word processor the user must first have a concept of mail merge. If a user understands the concepts entailed in an application and can use them to discriminate between different conditions in the environment, then it is quite easy to follow a set of written procedures to attain a goal. Without a clear understanding of the concepts, written procedures must contain wordy explanations which are often avoided by the user. A good practical strategy for most intermittent computer tasks is to teach concepts in an introductory training session, since these will be remembered, and then to provide a well-structured help facility or user manual. This is illustrated later on in case 2.

Third, the structure of HTA lends itself to *controlled development* of training. Where parts of a task can be practised separately, the trainee is able to master and consolidate component skills, free from the complexity of the whole task. One practical application of this, which can be readily applied in many IT situations, is to encourage supervisors to simplify the duties assigned to a new starter, or to control the flow of work so that the new starter may operate within his or her level of competence. As experience is gained, the range of duties can be expanded and the flow of work made richer. This control of a trainee's experience is a very practical and effective training strategy and can be exploited in a range of contexts, from management development to computer-based training. An important aspect of controlled development is *adaptive* training. The expansion of the task can be linked to how an individual progresses. If an individual learns quickly, he or she can move on quickly. If the individual already possesses a range of constituent skills, then he or she can be given appropriate responsibities, under supervision, to determine whether they are indeed competent in the real context. Case 3 will describe the application of these ideas in an IT context.

4.1.3   Redesigning work for trainability and operability

Jobs may be designed without due consideration of whether they can be carried out effectively by human beings. These issues fall mainly under the headings of work and job design, but they must sometimes be addressed in the context of training. Tasks are sometimes offered for training which cannot be carried out effectively; training on its own cannot solve these problems. HTA is helpful in the context of work design in two main ways. First, jobs can be partitioned according to the HTA structure to ensure that groupings comply with a sensible job design. Second, the information in plans necessary to make decisions and the feedback implicit in every operation stated in the analysis must be present in the array of information available to the user or operative. Without these two sources of information, tasks cannot be carried out effectively. In this respect, HTA can be used to prescribe the information content of screen design in HCI tasks. The application of HTA to HCI tasks is the central theme of Chapter 2 by Carey *et al.*

4.2   Examples of cases for training in HCI

The following five applications have been selected to illustrate the points made about training and support.

4.2.1   Case 1: Writing a simple user manual

The following case is an example of applying HTA to develop a user manual. The benefits of using HTA for this purpose have been described above. The example is taken from D'Souza (1988) and is concerned with development of a manual for a communications package called 'Z-TERM' which is used for file transfer between the Cambridge Computers' Z88 and other systems, such as PRESTEL or other microcomputers. The package consists of hardware, in the form of a ROM that is plugged into the Z88, a communications link, and software which presents the user with options and controls the communications. It is a commercial package for use by people with limited IT expertise, and so must be quite straightforward and non-technical. Only a small sample of the HTA and resultant manual can be included here.

The analysis. The analysis for this task was quite straightforward. It involved examining existing documentation, questioning the suppliers about points of ambiguity and trying out certain procedures on the package itself. Table 1.2 shows part of the resultant HTA. As with many task analyses concerned with computer application, the plans are almost exclusively choices or options and procedures.

Synthesis. Fig. 1.4 shows the part of the manual which corresponds to the

Table 1.2 — First two redescriptions of HTA of a communications package
from case 1 (adapted from D'Souza, 1988)

Superordinate	Task analysis — operations–plans	Notes
0.	Use the Z88 and Z-TERM for file transfer	Once the equipment is set up you may use it to either save data from PRESTEL or communicate with other users.
	Plan 0:1–2 then, according to choice: to record data from PRESTEL — 3; to communicate with other users – 4; to log off – 5. 1. Set up hardware and Z-TERM ROM 2. Configure Z-TERM 3. Record from PRESTEL 4. Communicate with other MODEM users 5. Log off	
1.	Set up hardware and Z-TERM ROM *Plan: 12–2–3–4–5.* 1. Switch on Z88// 2. Ensure Z88 Index Screen is on — if other applications are on, SAVE and KILL// 3. Insert Z-TERM ROM into a vacant ROM slot under Perspex cover at front of computer// 4. Connect Z88 to MODEM by using 9 pin connector to right hand side of Z88, 24 pin connector to modem// 5. Connect modem to telephone lines — using either a single or a double socket in the telephone wall-socket/ /	Remove RAM cartridge if necessary — do not forget to save RAM contents!

This analysis links to the user manual excerpt in Fig. 1.4.

part of the HTA in Table 1.2. Note that 'page 1' corresponds to the first level of redescription in the task analysis in Table 1.2, and serves as an index to the rest of the document. Translating from an HTA to a user manual is not constraining for the author and provides considerable opportunity for design. Comparison between 'page 2' and the redescription of operation 1 shows this. The basic instructions correspond to the operations in the task analysis, but include certain embellishments that the author favoured. Note also the plan is not separate, but has been incorporated into the main text for easier reading.

4.2.2   Case 2: Analysis of a word processor
Word processors provide good examples for demonstrating the application of HTA to computer applications.

The analysis. The main problem facing the analyst is in deciding what task to analyse — a computer application is a tool and not a task. We may choose a

HOW TO USE Z-TERM WITH THE Z88

Z-TERM is a program which can be run on the Z-88 portable
computer to enable you to communicate with other users via
telephone lines or to link into PRESTEL or other computers
using a modem.

For any applications you must first

**Set up your hardware and the Z-TERM rom
- see page 3**

To record from PRESTEL - see page 9

To communicate with other users - see page 11

**When you have completed the transfer of
files you must log off - see page 12**

page 2

Set up hardware and Z-TERM ROM

To set up the Z88 to communicate with other systems, follow
these instruction:

1. Switch the Z88 on by pressing both shift keys.

2. As a safeguard, save all SUSPENDED ACTIVITIES.

3. Insert the Z-TERM ROM into a vacant slot at the front
of the Z88. See Appendix 2 for guidance.

4. Connect the Z88 to the MODEM by connecting the
9 pin connector to the right hand side of the Z88 and
the 24 pin connector to the MODEM.

5. Connect the MODEM to the telephone line either
directly or via a T-junction double socket in
the telephone-wall socket.

page 3

Fig. 1.4 — Two pages from Z-TERM manual, related to the analysis in Table 1.2
(adapted from D'Souza, 1988). The form of instruction in the manual preserves
the description developed in the HTA.

task such as 'use a word processor', but it is not easy to make sense of something so broad. A good strategy is to start off with something more specific, for example, 'prepare and print a letter using a word processor'. Analyzing this task becomes tractable and will cover many of the main word processor functions, including 'entering text', 'editing', 'formatting' and 'printing'. This then provides a basic structure against which to extend understanding of the word processor. By next looking at, say, 'write a report with a word processor', we may rely on many of the functions required in 'write a letter' but introduce new features such as 'pagination', 'creating footnotes' and 'formatting tables'. One might then move on to, say, 'create a mail-shot', which will introduce the mail merge facilities. In this way, additional features may be added to the core word processor analysis. The result will be a hierarchical task analysis of word processing, with a particular feature that its plan statements can link to the kinds of goals for which a word processor might be used.

Fig. 1.5 shows the start of an HTA for the word processor Microsoft Word. As this analysis unfolds, it becomes clear that there are many general skills and concepts to be grasped in order to select the procedure to invoke commands. For example, plan 0 offers a number of choices, including 'entering text', 'formatting text', 'editing text' and 'printing'. It makes no sense to be definitive regarding when each of these is done. The whole point of the word processor is that it is a tool for people to use according to their requirements. To use the word processor, the user must know what 'entering', 'formatting', 'editing' and 'printing' imply, so that they can match these options to the goals they wish to attain. Similarly, the user needs concepts of 'entering text', 'loading existing files' that are being worked on, and 'merging text', so that it can be added from existing files. These concepts are required to carry out plan 2. An interesting, and potentially confusing, concept is that of a 'paragraph'. In normal text, a paragraph is characterized by a space between blocks of text or a first-line indent. Paragraphs help signify to a reader that, for example, a line of argument has changed, i.e. paragraphs have a distinctive function in aiding the readability of a piece of text. In Word, paragraphs have a particular definition, namely that they are blocks of text terminated by a paragraph-end control character. Pressing the 'enter' key creates the end of a paragraph, forcing a new line. This is understood as a normal paragraph by the reader. However, the same visual appearance is created by pressing 'shift–enter' to insert a line-feed command, which does not have the same properties of the full paragraph-end command. The practical difference is that several blocks of text separated only by the line-feed character are treated as only one paragraph from the view point of formatting paragraphs. Knowing this distinction provides considerable power for the user wishing to format text in operation 3.2; not knowing it can be quite confusing to the user, since the paragraph-formatting command can appear quite inconsistent.

Inspection of other aspects of the task indicates a number of procedural concepts associated with commonly occurring procedures, such as entering commands via the command line of Word. Thus the redescriptions of

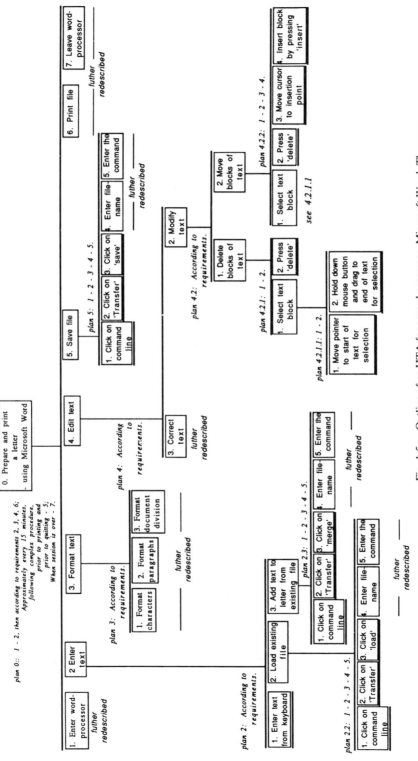

Fig. 1.5 — Outline of an HTA for a word processor, Microsoft Word. There are similarities between this analysis and an HTA for another word processor. However, this should always be checked out. For example, within Word, it is possible to commence work without naming a file, whereas this does not apply to other systems.

operations 2.2, 2.3, 5 and numerous others which have not been included in this example utilize the concept of the 'command line', the use of the mouse, and the concepts of 'fields' to enter data.

There are similarities between Word and other word processors and there are clear differences. Word enables the user to work on new files without previously specifying a file name. This cannot be done in other packages, where the filename must first be specified. Often the similarities are reflected in the concepts and the task structure- the differences are reflected in the procedures. Thus, *concepts* are the basis for transfer between different word processors, while *procedures* must be described for each application. It is advisable to be as specific as possible about the system under study and to allow similarities to emerge naturally.

Synthesis. The HTA can be used in three main ways to promote learning. First, it can be used to identify *concepts* and basic procedures that can be taught in an introductory training session or a computer-based tutorial. These can be remembered until they are needed when a particular function needs to be invoked. The kinds of concepts to be invoked here were described in the previous paragraph. The basic procedures are the commonly occurring low level routines, such as those concerned with using the command line in Word, e.g. 'load existing files' (operation 2.2 in Fig. 1.5). It saves a great deal of time and frustration if these can be taught at the beginning in a course or tutorial. Such basic procedures also typically transfer to basic procedures of a similar type and so enable the user to cope with circumstances never encountered in the introductory session or the manual.

Second, the HTA can be used to devise *manuals* or help facilities which enable users to locate the goals they wish to attain and to provide the procedures necessary to realize their goals, within a structure which can be adapted to the level of help the user chooses. This can be used at point of need. Procedures are easily forgotten. It makes little sense to waste much time on teaching procedures during initial training unless it is known that they will be used frequently and soon by the trainees in question. A well-designed manual is a more effective method of providing procedures. Procedures will thus be learned as they are practised.

Finally, learners can be helped by scheduling work which is consistent with a subset of skills to be practised, and then expanding demands as the learner gains experience. We exploit this last feature ourselves in teaching students word processing. First of all, they are provided with a simple manual which covers 'text entry', 'simple editing', 'saving and loading files' and 'printing'. They use the default formats provided in the word processor — but this enables them to produce complete documents. As experience is gained and skill and confidence grow, we expand the manual to encompass 'formatting of characters, paragraphs and document layout'. If students want to go further, they can use the manufacturer's manual — by this stage they are reasonably confident and can make sense of such documents — but we could extend the course if we needed to. The progression is thus based on the HTA. This approach is similar to the training wheels idea described by Carroll and Currithers (1984), in that the trainee is limited in the functions that can be used. Carroll and Currithers prevent their trainees from having access to these functions through software modification to prevent them from making errors. Our trainees are not constrained from making errors. This may be a disadvantage, but our part-task training method provides a cost-effective solution to a real training problem.

4.2.3   Case 3: The revenue-recording task

This example is of an office-based accountancy task. A fuller account is given in Shepherd (1989). The example demonstrates how a real training solution should include a mixture of effective training supervision, better user manuals and some conceptual training. It also demonstrates that HCI tasks should be considered within the context of a full job; focusing on IT aspects to the exclusion of other facets can be misleading.

The Post Office offers, on a contract basis, a wide range of services, such as bulk parcel services and business reply facilities. Customers are provided with docket books to indicate when and how much they use each of these services and voucher books in which to enter the payments they make for services used. Keeping track of the services used and the monies paid is a crucial task for which a *computer-aided revenue-recording system* has been developed.

The analysis. The environment in which this work is carried out is a typical large office space. Operators work at terminals, deal with telephone calls and make use of a paper-based filing system. The main parts of the HTA are shown in Fig. 1.6. Of these operations, it is only necessary to discuss the

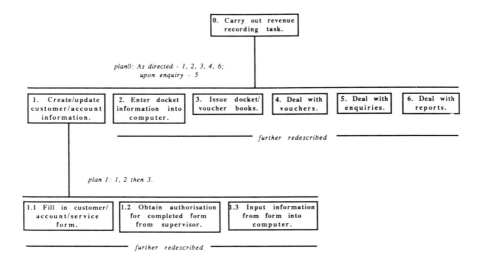

Fig. 1.6 — Part of the task analysis of the revenue-recording task.

redescriptions of operation 1 (i.e. 1.1, 1.2 and 1.3) and operation 5 to cover the critical features of the task. Operations 2, 3,4 and 6 are each computer input tasks and are similar to operation 1.3.

Operation 1.1 — fill in customer/account/service form. The operator has to prepare a form for computer input from information sent from the postal sales department, containing details of a new customer, a new account for an existing customer or a new service within an existing account. There will be mistakes in entering information into the computer (operation 1.3) if this is not done properly. However, this is a non-computer task element.

Operation 1.2 — obtain authorization for completed form from supervisor. Operators are required to seek confirmation from their supervisors that they have carried out operation 1.1 properly. This is a non-computer task element.

Operation 1.3 — input information from form into computer. This task involves (i) locating a required screen by making correct choices in the menu hierarchy, and (ii) correctly following screen form-filling procedures. The same general procedures are required in operations 2, 3, 4 and 6. These are computer task elements. They had given managers the impression of extensive computer activity for which computer-based training would be necessary. However, there was ample time for the operator to locate and use a suitable manual. Computer-based training was unnecessary, but a better user manual was needed.

Operation 5 — deal with enquiries. Enquiries are initiated by customers querying the invoices and statement sent to them. Enquiries might be due to customers failing to understand the document sent to them, recognizing an inconsistency in the document invoice or statement (which might be correct, but appear wrong to the customer because of the way the accounting system works) or recognizing a genuine error in the account, for example, a miskeyed amount. The operator has to listen carefully to the customer's complaint, and then analyses the problem and explains the outcome to the customer. Analysis of a problem entails locating enquiry screens on the computer and making reference to documents filed away in filing cabinets. The diagnostic skills that operators require in these circumstances are substantial, as is their need to be able to direct the customer through paperwork, via the telephone, courteously and effectively. This activity represents probably the greatest training need of the entire task and it had little to do with the IT aspects of the job — although computer-based learning was probably useful here in helping trainees to learn system concepts effectively.

Synthesis. From the analysis the following general training recommendations were made.

On-job instruction. Many of the data routines can be taught satisfactorily on the job, especially with a suitable user manual. In addition, filing skills must be taught.

Computer-based training. CBT was recommended to teach important concepts of the system, for example, the distinctions between the different types of account. It was also recommended to teach operators a model of the system to explain how information flows through the system and is stored. Paradoxically, it was not seen as appropriate to use CBT to teach any of the computer-based task elements.

Customer service training. Operators must understand a customer's enquiry over the telephone and deal with it effectively and courteously. These are difficult skills to master, requiring diagnostic and communications training followed by simulated practice.

Supervisory training. Since both CBT and on-job training would be handled locally, there is a need to give first-line supervisors some training in how to make best use of these approaches.

Thus, the revenue-recording task showed that tasks must be examined on their merits. In spite of the prominence of computing equipment, it did not dominate training needs.

4.2.4 Case 4: Familiarizing operators with new displays
Shepherd (1985) describes a case where training was required to help process plant operators to adapt to a new computer-based display on their plant (see Fig. 1.7). The plant comprised three main interacting areas. Each panel in the new system displayed information from, and housed controllers for, one of these three areas; information was organized according to a geographical hierarchy. The original plant was controlled via a conventional instrument panel consisting of individual indicators, controllers and recorders. Because operators were experienced with this plant, management assumed training would be minimal, merely involving familization with the new display.

Analysis. An HTA was carried out to identify a range of situations that could be used to generate conditions on a simulation of the new display for the purpose of familiarization training. However, the anlaysis revealed that the display was unsuited to supporting effective human performance and so the simple training solution would have been quite ineffective.

The basis of the problem was that, when disturbance occurred in one area, the operator had to investigate whether the plant had to be shut down, or whether there were any alternative intermediate states that the plant could be 'moved' to in order to minimize the costs of downtime. This would happen frequently and so was important commercially. The HTA considered typical decisions that had to be made and examined what information would need to be considered by the operator. It transpired that, whereas a disturbance might be confined to one plant area, the information needed to optimize the plant had to be collected from all areas of plant. To make these decisions, therefore, operators had rapidly to examine information throughout the plant to decide what remedial action to take. In the original system, where all information was *displayed,* this was done quite

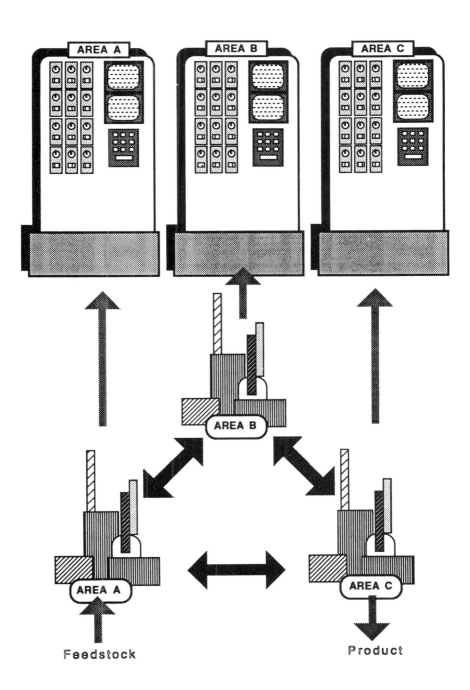

Fig. 1.7 — Representation of control panels and layout of plant in case 4.

easily, since operators could scan their control panels for the necessary information. In the new display system, however, operators had to retrieve individual items of information via a geographically organized menu hierarchy. Under this geographical organization operators would be subject to an extreme memory load, as they had to move around the menu structure and had to move between different display consoles to locate specific items of information, while remembering the information gained to date and the intermediate decisions they had made. Therefore, from the viewpoint of human decision making, introduction of this computer-based system was a retrograde step.

Synthesis. By redesigning the display to enable information related to specific types of decision to be collected and displayed on the same screen, the memory problem was abated, the task was substantially simplified and the required training became straightforward.

4.2.5 Case 5: A computer-controlled warehouse

This case is concerned with a computer-controlled pharmaceutical warehouse. Individual product lines were fed onto a conveyor belt in accordance with an order from a specific retail outlet which had been keyed into the computer controlling the warehouse. Between some items on the conveyor belt there were extra large gaps. These were either gaps between orders or gaps which had occurred because a particular product was out of stock. An operator was employed to identify the gaps between orders and to place in them a small tray, called a 'slug', which contained the order docket, used in subsequent packaging and dispatch operations. The problem was to distinguish between gaps between orders and those which had occurred because an item was out of stock. To identify these gaps, the operator was provided with a VDU which displayed the code numbers for the last five and first five of each order. Therefore the operator had to examine the code numbers on the boxes coming down the line and to ensure that there was a match between a chosen gap and the items displayed on the screen. The problem was confounded by the fact that some boxes fell onto the sides on which their code numbers were printed and so could not be identifed. The belt was moving quite fast and mistakes were a real nuisance because the belt had to be stopped and the incorrectly placed slug retrieved.

Analysis. The task analysis was quite simple and amounted to a cycle of operations as shown in Fig. 1.8(a) In principle there was no constraint on how the operator used the information presented, but stating the plan showed that there were two main strategies which imposed different loads on working memory. It was necessary to establish the most effective strategy before training could be prescribed.

Synthesis. These two candidates are shown in the plan in Figs 1.8(b) and 1.8(c). The plan in Fig. 1.8(b) prescribes that the operator looks first at the display, then at the boxes. In this case the operator is obliged to try to remember ten items from the screen, then to view the boxes on the conveyor

(a)

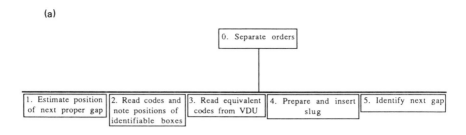

(b)   (c)

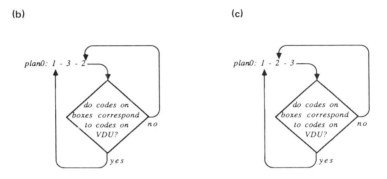

Fig. 1.8 — Operations and alternative plans for warehousing task in case 5: (a) the basic set of operations for the warehousing task; (b) plan requiring screen codes to be remembered, while searching for visable box codes; (c) plan requiring visible codes from boxes to be remembered prior to reading codes from screen.

belt to identify any items whose codes are readable, and then to judge whether they are in corresponding positions. If they are, the correct gap has been identified and the slug and docket can be dropped in. There is, however, a substantial working memory load for the operator and confusions are likely to arise. The other strategy in Fig. 1.8(c) appears to impose far less memory load and is therefore preferable. In this case, the operator looks up the line for the next gap, looks at the boxes on either side which are identifiable and, with three or four boxes identified from the ten, views the screen to see whether they correspond to the target gap. If they do not, the operator then looks further up the line for the next gap and repeats the process. The different plans impose different memory loads on the operator. The preferred plan can be used to shape a more robust strategy for the task.

Before concluding this example, I should like to add that there were lots of ways in which this situation could have been improved, and this operation effectively removed, but the management were adamant that this is how it had to be done.

5.   CONCLUDING REMARKS

The main aim of this chapter has been to show how HTA can be applied to deal with tasks associated with HCI. HTA was always intended to be versatile and to cope with tasks which demand cognitive skill as well manual skills. It is the writer's view that this claim for versatility is entirely justified.

A method of task analysis should not prejudge the task it is examining, so a task analysis method should be adopted which copes with both manual and cognitive elements. Through an analysis of goals that the user or operator is seeking to attain, HTA sets out to attempt an unprejudiced analysis. Obviously, when elements of physical activity or, more covert, cognitive activity are encountered, the analyst must vary his or her strategy in gaining information. Indeed, many so-called different approaches to task analysis might be better seen as helping the analyst to cope with different phases of data collection, to be carried out within the cohesive framework of a broad approach such as HTA rather than as a separate enterprise. Some critics of HTA, concerned that it fails to cope adequately with cognitive tasks, probably mean that it fails to yield a behavioural description in terms that would satisfy a cognitive psychologist. This does not matter if we are using a task analysis method to improve task performance, since we need a description in terms of the goals that have to be achieved. This can be a perfectly adequate basis for selecting methods to improve performance. There is no reason to presume that a description in terms of human cognition (if indeed it can be shown to be valid) will lead us to a more satisfactory solution to a performance problem.

There is a danger in naming techniques of analysis, because they become formalized and there is then the tendency to compare them, often unproductively, with other named techniques. In this chapter, I have tried to convey that the good analyst is sensitive to the context in which he or she is operating and should be prepared to adapt the approach in accordance with circumstances. The purpose of explaining terms and concepts is to provide the would-be analyst with an understanding necessary to make these modifications. For example, I have questioned the extent to which the $P \times C$ rule should be considered an integral part of HTA or just one rule appropriate to some training applications. Analysts should know what they are doing and why they are doing it. By the same token, there are many hierarchical approaches to task analysis which share the same ideas, but whose authors have chosen to formalize one particular aspect to help in the analysis of a particular class of problem.

I have stressed that procedural approaches to task analysis, such as the use of checklists or design guidelines, are rarely adequate for other than straightforward, stereotyped applications. Analysis of complex tasks requires skill that can only be acquired with practice. The skills in HTA involve gathering information to enable moving from a broad task goal to a description that meets the criteria for good task analysis. The analyst must also be skilled in moving from the task description to a method for synthesizing performance. One of the main effects of practice at HTA is the increased ability to recognize common task structures and techniques for examining and representing them. This enables the experienced analyst to work very effectively indeed. Applications packages, for example, benefit from an approach similar to that described in case 2. Many office-based systems share common features with case 3.

I should like to finish by emphasizing that the need for the various concepts and ideas in HTA becomes most clear when the technique is actually used. There is a concern that written accounts deter the would-be analyst as there seems to be so much that needs to be remembered. The would-be analyst will make rapid progress by trying to carry out the ideas on a simple task at first, and then moving to something more ambitious and meaningful, where real design decisions need to be made. The contents of this chapter are intended to serve as a source of ideas and models for task analysis in HCI applications to training.

2

Human–Computer Interaction design: the potential and pitfalls of Hierarchical Task Analysis

M. S. Carey*, **R. B. Stammers** and **J. A. Astley**†
Applied Psychology Division, Aston University

As computing applications increase in scale and complexity, the difficulties involved in the organization and management of the design process have multiplied. Within the domain of software engineering, structured analysis and design methologies are in use, enabling logical design to be decoupled from the physical design of systems while providing a means for large development teams to coordinate and control their activities. In contrast, the emphasis within the discipline of human–computer interaction in recent years has been upon iterative and evaluative approaches to design as opposed to top-down analytic methods. There is clearly a need in the future to complement evaluative approaches with structured analytic techniques in the early stages of system design.

Despite the obvious demand, there is considerable confusion evident in the area regarding the merits and applicability of individual techniques. Wilson *et al.* (1988), for example, review 11 individual task analysis methods that may be applied to human–computer interaction. These range from techniques which are intended to be used as design tools, through techniques which are designed to illustrate theoretical aspects of human–computer interaction, to task analysis methods which have been developed to contribute to cognitive models of human information processing. While it is true that they all focus upon user task activity and that they subject that activity to some form of systematic analysis, there is a wide diversity in their purpose, approaches and maturities (see also Chapters 1, 5 and 6).

Unfortunately, this is not a new problem or one that has been solved in the older, more general discipline of ergonomics. Duncan (1972) stated 'task analysis is not without its difficulties. The techniques which have been advocated are legion and poorly developed'. In this case, he was highlighting the need for task analysis in the development of programmed instruction, but the problems were basically the same. New techniques were continually being suggested, but few were taken further and developed into rigorous

* Now with R.M. Consultants, Warrington.
† Now with Technika Ltd., London.

techniques. Duncan advocated the use of Hierarchical Task Analysis (HTA), which had undergone development in the context of training for industrial tasks since its introduction five years previously (Annett and Duncan, 1967). The emphasis in the development of the techniques was very much upon the pragmatics of the technique as a way of providing an explicit and legible model of operator task activities, though the overall structure of the technique was based upon theoretical models of human information processing. Since these early beginnings, HTA has been in constant use within the general discipline of ergonomics, undergoing some minor modifications (Shepherd, 1976; Piso, 1981), but otherwise being substantially unchanged, applied primarily to industrial process types of tasks (see Drury, 1983).

This chapter begins by examining the role of task analysis methods in the design of human–computer interactions. A partial model of the cognitive processes involved in interaction with computers is presented first, forming the basis for a discussion of the mapping and analysis processes underlying task analysis methods. The second part of the chapter then examines the use of HTA in the design of human–computer interactions. Recently, we have had occasion to apply HTA directly to human–computer interactions and it is our experiences with using HTA in this context which form the remainder of the chapter.

1.   THE ROLE OF TASK ANALYSIS METHODS IN THE DESIGN OF HUMAN–COMPUTER INTERACTIONS

Before specifically discussing HTA, it is useful to examine in general terms the roles that task analysis can play in the design of human–computer interaction. This requires some examination of the cognitive processes involved in human–computer interaction and consideration of the stages of the design process to which task analysis can contribute.

1.1   Cognitive processes involved in human–computer interactions

At the outset it must be stated that human interaction with computing devices is a complex process which is still only vaguely understood, but a number of commonly accepted principles do exist upon which this account is based.

1.1.1   *System designers' conceptual model of a computing system*

A useful starting point is to consider the nature of the computing system itself. From the designers' point of view, the system is logically organized around data structures and the processes which operate upon those structures. Actions at the interface initiate processes which make modifications to internal data structures, which then may or may not result in a visible change on the user's display. At one level, therefore, the designers' conceptual view of the computing system operates at the machine level of functioning, in terms of bits, bytes, arrays, offsets, exception handlers, etc. It is hoped that the designers also have developed and employed a complete and consistent conceptual view of the system which operates at a higher level of abstraction. It should be possible to describe the system's functioning in terms of objects such as documents and mail-boxes, and processes such as modifying paragraph attributes and sending a mail message. The combination and interrelation of both conceptual views of the system forms the designers' mental model of the system (see Fig. 2.1).

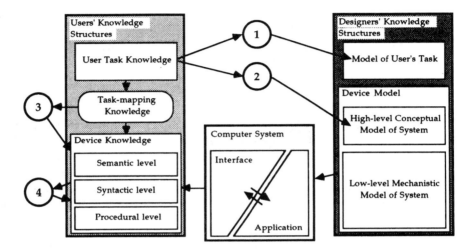

Fig. 2.1 — Role of task analysis in the design of human–computer interaction (numbered arrows indicate the various different roles for task analysis in the design process and are explained in section 1.2.1).

1.1.2 User's conceptual model of a computing system

The user's conceptual model of the system may operate at a number of different levels. Three particular levels of knowledge are identified here; the procedural level, the syntactic level and the semantic level.

1.1.2.1 Procedural level of user knowledge

At the lowest level of sophistication, the user may have been taught or have learnt strict procedures and operate the system by matching command sequences to immediate goals. In this mode of functioning, the users essentially treat the system as a 'black box'; they know what they want to achieve and they know which interface operations achieve that goal, but they have little conception of the precise effects of the commands upon the internal states of computing system. However, most users are unlikely to operate without attempting to form some type of mental model of the system's operation. Without guidance or instruction, this model is likely to be superficial and simplistic and to contain errors. In some cases, such models may involve anthropomorphization of the system, attributing to the system human characteristics and motivations. Such models are also often 'explanatory' in nature, allowing the user to rationalize why observed actions occur, rather than 'predictive', providing the user with the basis for constructing composite or novel commands.

1.1.2.2   Syntactic level of user knowledge

As the user gains experience, he/she may begin to perceive the nature of the internal structure of the system's command language. The consistencies in the syntax of commands, once they are appreciated, are utilized to construct more complex, combined commands or to diagnose input errors. The user may still not understand the more sophisticated aspects of the system's configuration of objects, processes and states, but is now able to step outside of his/her immediate knowledge of command operations to explore the effects of modified or alternative command operations. The users' knowledge now incorporates both the procedural knowledge relating to which command performs what function and additional 'meta-knowledge', defining principles of grouping and syntactic structure. This latter aspect of their knowledge is to some extent predictive in nature, allowing for more advanced forms of interaction.

1.1.2.3   Semantic level of user knowledge

At the highest level of sophistication, the user is made aware of the internal conceptual structure of the computing system. The user's knowledge now extends to cover an understanding of the conceptual objects within the system, the attributes and possible states of those objects and how commands operate upon those objects to modify their attributes and states. It is hoped that the user's conceptual understanding is complete and totally consistent with the design model employed by the system designers. If this is the case, the user is able to reason about the system both to diagnose problems that occur during its use and to plan complex operations.

1.1.3   Users' device knowledge — designing for effective learning

In most circumstances, it is clearly desirable that users are able to acquire rapidly system knowledge at the semantic level. Recent trends in the design of user interfaces have been directed towards that goal. For example, the desktop metaphor (Canfield Smith *et al.*, 1982; also discussed by Johnson in Chapter 5) was an explicit attempt to induce concrete conceptual models within users by the metaphorical use of everyday office objects and the reinforcement of the metaphor by the use of visual representation and direct manipulation.

In order to facilitate learning at the semantic level, there are a number of important rules that must be followed:

- Firstly, the system designers must develop and utilize a complete and self-consistent conceptual model of the system (Moran, 1981).
- The conceptual model and the interaction language that operates upon it should be efficient from the user's viewpoint. Unnecessary diversity in the types of conceptual objects, types of conceptual actions and the

wide-spread use of exceptions to rules is likely to result in a system which is difficult to learn.

- The model should be in terms which the user is already familiar with, or could be taught easily. It should be noted that this does not necessarily imply that metaphor should be used. In fact, there are strong arguments for avoiding metaphor in some cases (see Halasz and Moran, 1982).
- The model should be explicitly reinforced in the system interface, in supporting documentation and during training. As implied above, visual representation and direct manipulation may help.

The onus is upon the system designers to consider very carefully the type of conceptual model thay want the eventual users of the system to adopt. Unless the system is specifically designed for programmers, understanding of the system should not rely upon knowledge of low-level computing concepts that have direct or indirect influence upon the interface image the designers wish to communicate to system users. An example of where this can be a problem is where hidden control characters are employed in word-processing systems for formatting purposes. The characters directly affect the visible representation of the text and yet the computing-naive user is frequently unaware of their existence. This can result in confusion and loss of confidence in the system, as the visable representation of the text appears to respond in an unpredictable manner. Many word-processing systems now provide an option to 'show invisibles' which introduces a whole new class of objects to the user's conceptual model of the system, increasing the initial learning load whilst ensuring the integrity of the user's conceptual model.

1.1.4   Users' task knowledge — designing for effective use

The designers can clearly exercise some control over the user's cognition regarding the structures and operations within a computing system, but this is only part of the cognitive processes in operation in human–computer interactions. Most computer systems are employed within occupational contexts, where the users have specific tasks to complete within a framework of task-related goals and objectives. In this respect, computer systems can be viewed as just another tool in the workplace, similar in their status to typewriters, photocopiers and so on. Users bring tasks to the system which have been defined within their occupational role, such as 'write a letter', 'send a message to a colleague' or 'perform statistical tests upon a set of numbers'. They may also have criteria of satisfactory task completion which they apply in the selection of the appropriate computer system and software package, such as 'the letter must look professional', 'a quick reply is required to this message' or 'the statistical tests would benefit from a graphical presentation of results'. Therefore, task cognition impinges upon the design of a computer system in the degree to which it defines the required functionality of the system, in the extent to which working practices in the external task domain must be accommodated within the internal system domain and the degree to which task-specific assistance can be given.

The relationship between user tasks and system functions, however, is rarely as simple as has been implied (this is also discussed in Chapter 4 and 6, in particular). Computer systems frequently introduce additional functions and options which expand and amplify task objectives. For example, it may no longer be considered satisfactory to generate typed reports in single drafts with hand-drawn graphics, when word processors enable multiple drafts to be produced easily and can incorporate high-quality computer-generated graphics. In other contexts, computers are rapidly becoming an essential and integral component of the task, through which medium the majority of task actions are performed. There is no aspect of choice in these circumstances, though task objectives may still be defined in a manner which is external to the system context (for example, process operation is largely computer based, though objectives are still stated in terms of overall system objectives such as 'maximize efficiency', 'minimize loss', 'maintain safety' and in terms of specific tasks such as 'start stand-by pump', 'reduce pressure', etc.). Only in a few limited cases are user tasks entirely defined within the context of the computer system such as the task of a computer operator or data-processing operator.

At this point, it is worthwhile drawing attention to a fundamental difference that exists between interaction in command and control systems and interaction in other types of systems. In command and control applications, most user or operator tasks involve interaction with objects external to the computer system in the form of process plant, aircraft, vehicles, ships or personnel. Task cognition, therefore, is related to objects and states external to the system. In contrast, in most other contexts, the objects the user interacts with can be conceived of as being internal to the computer system. Such internal objects are open to modification and redefinition as appropriate and form the elements of the system conceptual model with which the user interacts.

The use of a computer system involves the users in 'mapping' their task-related goals onto their understanding of the structures and functionality of a computer system. They will possess task-related knowledge providing task goal structures and skills, along with system-specific knowledge to some degreee of sophistication. In addition, they will gradually accumulate special knowledge regarding how to map task goals onto the structures provided by the system. The complexity of such 'task-mapping knowledge' depends partly upon the efforts of the system designers in understanding user task needs. It follows that system use may be convoluted in circumstances where the designers have designed a system around their personal and limited view of user task requirements. However, there are exceptions where a complex task mapping may be considered legitimate:

- With the goals of producing a concise and consistent system conceptual model in mind, in some circumstances it may prove to be more efficient to employ a system structure which is radically different to existing computer or paper-based versions.

- Many systems are designed to be general purpose and to meet the needs of wide variety of users. While it is expected that the designers would carry out some form of user requirements analysis, the resulting system is unlikely to meet all the requirements of all the users all of the time.

However, neither of these two exceptions changes the general rule, that in designing efficient human–computer interactions, it is a necessary part of the design process to investigate and document user task knowledge, in order to contribute both to decisions regarding the functionality of the future system and in the optimization of user–system interaction.

1.2 Contribution of task analysis methods in the design of human–computer interactions

1.2.1 Applications at different stages of system design

Based on the description of user knowledge given above, analytic techniques may be applied in a number of different stages in the design of human–computer systems.

1.2.1.1 User requirements (Arrow 1 in Fig. 2.1)

During the initial stages of design, task analysis methods are needed which capture the overall basic dimensions of current and future user tasks. For example, the MOD–DTI Human Factors Guidelines (Gardner and McKenzie, 1988) recommended that each task function is documented ('users' models') along with performance targets for each function ('goal specification'). Such analyses form the basis for stating user requirements as an early input to system design. They may help in decisions regarding the allocation of overall system functions between human and machine and establish the required functional scope of the computing component.

1.2.1.2 Conceptual design (Arrow 2 in Fig. 2.1)

The next stage involves mapping the task description onto the detailed design of the computer system interface. Ideally, the mapping will be carried out in a 'top-down' manner, beginning with task description, then specifying the mapping between task goals and operations upon system objects, continuing through successive levels of refinement until the details of individual input actions have been specified. This is the rationale behind Moran's Command Language Grammar (CLG) (Moran, 1981) which, despite its complexities in use (e.g. Sharratt, 1987), still provides a valuable role model.

In some circumstances, it may be possible to map directly between the task description and the system conceptual model, representing existing objects in the task domain as conceptual objects within the system domain and allowing analogous object manipulations to be performed wherever appropriate. In these cases, the task description will need to contain a great deal of detail regarding user task cognition, in the form of user knowledge relating to task goals, objects, actions and cognitive skills (e.g. TAKD in

Chapter 4; KAT–TKS in Chapter 5 and ATOM in Chapter 6). In other cases, the mapping may be much more superficial, simply mapping task functions onto the structure of system functions.

1.2.1.3   Evaluation of conceptual design (Arrows 3 and 4 in Fig. 2.1)

Once the interface design is complete, it is possible to evaluate the demands it makes upon users. A range of analysis methods exist which essentially analyze the task of using the system. A limited group focus on the analysis of the efficiency of the task to system mapping by measuring the extent of 'task-mapping knowledge' required (e.g. ETIT: Moran, 1983). A much more substantial group focus upon an analysis of user device knowledge (e.g. Reisner, 1982; TAG Chapter 3; GOMS: Card et al., 1983; CCT: Kieras and Polson, 1985; and this is also discussed by Johnson in Chapter 5).

1.2.1.4   User evaluation

There is use for task analysis in the later stages of evaluation in the design and interpretation of data from user evaluation trials. With the availability of a full tasks description, it is possible to ensure that a representative range of user tasks are subjected to rigorous evaluation. At the same time, behavioural data from the trials can be more easily interpreted when there is a detailed task analysis acting as a normative description of behaviour.

1.2.1.5   Documentation and training

Once the design of the system has stabilized, the task analysis information may be utilized in the development of documentation, tutorial materials and training programmes.

1.2.1.6   Support in use

Task analysis documentation is also likely to be of great use during the processes of system maintenance. Without a clear statement of the reasons behind the incorporation of each system feature and a description of the conceptual design of user–system interaction, modifications are likely to be made which violate the original design intention.

1.2.1.7   Post-mortem analysis

Finally, fully detailed task analysis documentation would also be valuable for the process of 'reverse engineering', where reasons for the particular success of a system, or, as is more likely, reasons for the failure of a system, are established by tracing back decisions throughout the process of system design.

1.2.2   The complexities and opportunities in task–system mapping

Our involvement with task analysis and the design of human–computer systems has primarily been concerned with the first two stages described above; user requirements definition and conceptual design. The key element in both of these stages is the process involved in mapping the collected task information onto the conceptual and detailed design of user–system interaction (note: this issue is discussed further by Diaper in Chapter 4 and is the main theme of Chapter 6 by Walsh). In an ideal world, this mapping would be totally 'prescriptive' such that, once an accurate and complete task description has been produced, it would be possible to apply logical, defined rules to transform it directly into a detailed system specification (Fig. 2.2).

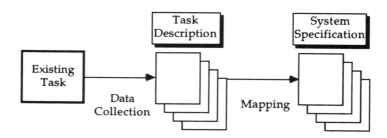

Fig. 2.2 — Idealized mapping between user tasks and system design.

Unfortunately, the reality is far from the ideal. This assumes that the objective of system design is to duplicate existing task practices in all their detail, even when they are inefficient or limited in scope. Additional functionality, the provision of new or synthesized information or increases in the speed and responsiveness of the system can each result in significant changes in task configuration and content. In this respect, user requirements and tasks are a moving goal: a new system provides new task opportunities which in turn generate a new additional set of requirements. Within SSADM (e.g. Downs *et al.*, 1988) this problem is refered to as 'the paradox of change' and has been extensively commented upon by others:

> *Current practice in a task is frequently tied to the existing techno-*
> *logy employed in the task and it is therefore difficult to produce a*
> *creative, novel solution to system design based on such methods.*
> *(Diaper, 1986, 1987)*

Furthermore, as has been mentioned earlier, the most efficient form of system conceptual model may not be one that directly reflects the object and action structures of the existing task configuration. However, while bearing these constraints and conditions in mind, there are aspects of task information that can potentially be mapped directly from a task description to a system design.

1.2.2.1 Task functions
The most basic form of mapping is between the functional components of user tasks and the functionality of the system. This is achieved in the process

of allocating functions between human and machine, where individual task functions are allocated to the machine component, retained as a human task or subdivided to form interpendent human and machine subtasks. Unless the overall scope of user responsibilities is reduced or expanded as a planned part of system development, the description and allocation of task functions provides a very useful framework in defining system scope.

1.2.2.2   Information input and output requirements

In describing user tasks, it is possible to identify where information in generated or communicated by the task incumbent and where it is sought or received. In most cases, information output from the user will define information input to the computer system and vice versa. This is unlikely to define the totality of system input and output, since further system-specific input and output relating to the control of the system itself will be required and, in addition, changes in task responsibilities resulting from the allocation process may alter information input and output requirements. For this form of analysis, the task attributes approach of Smolensky et al. (1984) appears to hold promise.

Further to the identification of inputs and outputs, it should be possible to characterize the nature of both the information input into the system and the required outputs. For information input, it should be possible to establish the type of information that is entered (numerical, locational, alphabetical) and its major quantificational variables (volume, frequency). This form of data is useful in the specification of input devices and dialogue type (Carey, 1985). For information output, the type of information, the amount of information and the task use to which it is to be put largely defines the form and presentation of the display (a modification of HTA for such purposes is described later in section 2.2.2.3). The processes involved in this type of mapping are fairly well developed for discrete control and display interfaces (Meister, 1971; Chapter 3), but still requires development for interactive controls and displays.

1.2.2.3   Task objects

Part of the task analysis process can involve the identification of the specific objects and classes of objects that are acted upon, generated and interacted with during task performance (note: with some variations in definition, the concept of task objects is dicussed by all the chapters in this book). Some of these objects will, of course, remain outside of the scope of the computer system, but others will need to be accounted for within it. In this respect, establishing the class structure, behaviour and instantiations of task objects is very important. In some cases, identified objects will be mapped directly onto objects within the conceptual structure of the system. In such circumstances, it is vital to replicate the behaviour and class structure of the objects faithfully, clearly signalling any unavoidable divergences where they occur. Alternatively, an entirely different conceptual object structure may be implemented, but the relationship between the task object structure and the conceptual structure of the system still needs to be established.

In command and control applications, however, it can be argued that a good interface would be largely transparent to the user. This goal requires the system to have a minimal conceptual structure, since user device knowledge should primarily be related to the external system under the user's control. Under these circumstances, the most obvious method of interface implementation is to provide a replica of each external physical object at the interface (note: this is not always optimal; Duncan *et al.*, 1989).

1.2.2.4   Task methods
For most task domains, the introduction of a new computing system will result in new methods of working being developed in order to achieve task goals. However, some existing methods and procedures will still remain valid, either because the ordering of tasks is externally controlled (e.g. legislation, standard procedures, imposed timescales) or because of logical precedence and causality. In these cases, it is possible to consider mapping the sequence of operations within a task method onto sequential constraints of procedural aids in the system (e.g. task displays and computerized operating procedures for use in power stations (Umbers and Jenkinson, 1989); also, task sequences are discussed in most of the chapters of this book). For the remainder of the task methods, it is at least possible to take into account existing methods of working in deriving prototypes of their replacements.

In summary, the complex interaction between task behaviour and the tools employed renders it virtually impossible to derive the conceptual design of a human–computer system directly from task information. However, it is possible to make partial mappings along the four dimensions described.

2.   HTA IN THE DESIGN OF HUMAN–COMPUTER INTERACTIONS
The use of HTA in the development of training programmes is well established (see Chapter 1 by Shepherd), but its use in the design of interfaces and its application to human–computer systems is poorly documented. There are a few notable exceptions such as the analysis of air traffic control tasks (Crawley *et al.*, 1980), the investigation of tasks in process control (Piso, 1981) and the design of control panels (Hodgkinson and Crawshaw, 1985). Though our experience has indicated that many individuals within the disciplines of ergonomics are familiar with HTA and many report having used it within projects, there is little actual documented evidence of its use. In addition, even though HTA is better documented than most comparable task analysis techniques (e.g. Annett *et al.*, 1971; Patrick *et al.*, 1985), there is a paucity of worked examples and limited practical guidance on applying HTA outside of its training context. It is therefore difficult for those unfamiliar with the technique to evaluate its potential in a particular design context without applying it first. Many of the chapters in this book make a similar point and this is, in part, the *raison d'être* for its publication.

Research at Aston, focused primarily in the domain of command and control systems, has made wide use of HTA. The technique was found useful in isolating air traffic control tasks by Crawley *et al.* (1980). These tasks were then assessed by controllers in terms of skill content and job satisfaction. An HTA of a simulated naval command data-handling system provided the basis for studies of human–computer dialogue design and of training provision for users of that system (Stammers and Morrisroe, 1985; Hallam and Stammers, 1985). Recent projects involving process control and military command and control applications have been directly concerned with the design of human–computer interaction in these contexts. In both cases, we have had occasion to utilize HTA, applying it to establish task overviews through direct interaction with operators and developing extensions to the method to facilitate the mapping of task information onto display design. Through these efforts, we have had considerable opportunity to evaluate the strengths and weaknesses of HTA in relation to human–computer interaction, albeit within the limited context of command and control systems. The remainder of this chapter explores the issues raised and considers the future prospects for the development of HTA and other similar techniques.

2.1   Extent and limits of HTA in the representation of cognitive task behaviour

As has been explained previously by Shepherd (Chapter 1), there are two main interrelated forms of task representation within HTA. The most familiar of the two forms of representation is the hierarchical diagram, this indicates how an overall task can be decomposed into component operations. However, far more information is contained within the accompanying tables which present descriptions of the plans that govern the sequencing and selection of subordinate operations within the task and may include a variety of other information such as explanatory notes, information on decisions regarding the grain of analysis, direct analysis statements regarding interface or system requirements, task inputs and outputs. HTA therefore has the potential to incorporate a wide variety of task information within its representational format, assuming that the information can be related to its fundamental hierarchical view of behavioural organization.

The hierarchical structure of HTA is based upon the decomposition of an overall task into subtasks, each task described in terms of its objective. The tasks can be concerned with physical or cognitive activity, embedded within the universal 'goal hierarchy' provided by the technique.

The theoretical underpinnings for the hierarchical organization of HTA are given by Duncan (1974). Referring to the then current theories on the acquisition of skills, he notes how the learning process tends to involve changes from smaller to larger units of performance. Studies of Morse telegraphists and typists indicated a progression from operating with single letters, to syllables, to words and finally to phrases. A theoretical model accounting for the hierarchical nature of skilled behaviour was available in the influential work of Miller *et al.* (1960). The idea of behaviour having an underlying hierarchical organization still has its proponents within cognitive psychology. For example, Anderson (1983) suggests how declarative task knowledge is gradually aggregated into units of procedural knowledge during the process of learning. The concept of goal hierarchies is integral to other task analysis techniques such as GOMS (Card *et al.*, 1983) and has been the subject of psychological investigation (e.g. Robertson and Black, 1983).

In this respect, HTA is related to many of the other techniques described in this book which claim some degree of psychological validity. For example, in TAKD (Diaper, Chapter 4) it is claimed that the task descriptive hierarchy (TDH) has an isomorphic structure with respect to the validity of the TDH's contents. Similarly, within TAG (Payne and Green, Chapter 3) it is claimed that 'simple tasks are a psychological construct'.

However, the assumption underlying HTA that behaviour is hierarchically organized has not been adopted without challenge. Becker (1975) provides some very powerful counterarguments, suggesting that hierarchical organization is artificially imposed upon streams of human behaviour and that current notions of goals have been the result of a considerable amount of undisciplined thinking. It is unclear whether writers on HTA have necessarily assumed that the hierarchical representation was anything more than a convenient structure imposed by the analyst on information generated from task incumbants.

In addition to the hierarchical structure of HTA, the other major components of behavioural description which it contains are in the form of plans. These describe how component suboperations are combined to produce the behaviour described by the superordinate operation or task. Often represented in the form of a flow chart (refer to Shepherd, Chapter 1, for examples) or in the form of prose, plans state how suboperations are performed in sequence or in parallel or how one operation is selected from amongst alternatives. The combination of plans and operations can be used to describe quite complex behaviour, such as problem solving, where the plan would describe the heuristics applied and the operations would describe the fundamental range of operations that could be applied according to the heuristic in the problem solving process. In this manner, classic problem solving behaviour such as the solution of cryptarithmetic problems (Newell and Simon, 1972) could be described in terms of the means–end analysis heuristic and the set of potential operators which could be applied to generate a transformation of state in the problem space.

HTA clearly has the potential to represent a wide range of behaviour, including goal structures and cognitive decision-making activities. In fact, its features directly parallel the structures of early cognitive task analysis techniques such as the BNF formulation of Reisner (1982) and GOMS (Card *et al.*, 1983). Both the BNF and GOMS techniques are decompositional and represent the sequencing and selection of suboperations (note: the BNF notation underlies the TAG methodology as described by Payne and Green in Chapter 3 and the GOMS approach has been used as the starting point by many of the methods described in this book, such as Johnson, Chapter 5). In addition, the selection rules component of GOMS is directly equivalent to the plans within HTA. However, HTA does have some significant missing components when applied as a general technique to human–computer interaction.

Unlike the other methods described in this book (TAG, TAKD, KAT–TKS and ATOM; Chapters 3–6 respectively), HTA has no formal means of representing objects within the task domain. Apart from the definitional value of object descriptions, the combination of structured action and object representations provides a means of generating 'generic' task descriptions, allowing common behaviours to be identified and task information from a range of users to be rationalized.

In command and control applications, the requirement for an object representation is even more stringent. The object is a dynamic system in this case, and one that can change state or generate events outside of the direct control of the operator. However, the dynamic system can be considered to be part of the operator's task environment and it is extremely difficult to describe operator actions without linking them to present and potential future system states and events. Piso (1981) recognized this problem and preceded the use of HTA by an analysis of the process itself, but the process analysis was not linked in to the HTA as an integral element. In contrast, new cognitive task analysis methods are being developed for process control applications that explicitly model process states and link them to operator actions (Hollnagel, 1984). In a similar manner, an analytic technique developed for describing air traffic control tasks explicitly links behavioural sequences to airspace events (Phillips and Tischer, 1984).

Finally, as mentioned earlier, HTA has difficulty in representing global goals or responsibilities such as 'maintain safety', 'minimize aircraft fuel consumption' or 'maximize visual impact' that might apply respectively to process operation, air traffic control and document production. Such goals can be essential constraints in the planning and organization of behaviour and yet are difficult to fit within the hierarchical structure of HTA or to incorporate within plans.

In summary, HTA has a wider application to cognitive tasks than is often implied, offering an action-oriented approach to behavioural description that incorporates goal structures and means of specifying the sequencing and selection of actions. It does not claim to be a knowledge representation technique and is limited in its inability to adequately represent domain objects and global goals.

2.2   The role of HTA in the design of human–computer interactions

Apart from its classic role in the development of training programs, HTA may be applied in the first two stages of the design process as defined earlier; establishing user requirements and in contributing to conceptual design.

2.2.1   User requirement definition

The most effective use of HTA is at an early stage in the design process, where the requirement is to establish the scope of user tasks as part of the basic functional specification of the proposed system. There are a number of advantages in HTA when used in this way:

- The decompositional nature of the hierarchical task descriptions can assist the analysts in structuring their data collection and documentation activities. It is possible to focus on parts of the task description without losing an appreciation of the overall picture of task activities and the top-down nature of the method assists in ensuring completeness.
- HTA can be applied as a rough-and-ready tool at this stage of the design process, with little need for extensive detail in the grain of analysis or in the plan elements.
- The hierarchical diagrams are relatively easy to understand by the task incumbents, enabling the diagrams to be used as a tool for initial data collection and for subsequent confirmation.
- The clarity and structure of the hierarchical representation is also of assistance in providing information for system designers. At this early stage of design, it enables the breadth and diversity of task activity to be appreciated, whilst the numbering system for tasks may help in systematizing the decision-making process.

Three aspects of the task analysis process are important at this stage; rapid completion, clear communication and overall completeness for accurate specification. With regard to rapid completion, it may be used in an outline form at this stage, speeding up the development process, but the production of the diagrams can cause a bottleneck. Fortunately, generic computer-based tools, such as graphics and outlining programs, are increasingly becoming available, these can significantly reduce the effort involved. Once produced, the diagrams are an aid to communication compared with grammar-based representations, but they can cause some problems of understanding, since accurate comprehension of the meaning of lower level tasks often requires an appreciation of the position of the task within the overall hierarchy which can be difficult to achieve. Also, an appreciation of the relevant plan is required for the interpretation of each subhierarchy. The addition of plan graphics to the hierarchical diagram can be of assistance in this respect (e.g. Shepherd's modifications as described in the Chapter 1). HTA scores most strongly on the completeness criteria.

2.2.2 Conceptual design
As design progresses, the level of detail and the accuracy of the task description increase in importance. Ambiguities, missing information or errors may result in costly mistakes during design. The representational technique, therefore, needs to possess a high degree of rigour in specifying how information should be recorded and subsequently interpreted. The technique should also specify how the multiple, and possibly competing,

views of those contributing to the task description are to be resolved in order to generate a generic task description. Finally, there should be some guidance provided on how to map from the task description onto the design of the system.

2.2.2.1   Rigour of representational techniques

HTA possesses a number of potential shortcomings with respect to its rigour in defining how the task hierarchy should be constructed. Ideally, the decomposition of tasks would be a carefully regulated process, so that the resulting structure reflected the actual underlying organization of task activity. However, without precise guidance, the process of decomposition tends to be unduly influenced by the desire to produce a 'neat' hierarchy. Patrick *et al.* (1985), for example, suggest that each task should be divided into about four to eight subtasks, which makes no allowance for the case where a task is clearly identified as containing either less than four or more than eight component subtasks. In such a case, the analyst is tempted either to aggregate together or to subdivide tasks for the purpose of creating order. There is also a tendency to attempt to achieve symmetry across the levels of the hierarchy such that closely related tasks at the level of the hierarchy are at an approximately equivalent grain size. The earlier guidance on applying HTA (Annett *et al.*, 1971) had envisaged application of the redescription rule leading to breakdown ceasing at a number of different levels of description. At present, the procedures adopted by analysts in generating task hierarchies in HTA are idiosyncratic and open to widespread variation. There is a need for a set of rules, similar to those developed by Diaper (1988a) for use with TAKD (see also Diaper, Chapter 4), that would standardize the approach adopted to the decomposition of tasks.

A further problem of lack of rigour exists in the naming of tasks. HTA does possess a convention for task naming, specifying an activity verb followed by a noun phrase, such as 'monitor pressure' or 'enter client data'. It is advised that vague words such as 'understand' or 'know' are avoided, but it is still possible to end up with ambiguous names. Patrick *et al.* (1985) suggest that a list of activity verbs with their definitions be maintained. Duncan (1972) advises that the natural language of the task environment should be used in the analysis. These terms may subsequently have to be learned by trainees and other involved in the system. The problem stems from the ambiguities in natural language and is solved in other analysis techniques by the use of more precise grammatical representations.

2.2.2.2   Generic task description

HTA offers no solution to the problem of how to combine multiple task descriptions from different users to form a generic task description. In contrast, TKS (Johnson, Chapter 5) incorporates a well-specified procedure for the generation of a generic knowledge description from the data provided by individuals from the target population.

2.2.2.3 Task–design mapping

The mapping from task information to the design of target system is the primary objective of the task analysis process. This topic is addressed by most of the chapters in this book and is the central concern of Walsh's ATOM methodology (Chapter 6). However, in the published accounts of where HTA has been used in interface design, the method of mapping is generally left unspecified (e.g. Hodgkinson and Crawshaw, 1985). There is a significant gap between the data in the form of task description and the derived solution. In such cases, the link between data and solution was probably more inductive than deductive, drawing upon the analyst's background knowledge and design skills. For simple panel interfaces this is probably sufficient, but the complexities of human–computer interactions demand a more rigorous, deductive approach.

Referring to the four methods of mapping identified earlier in the chapter. HTA has the potential to provide the information for three out of the four methods. Firstly, the task hierarchy within HTA provides a clear description of all task functions for mapping on to the new human–computer system. Secondly, HTA is ideally suited to the identification and mapping of information input and output requirements in system design. Additional columns can easily be added to the table within HTA to accommodate abstracted information on task inputs and outputs. Finally, HTA supports the identification and mapping of task methods onto system design through the clear description of methods given in the form of plans. The major shortcoming of HTA with respect to its value in interface design is its lack of any independent representation of task objects which may be mapped directly or indirectly onto conceptual objects within the system.

As an example of adapting the technique for determining input and output requirements, some work we have conducted in a process control context can be briefly described (Astley and Stammers, 1987). This work was aimed at developing a technique for extracting task information in order to improve computer system display design. A survey of existing techniques suggested HTA as the most appropriate approach, but also one that has some shortcomings for extracting user information requirements. Whilst the basic form of HTA provided a useful structure for the task information, it failed to make all the necessary information available.

A first modification was a change in the redescription rule during the initial breakdown. The $P \times C$ stopping rule was not found relevant to this context (see Shepherd, Chapter 1). Tasks were broken down to the point where the relevant individual items of information could be specified (cf. Piso, 1981). It was also not found to be appropriate to 'err on the gross side', as had been recommended in a training context for deciding an appropriate level of description (Annett et al., 1971). The aim was a complete analysis of information needs and as such it was felt more appropriate to err on the side of caution.

The basic HTA could be used to represent information on what were the conditions governing the execution of operations and also what was their temporal ordering. This was achieved by using the Shepherd (1976) method of representing 'plans'. The table format suggested by Shepherd required three extra elements to be introduced. There was firstly the need to specify the nature of the information flow across the interface. The information the operator needs from the system to carry out the operation was recorded here. In turn, the information that the operators communicated to the system was also specified. An additional column was added to the table for this. A second additional column was introduced to enable the analyst to specify a 'context' for the information. In this column, the analyst had to make a statement on the information that it must be assumed the operator needs at this stage in the task. Such information may be possessed by the operator as a result of previous training, be obtained from manuals, etc. or be available from the displays in the system. The final column involved the classification of the operation in terms of a taxonomy of process control task types (e.g. monitoring, prediction, etc.). This provided additional context information for the subsequent design activities. Although Duncan (1974) has argued against the use of psychological category schemes as being premature, in this context the taxonomy was invoked in the spirit of Miller's (1967) working tool idea. The aim was to produce a scheme to aid design decisions and not be concerned with its theoretical soundness. The analysis document thus produced then formed the basis of mapping activities from task classification to display type.

2.3 The future of HTA as a method for Human–Computer Interaction design

HTA is now over 20 years old and is still widely used within ergonomics. The strengths of the technique lie in the outward simplicity of the form of its hierarchical diagrams, coupled with the flexibility of the associated tables. This has enabled successive users to make minor modifications as and when necessary to suit particular application requirements. It also has the benefit of being capable of application at different levels of detail to suit the occasion. There is no reason to doubt that it will continue to survive as a general technique for some years to come.

The future applicability of HTA to Human–Computer Interaction design, however, it much more in question. Two trends in particular are likely to affect its future prospects: the gradual integration of task analysis techniques into the structured analysis and design methods of software engineering, and the development of computer-based tools for Human–Computer Interaction design. While HTA is useful in the user requirements definition phase of system design, there is nothing particularly remarkable about any single aspect of HTA that it cannot be replaced by other representational methods which are more compatible with current practice in software engineering (e.g. Walsh, Chapter 6). The development of computer-based tools has already had an effect in the short term on the prospects for HTA, since text outlining tools are ideally suited to the quick production and revision of hierarchical analyses. In the longer term, computer-based tools will also have the effect of facilitating the use of other much more sophisticated cognitive task analysis methods, reducing the usability and legibility advantages that HTA possesses at present. Shepherd (Chapter 1) suggests the use of currently available software tools to aid HTA analysis and Diaper (Chapter 4), supported by Johnson (Chapter 5), discusses the need for the development of specialized software for specific task analysis techniques. It is hoped that the wealth of practical lessons that have been learnt from using HTA in a wide range of applications will not be lost in the process of transition to new approaches.

3

Task–Action Grammar: the model and its developments

Stephen J. Payne
Departments of Psychology and Computing, University of Lancaster
T. R. G. Green
MRC Applied Psychology Unit and Rank Xerox EuroPARC, Cambridge

The first five sections of this chapter are reprinted (with minor edits) from Payne and Green (1986), in which the task–action grammar (TAG) model is motivated and described. The final two sections are new. The penultimate section of the chapter reviews recent research on TAG, by the authors and by others, that has been developed since the model was initially proposed. The final section briefly sketches some assessment of progress, and some future directions.

1. INTRODUCTION

The definitions of programming languages have frequently been formalized, often in Backus–Naur Form (BNF), a notation which describes generative context-free phrase structuring grammars. The virtue of BNF was originally seen as its unambiguity. Whereas programming languages had previously been described loosely in English, BNF allowed the syntax (though not the semantics) to be expressed precisely. A second virtue was soon found to be that BNF descriptions could be executed by programs, guaranteeing a correspondence between the documentation and the compiler. Yet a third virtue emerged: the descriptions of different languages could be compared through their expression in a uniform, limited meta-language.

Reisner (1977) introduced the term *action language* to describe the command system of interactive devices, and attempted to transport the virtues of BNF into this realm. She also hoped to achieve a fourth virtue, namely, to predict the psychological complexity of the language:

A natural index of the complexity (of a statement) might be the

number of rewrite rules . . . used to describe it . . . By this we mean
to suggest that a BNF description of a language, usually intended to
describe a set of valid statements, may have a *psychological* validity.

Reisner went on to propose an experimental search for a 'single,
consistent, psychological BNF'. To some degree her claims were vindicated;
her analysis of two graphics systems (Reisner, 1981) signposted areas of
complexity in one of them, which were confirmed by empirical observation.

In this article we, like Reisner, offer a formalization of interface
languages. Our formalism is intended to model the mental representation of
the interface language and so to allow a formal specification of the language
as perceived by the user. Of course, this goal is ambitious; we will be
satisfied if our formal specifications reflect some important aspects of the
perceived structure. This formalism must therefore readily express those
characteristics that are salient to the user, and will thus address many of the
characteristics that determine usability, particularly configural properties.

We aim to capture the notion of regularity or *consistency*. Consistency is
difficult to define and therefore difficult to measure, but it is informally
recognized to be a major determinant of learnability. The advantages of
consistency lie in facilitating generalizations by the user, who having learned
some parts of the system can then infer others.

A language can be consistent at several different levels, but at each level
the key properties that determine consistency are *configural*, in that they
relate to the overall structure of the language, rather than to the nature of
individual task–action mappings.

To illustrate the notion of consistency, and describe informally the space
of phenomena we intend to address, we present a series of examples.
Although we have labelled these examples according to the level of linguistic
description at which the interesting properties seem to emerge, we do not
pretend to offer a taxonomy of consistency. We recognize that the boundaries between syntax and semantics are fuzzy and theory dependent, but we
have chosen examples which seem comfortably classifiable. A really useful
taxonomy of consistency must wait to be stated in terms of a psychological
theory, rather than linguistic abstractions.

Syntactic consistency. Some forms of consistency are syntactic in nature.
BNF can only capture a weak version, namely the consistent use of one
expression as a common element in other expressions. The term *arithmetic
expression*, for instance, might well be an element common to rules for
assignment statements, array bounds, Boolean expressions, and statements.
In command languages it is sometimes the case that every command has an
identical form, perhaps a single letter followed by carriage return. This is a
second example of *common structure*, a syntactic consistency that BNF
grammars can display

However, there are often *family resemblances* between syntax rules that
are simply not expressible in BNF. An example of family resemblance is
shown in Fig. 3.1. The three separate types of sequence exhibit a clear

⟨**declaration sequence**⟩   ::– ⟨**declaration**⟩
                                    | ⟨**declaration sequence**⟩ + ⟨**declaration**⟩
⟨**statement sequence**⟩   ::– ⟨**statement**⟩
                                    | ⟨**statement sequence**⟩ + ⟨**statement**⟩
⟨**letter sequence**⟩   ::– ⟨**letter**⟩
                                    | ⟨**letter sequence**⟩ + ⟨**letter**⟩

Fig. 3.1 — Family resemblances between syntactic rules. The three rules express a small fragment of a progamming language in BNF. The rules have an obvious resemblance, but that is not directly represented in the grammar, which has no generalized notion of a sequence.

similarity (to the human eye), yet require completely separate BNF rewritings. This kind of syntactic consistency can only be captured by notations that have more expressive power.

Lexical consistency. In natural languages it is usually assumed that lexemes are tied to their meaning by arbitrary connections. For computer languages, in which the lexemes are often English words (or icons, e.g. arrows or waste bins), the relationship is clearly nonarbitrary. The relationship between the extended meanings of words and their use in command languages is complex, but one configural aspect which has been shown to benefit learners is *congruence* — the matching of lexical (external to the command language) and semantic (internal) relations (Carroll, 1982). Congruence is discussed in detail below.

Semantic–syntactic alignment. In the ideally consistent language, semantic relations will be mirrored not only in the lexical or symbolic relations, but also in the structure of commands. If a 'copy file' command requires the existing file to be specified before the new file, then a 'copy disk' command should require the source drive to be specified before the target drive: the task semantics should map onto the language syntax in a consistent way. This point is developed at greater length in section 4.2.

The inverse is also true: a single linguistic element will ideally perform the same semantic function in any context. Green and Payne (1984) noticed that, in a commercial word processing system, the control and escape keys were used to organize the cursor movement semantics, but according to two conflicting *organizing principles*. For some pairs of commands, 'control' and 'escape' would switch between small and large units; in other cases, 'control' and 'escape' determined the direction of movement of the cursor. A language learning experiment confirmed that this conflict troubled learners, to the extent that a language with no meaningful mnemonics, but a single organizing principle, proved reliably easier to learn. A small subset of both of these experimental command languages is shown in Fig. 3.2. (A third language from the experiment, the most easily learned of all, is described later, in Fig. 3.4).

Commands	Language 1	Language 2
Move cursor forward one character	ctrl-F	ctrl-L
Move cursor backward one character	ctrl-B	esc-L
Move cursor forward one word	esc-F	ctrl-E
Move cursor backward one word	esc-B	esc-E
View next screen	ctrl-V	ctrl-C
View previous screen	esc-V	esc-C

Fig. 3.2 — Example commands from two experimental test-editing languages (Green and Payne, 1984). Language 1 is a subset of a commercially available editor, but has conflicting organizing principles. Language 2 has no mnemonic coding, but is organized according to a single principle. [ctrl=control key, esc=escape key.]

Semantic consistency. Our final examples of consistency are properties of the extensional semantics of a language. Again, the key issue is that one part of the language prompts expectations about the remainder. For example, if a word processor allows search for a character string both forward and backward through a file, then we expect it to allow a similar flexibility for a search-and-replace operation. Similarly, in the programming language Pascal, we are disappointed that one can read in values for real identifiers, but not for Boolean identifiers. We term the consistency principle that is being broken here *completeness*. Some richer examples of semantic consistency will be discussed below.

Our central goal in this article is to present a notation for the description of languages which has something to say about all these various aspects of consistency. We attempt to capture generalizations in a psychologically valid manner, and so identify consistency with observable properties of notational descriptions.

Our first efforts toward this goal modelled syntactic generalizations, addressing the family resemblances illustrated here (Payne and Green, 1983). We proposed a context-free variant of van Wijngaarden's two-level grammar (for a good description, see Pagan, 1981), which we called *set-grammar*, because the rewrite rules operated on sets of grammatical objects rather than individual non-terminal or terminal symbols (Payne and Green, 1983). Fig. 3.3 shows the set-grammar representations of the syntactic family resemblances illustrated in Fig. 3.1.

Consistent languages, we argued, could be expressed by a small number of set-grammar rules, whereas inconsistent languages, in which some syntax constructions had little in common with other constructions, could not be reduced to a small number of set-grammar rules. The set-grammar achieved some success as a model of syntactic perception, predicting several laboratory results on the learnability of command languages and miniature artificial languages (Payne, 1985, Payne and Green, 1983). Payne (1985) gave some support to the specific type of family resemblance that was

---

SET
SEQ-ITEMS ::| declaration, statement, letter |
RULE
SEQ-ITEM sequence→**SEQ-ITEM | SEQ-ITEM sequence+SEQ-ITEM**
SELECTION RULE
Uniform replacement — the same element is chosen from the set of **SEQ-ITEM**
throughout the rule

Fig. 3.3 — Set-grammar treatment of family resemblance. The fragment of a
programming language shown in Fig. 3.1 is represented here in the set-grammar
notation (Payne and Green, 1983). The family resemblances are captured by
collapsing three rules into one higher-order rule.

expressible in set-grammars by showing that, of two miniature artificial
languages, the easier to learn was the one predicted by set-grammar,
because fewer set-grammar rules were needed to express its grammar. This
result was promising because the languages were carefully devised so that
their BNF representations predicted the opposite result. However, the
utility of set-grammar as a cognitive model and for the analysis of usability
suffered from a severe shortcoming: it possessed no mechanisms for relating
the syntax of a language to its semantics. Many of the most important
determinants of consistency rely on semantic properties.

The notation presented here supersedes set-grammar and extends its
explanatory power beyond the syntactic realm into the semantics of tasks.
The notation is a grammar describing a mapping from the user's tasks onto
sequences of actions. Because the starting symbols of our grammars are
tasks and the terminal symbols are action specifications, our notation is
called Task Action Grammar (TAG). We use the term *task language* to
describe the intended domain of application of Task-Action Grammars. A
task language is any task action interface between a person and a machine,
including lexical command languages, direct manipulation interfaces, and
knobs-and-dials control panels.

Like other grammars, TAG models competence rather than performance, but we offer sketches of related learning and performance theories
in this chapter. Many of our notational devices, such as the use of a feature
grammar, the representation of concepts as sets of semantic components,
and the notion of a simple or an atomic task, have a basis in cognitive
psychology and psycholinguistics. This basis will also be discussed.

2.   THE AIMS AND NOTATIONAL STRUCTURE OF TAG

In this section we first illustrate the general principles of our notation, which
are those of a feature grammar. This feature grammar describes the
mapping from the task level to the action level. The central aim of TAG is to
formalize that mapping in such a way that simple metrics over the grammar,

such as the number of rules, will predict aspects of the psychological complexity of the mapping. These aspects of complexity include time spent learning, intrusive errors during learning, and the ability to generate a forgotten or unknown part of the language from the remainder. (We discuss metrics and predictions in section 4.) A secondary aim of TAG is to help the analyst to appreciate the structure of a task language.

A TAG is a formal device. Its input is a description of a task as a set of semantic components. (A semantic component is a particular value on a featural dimension; if **Direction** is a feature, then **Direction=right** is a particular value which might be a component of a task definition, such as **move-one-character-to-the-right**). Its operation is that of a generative grammar, and its output is a list of the actions required to perform the input task. Thus TAGs describe not just the syntax of operations used to control the device, but also the relationship between the actions and commands and the user's view of particular tasks.

Obviously, the users of interactive systems have the ability to perceive certain regularities in task action mappings, but not others. When regularities exist and can be perceived, thay can be used to simplify the structure of the mapping, to replace a number of unrelated mapping rules by a single, more general rule. Our choice of formalization makes an implicit theoretical statement about the limits of that ability. For instance, using a standard context-free phrase structure grammar as a representation of the mapping would postulate that users could perceive a hierarchical structure of rules and subrules, but that they were blind to family resemblances between rules.

In describing the general principles and the particular notational conventions, we will show how TAG representations capture the following important attributes of particular mappings (including aspects of consistency discussed in section 1):

- family resemblances, or the overall sentence structure of commands;
- the degree to which a task language relies on well-learned 'world knowledge', in particular on familiar names, such as 'up' for the concept 'upward direction';
- the 'completeness' of a mapping, as opposed to arbitrary absence of expected components;
- the notion of 'congruence', or the representation of semantic relations by equivalent lexical relations (notably, semantic opposition by lexical antonymy);
- the organization of tasks and subtasks, and the alignment of semantic and syntactic aspects of the task language.

2.1   The TAG framework — simple-task dictionary and rule-schema expansion

Fig. 3.4 presents a TAG description of a fragment of an experimental text-editing language used by Green and Payne (1984) and introduced already in Section 1. The description consists of a *simple-task dictionary*, in which simple-tasks are identified and defined by their semantic components, and a

List of commands

Move cursor one character forward	**ctrl-C**
Move cursor one character backward	**meta-C**
Move cursor one word forward	**ctrl-W**
Move cursor one word backward	**meta-W**

TAG definition

DICTIONARY OF SIMPLE TASKS

move-cursor-one-character-forward {Direction=forward, Unit=char}
move-cursor-one-character-backward {Direction=backward, Unit=char}
move-cursor-one-word-forward {Direction=forward, Unit=word}
move-cursor-one-word-backward {Direction=backward, Unit=word}

RULE SCHEMAS

4.1   **task [Direction, Unit]→symbol [Direction]+letter [Unit]**
4.2   **symbol [Direction=forward]→"ctrl"**
4.3   **symbol [Direction=backward]→"meta"**
4.4   **letter [Unit=word]→"W"**
4.5   **letter [Unit=char]→"C"**

Fig. 3.4 — TAG's treatment of cursor control in an experimental text editor.

feature grammar in which the dimensions of those components serve as features. (In more complex examples, it aids exposition to add a third component, an explicit list of possible features and their values. This redundant device has been omitted here.)

The TAG description models the mental representation of a user who has learned the four commands. The simple-task dictionary represents all the tasks the user can routinely perform, and defines each as a set of semantic components. These components are to be used in guiding the *rule-schemas* into generating the required actions for each possible task.

The rule-schemas generate action specifications from simple-tasks in a similar manner to standard phrase-structure grammars, but they have the additional notational power of encapsulating several standard phrase-structure rules in a single rule-schema. In this example, the general task-action rule-schema (rule 4.1) is expanded by assigning the values to all the features in the square brackets, with the constraint that a feature must be assigned with the same value wherever it appears in the rule. A possible result of these assignments is the single-level rewrite rule:

Task [Direction=forward, Unit=word]→
symbol [Direction=forward]+letter [Unit=word]

All tokens now refer to unique grammatical objects (they must; this is a constraint on the features in the square brackets). The simple-task object can be found by looking at the simple-task dictionary; the symbol and letter objects are expanded by further rewrite rules (in this case, rules 4.2 and 4.4), using the standard production-rule grammar mechanism. These operations yield, in the example:

$$\textbf{move-cursor-one-word-forward} \rightarrow \textbf{``ctrl'' + `W'}$$

which is one of the represented commands.

This simple example illustrates most of the important mechanisms of a TAG grammar. The most novel mechanism is the consistent assignment of values to features, combined with the looking up of simple-task descriptors in a dictionary. The strength of the grammar which we have used as this first example is that it allows the basic form of all the task action mappings to be represented in a single higher-level schema (rule 4.1). It captures the observed consistency in the organization of the language due to an organizing principle in the semantic–syntactic alignment.

It is intuitively clear that the design of this language could be improved further by the use of mnemonic codes. Just such an improvement was validated in the experiment of Green and Payne (1984). The TAG description of the advantage is illustrated in the following section.

2.2 Sentence structure, completeness and world knowledge

An important type of consistency in a task language occurs when every command has the same sentence structure. Frequently this structure is a single keypress, which is trivial. A less trivial sentence structure is the postfix-style language structure, as used, for instance, on the Apple Macintosh. Another non-trivial structure is the list of operations, followed by a terminator, familiar to users of TECO and its descendants.

We start by considering an example of a system in which every simple-task is performed by entering a single command name, followed by a carriage return. In this particular system, there are only three commands which are used for moving some object around the screen. The entire task world, therefore, comprises three simple-tasks, which we can denote as follows:

> **move-up {Direction=up}**
> **move-down {Direction=down}**
> **move-right {Direction=right}**

The featural description of each simple-task concept arises from a straightforward *categorization* of the task world. A user who has learned the entire language will represent the dictionary of simple-tasks in this way, reflecting the natural categorization. The features are chosen to describe the important discriminations in the set of simple-tasks; if the current language were extended to include commands that have no movement function, then the direction components of our three tasks would need to be supplemented with a new feature, allowing their specialized movement function to be represented.

If the commands chosen for the three tasks were, for example, **N**, **V**, and **G**, then the user may represent the task-action mappings as follows.

0.1	**task [Direction]→name [Direction]+"RETURN"**
0.2	**name [Direction=up]→"N"**
0.3	**name [Direction=down]→"V"**
0.4	**name [Direction=right]→"G"**

We use this trivially simple grammar to make three points. First, we note that the mapping is incomplete. Because TAG descriptions include a dictionary of simple-tasks and their associated semantic components, it is easy to spot combinations of features that are semantically acceptable but have no associated simple-task. In this example, there is no simple-task with the component {**Direction=left**}. Of course, it is hardly necessary to use a Task-Action Grammar to reveal this particular incompleteness, but, in general, incompleteness can be much harder to spot. Highlighting completeness is a small example of TAG's potential as an analytical device for appreciating the structure of the task language, separate from its main role as a predictor of relative learnability.

Next, the TAG description captures a strong intuition about sentence structure. If a fourth command were to be added, for moving to the left, we would be perplexed if it were not accomplished by typing a single letter followed by **RETURN**. According to the TAG, our difficulty would spring from the fact that a new top-level schema would need to be formed: a special one for the move left command. (Actually, we have not yet represented the fact that every command name in this system is a single letter. TAG can express this, but it depends on a notational device which we have yet to describe.)

Finally, and the main point of this example, we can contrast rules 0.1–0.4 with rules 0.5–0.9 which describe a language in which the arbitrary letters have been replaced by **UP**, **DOWN**, and **RIGHT**.

0.5	**Task [Direction]→name [Direction]+"RETURN"**
0.6	**name [Direction]→known-item [Type=word, Direction]**
0.7	***name [Direction=up]→"UP"**
0.8	***name [Direction=down]→"DOWN"**
0.9	***name [Direction=right]→"RIGHT"**

Since English-speaking users will know that **UP** is the name for the concept, we wish to find a way to differentiate between arbitrary and well-learned names. We do so by constructing a TAG that contains only two effective rules, 0.5 and 0.6, of which rule 0.6 says, 'The subrule for determining the name for a given movement is: use the word that shares the direction feature of the intended movement'. We assume that lexical access to well-learned names is essentially effortless; as long as the semantic components of the task genuinely do bring to mind the required words, the size of the vocabulary is not important. Rules 0.7–0.9 are therefore marked with asterisks to indicate that they should not be included in any simple metrics over the grammar, such as counting the number of rules. We choose to include them in TAG descriptions because all the terminal symbols of the language are then visible, and because assumptions about world knowledge are then open to inspection. (We can determine, for instance, what aspects of a language might give trouble if users come from a different population from the one envisaged by the designer.)

Rules such as 0.6 are called world knowledge rules. Naturally, they need not be exclusively lexical; their right-hand sides can refer to any entities that exist, independently of the task language, in the user's semantic memory. Spatial features of the keyboard or screen are powerful examples. World knowledge rules serve two purposes for the user: they increase the robustness of the grammar in the head, so that a forgotten rule can be regenerated from a world knowledge schema, and they ease the learning load, allowing unlearned rules to be hypothesized from existing ones.

A notational device similar to world knowledge rules is used to denote *action variables* — action specifications that require a feature value to be determined by the user's current goal. Action variables are quite common in command languages. For example, most text editors allow the user to search through a file for any string of characters. The search command will have a set syntax, but the particular string to be searched for is an action variable, whose value is determined by the current goal. Often it is convenient simply to denote action variables with standard quoted terminal symbols, specifying the action weakly by a general label which needs to be replaced by an exemplar. Sometimes, however, if the organization of the task language is to be fully captured, it is necessary to specify features that take values from the goal. Using this convention, a TAG rule for a search command might be:

0.10   **Task [Purpose=search]**→
              "ctrl-S"+action [Type=key, String=value-from-goal]

2.3   Congruence: matching semantic and lexical relationships

An important paper by Carroll (1982) provided empirical evidence in support of a naming principle he called *congruence*. The idea can be illustrated by a small subset of two of his experimental languages, as shown in Fig. 3.5.

Carroll discovered that subjects learning a pencil-and-paper simulation game found the names of language A easier to learn than those of language B. He explained this with reference to the congruence of the name set and the task world; basically, opposite commands are invoked by opposite words. This is a good general principle, and intuitively likely to be a robust influence on usability, beyond individual differences and context effects.

It is not difficult to devise a notational device to express congruence. On the one hand, we have a set of tasks whose semantic components are identical in every respect except one; thus the tasks whose components are |**move,forward**| and |**move,backward**| differ only in the **Direction** feature. On the other hand, we have a set of names for just those semantic components. To express the idea of congruence between the names *advance* and *retreat*, therefore, we need a notation that describes the set of words, choosing between them on the basis of the **Direction** feature.

Rule 5.2 in Fig. 3.5 shows how we do this. It can be read as: 'the name for movement in a given direction is that word which has all the features of advance except the **Direction** feature, which it derives from the current task'. So, if the **Direction** feature is forward, the name is *advance*, if it is backward, the word is *retreat*. Thus, to express the idea of congruent sets, we pick an arbitrary member of the name set (*retreat* would have done just as well as *advance*), use the notation **F("advance")**† to refer to all the semantic components of that word, and then replace the **Direction** feature by the desired direction. Using a single symbol to denote a feature set defining a concept does not add formal power to the TAG notation, and it is, in fact, common practice in the linguistic and psychological literature (e.g. Tversky, 1977).

We are now in a position to compare the TAG descriptions of Carroll's two languages. Language A permits us to use the notational device we have described. Language B does not, because GO and BACK do not form a set differentiated solely by the relevant semantic component **Direction** (neither do **TURN** and **LEFT**). Language B will, therefore, require more rules. Simple metrics, such as the number of rules, suggest that language A will be easier to learn and remember, as Carroll found.

2.4   Task structure, organizational consistency and conflict

Having described the main features of the notation, it remains for us to show how the structure of a more complex interactive system is expressed in these terms. We hope to use this example to demonstrate the secondary function

---

† (Notational remark. Essentially, **F** is a function returning a set of components. We use parentheses to differentiate it from the feature marked non-terminal symbols of the grammar. Because rule 5.2 expresses the idea that 'advance' and 'retreat' share the same semantic attributes, varying only in direction, the notation could be said to embody a view of antonymy that is in keeping with some suggestions in the linguistic literature (e.g. Katz 1972). There is a debate surrounding such logical distinctions as contrast and opposition (Lyons, 1977), but we are merely suggesting that a good nameset will reflect differences and similarities between operations by providing names that vary along the same dimensions as the operators they represent.)

A subset of commands from the languages

	Language A (congruent)	Language B (non-congruent)
Commands the robot to move forward or advance one step	**ADVANCE**	**GO**
Commands the robot to move backwards or retreat (in reverse) one step	**RETREAT**	**BACK**
Commands the robot to change the direction it faces by moving or turning 90° to the right	**RIGHT**	**TURN**
Commands the robot to change the direction it faces by moving or turning 90° to the left	**LEFT**	**LEFT**

TAG descriptions

TASK FEATURES (the same for both languages)

Feature	Possible values
Move/Turn	**move, turn**
Direction	**forward, backward, right, left**

SIMPLE TASKS (the same for both languages)
move-robot-forward {Move/Turn=move, Direction=forward}
move-robot-backward {Move/Turn=move, Direction=backward}
turn-robot-right {Move/Turn=turn, Direction=right}
turn-robot-left {Move/Turn=turn, Direction=left}

RULE SCHEMAS, Language A
5.1   **Task [Move/Turn, Direction]→name [Move/Turn, Direction]**
5.2   **name [Move/Turn=move, Direction]→known-item [Type=word, F("advance"), Direction]**
5.3   ***name [Move/Turn=move, Direction=forward]→"ADVANCE"**
5.4   ***name [Move/Turn=move, Direction=backward]→"RETREAT"**
5.5   **name [Move/Turn=turn, Direction]→known-item [Type=word, F("right"), Direction]**
5.6   ***name [Move/Turn=turn, Direction=right]→"RIGHT"**
5.7   ***name [Move/Turn=turn, Direction=left]→"LEFT"**

RULE SCHEMAS, Language B
5.8   **Task [Move/Turn, Direction]→name [Move/Turn, Direction]**
5.9   **name [Move/Turn=move, Direction=forward]→"GO"**
5.10 **name [Move/Turn=move, Direction=backward]→"BACK"**
5.11 **name [Move/Turn=turn, Direction=right]→"TURN"**
5.12 **name [Move/Turn=turn, Direction=left]→"LEFT"**

Fig. 3.5 — Congruence. TAG's treatment of lexical consistency in two experimental languages from Carroll (1982).

of TAG, as a tool to help the analyst to uncover subtle aspects of the structure of an interface. An important feature to bring out is how subtasks are captured by subrules, thus:

Task→subtask 1+subtask 2

This procedure (which closely resembles subroutining) is assumed to model hierarchical task structure as perceived by the user.

The examples we draw on to illustrate the points must necessarily be rather larger than the smaller ones given previously. We have chosen to present an analysis of an idealized interactive graphics drafting system with a mouse-driven interface, based on Apple Computer's MacDraw program for the Macintosh. This program manipulates graphic objects, such as lines, circles, and rectangles. We suppose that the user perceives four main tasks.

- A new object can be created. The user chooses a 'tool' or object type, from a menu of line, ellipse, rectangle, and arc. The user specifies the location and size by positioning the mouse in the top left corner of the desired location, pressing the mouse button, and 'dragging' the mouse to the bottom right corner. The object is created inside the rectangle thus designated; for example, if an ellipse tool is chosen, an ellipse will be created inside the rectangle, with its origin in the center of the rectangle and its major axis either vertical or horizontal, parallel to the long side of the rectangle. 'Style' attributes, such as line width and filling, are set by default.
- The default style attributes can be altered. The user must point to the appropriate style menu and item within menu.
- The style attributes of an existing object can be altered. The user selects an object, then points to the appropriate style menu and item within menu.
- An existing object can be moved. The user selects an object, then drags it to a new position.

In the genuine MacDraw, users can also delete objects, resize the drawing, write text, and draw freehand. These abilities would add complexity to our description without revealing any further aspects of our notation. A knottier problem that we will not discuss is that users can also manipulate different groups of objects at one time.

2.4.1   Task structure

We first consider the modelling of hierarchical task structure. The main structure of the simple-tasks will be clear from Fig. 3.6, but how does one decide on the detailed structure? This problem confronts any model purporting to describe perceived structures. In the absence of any empirical data on perceived task structure (e.g. in the style of Robertson and Black, 1983), writers of a TAG must use their judgment. One solution to the problem is to base description on the structures presented in the training manual, as was done by Kieras and Polson (1985).

The solution we have adopted is to search for the most economical representation of a language that we can find. Although this representation may not be achieved by all users, it gives a lower bound on the psychological complexity. Observe that where alternative methods exist for achieving a particular task, the most economical representation will probably only describe one of the methods. This representation is a generative grammar, but not necessarily an acceptance grammar because it may not be able to describe an accurate parse of some users' action sequences.

When, however, the aim of the analyst is to predict confusions that a learner might encounter, the appropriate representation might well be an

SIMPLE TASKS
Create new object [Effect=create, Case=regular]
Create special object [Effect=create, Case=special]
Move object [Effect=move, Case=regular]
Move object along restricted path [Effect=move, Case=special]
Change default style attributes [Effect=change-default-style]
Change object style attributes [Effect=change-object-style]

RULE SCHEMAS
6.1   **Task [Effect=create, Case]→**
          select-tool
           +point-to-2-places [Case, Place1=value-from-goal,
                          Place2=value-from-goal]
6.2   **Task [Effect=move, Case]→**
          point-to-2-places [Case, Place1=value-from-goal,
                       Place2=object-location]
6.3   **Task [Effect=modify-object-style]→select-object**
                        +select-style
6.4   **Task [Effect=change-default-style]→select-style**
6.5   **point-to-2-places [Case=regular, Place1, Place2]→**
                   action [Type=point, Place1]
                   +drag-to-place [Place2]
6.6   **point-to-2-places [Case=special, Place1, Place2]→**
                   action [Type=point, Place1]
                   +"depress mouse button"
                   +"depress SHIFT"
                   +action [Type=point, Place2]
                   +"release mouse button"
                   +"release SHIFT"
6.7   **drag-to-place [Place]→"depress mouse button"**
                   +action [Type=point, Place]
                   +"release mouse button"
6.8   **select-style→**
          point-to-2-places [Place1=style-menu, Place2=menu-item]
6.9   **select-object→action [Type=point, Place=object-location]**
                 +"click mouse button"
6.10 **select-tool→action [Type=point, Place=tool-icon]**
                 +"click mouse button"

Fig. 3.6 — TAG description of an idealized MacDraw interface. In this grammar, the
Place features can take values from the user's current goal, denoting action
variables as discussed in section 2.2.

acceptance grammar, describing all reasonable routes to a task, so that
potential confusions between them become visible. We illustrate this
problem of *organizational conflict* in the following section.

In the present instance, it seems reasonable to suppose that experienced
users perceive the task structure in terms of pointing at places and selecting

tools, objects, or styles. If this task structure is directly used as a design basis, it gives the following method for object creation:

Task [Effect=create, Type]→
select tool+point-to-place+point-to-place

The designers of MacDraw foresaw, however, that this simple presentation created an extra and undesirable mode, in which a tool had been selected and the first place, but not the second, had been marked. To avoid this mode, they imposed the rule that whenever two places are to be marked in succession, the mouse button must be depressed at the first place, held down while travelling to the second, and then released. It is therefore necessary to introduce a subtask, **point-to-2-places**, to describe this generalized action sequence, giving the structure seen in rule 6.1.

2.4.2 Organizational consistency

The dragging operation also illustrates another neat piece of design, in which special cases are managed with a degree of consistency that is very high (but not perfect, as we will soon see). The graphic objects that can be created by MacDraw include lines, rectangles, ellipses, and arcs. Each of these objects has a special case: vertical or horizontal lines, squares, circles, and quarter circles. (Lines, of course, have more than one special case — we discuss that awkward fact in a moment.) It would be perfectly possible to design a system in which the command **create-a-square** was different from **create-a-rectangle**, and in this system the designer could arbitrarily decide not to include a special case for, say, arcs. In MacDraw the designer has opted to use general tools to create both ordinary and special cases, and has created a language that requires every object to have exactly one special case; pressing SHIFT during the dragging part of the **point-to-2-places** subtask will create the appropriate object. In the special case of lines, the line snaps to vertical, horizontal, or 45°, whichever is the best fit, so that three special cases are automatically subsumed into one to preserve consistency of structure.

The same constraints apply also to the movement of graphic objects and are treated the same way: By pressing SHIFT during the dragging operation, the movement of the object can be restricted to vertical, horizontal, or 45°. The task structure shown in Fig. 3.6 captures this consistent use of the SHIFT key by using the same subtask, **point-to-2-places**, for both creating and moving objects.

2.4.3 Organizational conflict

We have used the term 'organizational conflict' to refer to the situation in which two or more competing organizations can be perceived. We know of no test that could alert designers to possible misperceptions of this type, but one countermeasure might be to ensure that each task and subtask of the intended organization included a distinctive action.

TAG analyses help to unearth organizational conflicts, and examples can be found in our idealized MacDraw. One such conflict involves rules 6.5, 6.6, 6.7. Of these, rule 6.7 represents a standard **drag-to-place** method, which is utilized by rule 6.5. Rule 6.6 does not utilize the standard dragging subtask, however, because the mouse button and point sequence is interrupted by pressing the SHIFT key. An alternative perceived organization for rule 6.6 would be:

6.6a   **point-to-2-places [Case=special, Place1, Place2]→**
              action [Kind=point, Place1]
         +"depress SHIFT"
         +drag-to-place [Place2]
         "release SHIFT"

This would be simpler. Moreover, it is successful some of the time. We would therefore predict that some novices would discover rule 6.6a. However, it is only successful in one context, when an object-creation tool has been selected. So when the task is to create an object (rule 6.1), the alternative form of rule 6.6 will be successful. When, instead, the task is to move an object, the alternative form of rule 6.6 will have a different effect, because in that context pressing SHIFT will result in selecting multiple objects (or deselecting them, if already selected).

The most economical TAG grammar for the idealized MacDraw can ignore rule 6.6a, but an acceptance grammar would have to represent both that and rule 6.6. The result would be complicated. We would expect learners who discover the structure by experience, rather than tuition, to suffer some difficulties before they acquire the more economical form of representation.

A second conflict occurs because our idealized MacDraw supports a second organization for rule 6.2. (In fact, this second organization was the one held by the authors until performing this analysis.) To explain the second organization, we will start with the task of modifying the style attributes of an object. To do so, the user selects the object (which causes MacDraw to highlight it) and then chooses a new style attribute. Naturally, this is presented in Fig. 3.6 as **select-object** followed by **select-style**. It turns out in practice that many users seem to regard **move-an-object** as a task with a similar structure, in which the first subtask is to select the object. This gives them the following structure:

6.2a   **Task [Effect=move]→**
              select-object
         +drag-to-place [Place=value-from-goal]

Users then have a very consistent structure for all four tasks, because they all start by selecting something, whether tool, object, or style. There are two consequences of that perceived organization. First, unnecessary keystrokes are performed, although because these are no more than an otiose release and redepressing of the mouse button, they are not expensive in effort. Second, the consistent use of the SHIFT key is not visible in that organization, because it does not use the subtask **point-to-2-places**; the subtask **drag-to-place** might or might not make use of the SHIFT key to constrain direction of movement, entirely independently and apparently arbitrarily. It would therefore be quite possible to believe, as the authors did, that the SHIFT key produced special effects during object creation, but had no further uses in MacDraw.

2.4.4 Summary

In this analysis of MacDraw, we have attempted to demonstrate that TAG can capture quite subtle aspects of organizational consistency. Indeed, by performing the TAG analysis we have ourselves been led to perceive initially obscure subtleties. This observation might lead to a criticism that TAG is capturing properties of the language that are not salient to users, and so do not influence complexity. Our response to this criticism is twofold. First, we would argue that it is a mistake necessarily to tie salience and complexity to awareness — consistency may reap benefits for users without being articulated by them. Second, TAG's psychological validity should not be second guessed, but should be subject to empirical scrutiny. This theme is taken up in section 4.

3. FORMAL SPECIFICATION OF THE TAG META-LANGUAGE

The preceding examples illustrate all the notational conventions of the TAG meta-language and leave us in a strong position to define it precisely. We have chosen, however, not to offer such a definition, for two reasons. First, we do not regard the notation as fixed: It seems sensible to keep the way open for refinements and extensions. Other attempts at formal definition in computer science do suggest that case-driven development is likely to be necessary (e.g. Lee, 1972). Second, such a definition would add little to the precision of our case; if the examples given here are taken as definitive rather than merely illustrative, we are able to demonstrate the formal properties of TAG straightforwardly. It will be helpful, however, to offer a complete list of the symbolic expressions and operations used in the current notation.

A TAG has three parts: (a) an optional list of features for categorizing the simple-tasks, (b) a dictionary of simple-tasks, and (c) a set of rule-schemas. The list of features is redundant in the grammar's workings and is provided purely to aid exposition.

The dictionary of simple-tasks lists a label for each operation which the user can perform routinely, together with a featural description of that simple-task in terms of semantic components which categorize the entire task world. The component-set is denoted by braces, { }. Each component is denoted by a descriptive term for the feature, the equal sign, =, and a term for the value of that feature. The symbols + and − are used to denote presence or absence of binary features.

Every rule-schema contains a single element on the left-hand side (LHS); each LHS is a term consisting of an arbitrary label and a feature-set contained in square brackets, which may contain any number of unvalued or valued features (components). (The meaninglessness of all non-terminal symbols is a virtue not shared by earlier formulations of the TAG notation. It results from a simple change to the syntax of world knowledge rules, and was suggested by Tom Moran.) The LHS is separated from the right-hand side (RHS) by an arrow → which denotes rewriting, or definition, in the standard phrase-structure grammar sense. The RHS of a rule contains an ordered sequence of terms (in exactly the same format as the LHS) and of terminal symbols. Entire sets of features may be abbreviated by the symbol F(label), which denotes the set of defining features of the labelled token. Where a feature-set appears together with a specified feature, the specific feature takes precedence, and the feature-set is understood to denote only the unspecified defining features. Unvalued feature-sets may also be specified, denoted by F( ).

To expand a rule-schema, any unvalued feature must be assigned values uniformly throughout the rule, whether they are ordinary features or feature-sets. When this assignment is complete, every term must denote a unique grammatical object. If a term refers to a simple-task (given the generic label **task**), then the valued features will specify exactly one of the entries in the simple-task dictionary. Where the term refers to a non-terminal symbol, that non-terminal will itself appear as the LHS of a rule schema. The third possibility, if the rule is a world knowledge rule, is that the term (denoted **known-item**) refers to a unique object assumed to be in the user's semantic memory. Terminal symbols are action specifications, denoted by terms in quotation marks, or action variables (denoted **action**) which contain features whose value may be determined by the current goal.

The most important formal property of TAG is its generative power. It is easy to see that TAG only has context-free capability. Each ordinary rule schema can be explanded into a finite number of single-level (context-free) rewrite rules, simply by assigning values to features in all admissible ways. World knowledge rules do not affect this capability, as they meet the same constraint, albeit through the device of features and components that exist independently of the system being described. Nevertheless, as we have noted, it is inevitable that some extension to the core meta-language will be demanded as wider aspects of usability are considered.

4.   USING TAG TO ASSESS LEARNABILITY

Having described the workings of TAG and shown how it addresses some interesting properties of the interface, we now explain how to apply TAG in order to make predictions of task language learnability. First, we discuss some complexity metrics which allow direct comparisons between one TAG description and another. Next, we examine the empirical literature on command language learning to consider the extent to which TAG, allied to the complexity metrics, predicts the important results; this section is extended by summaries of two novel experiments testing central TAG learnability predictions.

4.1   Complexity metrics over grammars

The prime applied focus of TAG is to assess the relative learnability of different task languages. The central argument is that, because a TAG description models mental representation of the language, simple metrics over the grammar will reflect psychological complexity, and thus learnability. We have already mentioned these metrics; in this section we inspect them more closely.

This argument suffers two potential difficulties. First, in the absence of a specified learning mechanism one might argue that learnability is badly underdetermined, because a mechanism could be devised that learned complex grammars more easily than simple ones. Our response to this is straightforward: although we have not specified a learning mechanism, we simply assume one with the appropriate properties. Indeed, we are now more or less bound to such an assumption by the nature of our enterprise, for the status of any representation as an explanatory device depends crucially on implicit processing assumptions. If the empirical predictions made by TAG, through its alliance with learning assumptions, should fail, then we must modify the grammar, not the assumptions.

The second difficulty with our learnability argument is that any number of TAG grammars can be written to define a single task language. How do we know which definition to use? This degrees-of-freedom problem is an inevitable consequence of using a grammar as a competence model, but it also applies to other attempts at modelling human–computer interaction, such as the production systems of Kieras and Polson (1985). The problem in our case is rather less severe, for our express goal is the prediction of relative complexity, so that any consistent approach to choosing a single description can be justified. The approach that we choose is governed by our proposed complexity metrics over TAG descriptions.

Any grammatical decription has a large number of properties; which are the ones that determine complexity? The most important index of complexity derived from a TAG definition is the number of simple-task rule schemas, for these rules define the top-level configuration of the task language. For two langauges that possess the same number of simple-task rule schemas, complexity comparisons should utilize the total number of rule-schemas, including those that rewrite the non-terminal symbols of the grammar. Because of the prime importance of the simple-task rule schemas, our solution to the degrees-of-freedom problem is to base comparisons on descriptions of languages that minimize the number of simple-task rule schemas.

It is worth noting that the degrees-of-freedom problem potentially can be turned into a positive advantage. Because several TAG descriptions of a given language are possible, we have the means of modelling individual differences in perceived structure. We have already seen some benefits of using TAG in this fashion in our discussion of the MacDraw interface. In that case, by departing from our usual constaint of minimizing the number of simple-task rules, we were able to display interesting alternative structurings of the task language. Our complexity metrics depend on the assumption that although alternative TAG descriptions are necessary to model individual perceptions of structure, the minimal description models regularities that generally will be perceived and is therefore the best available approximate guide to the intrinsic complexity of the design.

4.2   Empirical support

TAG's main empirical prediction is that, of two similar task languages, the one that will be easier to learn and remember is the one with fewer simple-task rule schemas, or, should the languages be equivalent in this respect, the language with the fewer rules altogether (not counting rules that are captured by world knowledge schemas). This claim is supported in as much as TAG descriptions capture previous results in the command language literature, including those on command names by Black and Moran (1982), Carroll (1982), Scapin (1982), Green and Payne (1984); and those on command language syntax by Barnard *et al.* (1981) and Reisner (1981).

Furthermore, some experiments have been specially designed to test TAG's predictions. Payne and Green (1989) showed that a command language structure which reflected the semantic relations between simple-tasks was easier to induce than alternative structures, including one which utilized fewer different phrase orderings. Payne (1988) showed that an abbreviation scheme in which a different abbreviation rule applied in two task categories was better remembered than one employing the recommended 'secondary rule' scheme (Ehrenreich and Porcu, 1982).

5.   THE COGNITIVE SCIENCE BASIS OF THE TAG NOTATION

In this section we look at the particular devices utilized by TAG and examine their relation to various cognitive science concerns. We begin with the thorny question of task analysis, describing our approach to simple-tasks. We next discuss the use of semantic features to describe task concepts and to mark rewrite rules. We raise the issue of notational power, and finally dicuss a possible extension to TAG's notation.

TAG makes two novel contentions about the representation of tasks. First, it identifies the special simple-tasks that can be performed without any problem solving or iteration. Second, it represents simple tasks as concepts, whose semantic interrelationship plays a crucial role in the representation of the language.

5.1   Simple-tasks

We have defined a simple-task as any task that the user can routinely perform with no demand for a control structure, such as branching or iteration, that requires monitoring of plan progress. We believe that higher-level, more complex, tasks requiring coordination between task sequences are best handled by a separate planning component. Our motivations for this need a little unpicking.

First and foremost, we argue that this class of simple-tasks is psychologically important. Against this, critics may claim that, as simple iteration can be easily routinized (Card *et al.*, 1983) and as we distinguish iterative from non-iterative tasks, the class of simple-tasks cannot be a psychologically relevant category. This argument has some force for task performance, but for task language learning it is faulted. A novice user who has been told the command for, say, deleting words, will induce the iterative method for deleting sentences with little trouble. This point has been demonstrated empirically by Douglas (1983), who showed that novices could correctly induce how to perform any task that relied on a simple combination of tutored tasks. Our focus on the prediction of learning effort renders such distinctions crucial: simple-tasks are the set of tasks for which distinct action sequences have to be learned, or induced, from the particular structure of the task language.

We should note at this stage that if TAG is eventually to play a role in theories of performance, as we intend, simply ignoring iteration will not do. A tactic of 'leaving iteration to the planning system' may handle the repetition of entire task–action sequences, but it would be critically weak in one important respect: many tasks have iterable subcomponents. For example, to format disks on the CP/M operating system one must run the Format program, and respond to the prompt that yes, you really do want to format the disk in drive B. To format more than one disk, one could, of course, exit the Format program and loop through the entire sequence, but an option is supplied to allow users efficiently to repeat the last step only. Our current thoughts on planning with TAGs suggest tackling this problem by allowing control tokens on subtasks and action specifications, such as **can-be-iterated**. These developments will not be discussed in this article, because thay do not affect our central concerns with learning and learnability.

The concern with learnability also dictates the second property of simple-tasks. The simple-tasks for a given system are determined as much by the device as by the external task domain. In Moran's (1983) terms, simple-tasks are 'internal' rather than 'external' tasks. To adapt one of Moran's examples, consider a very simple cut-and-paste display editor. Although in the external task domain the user can distinguish between such entities as sentence and paragraph, in the internal world of the system this distinction may disappear; both words and sentences are treated as strings. For example, to delete a sentence one has to mark the beginning and end with the mouse and choose the cut command. The job of a TAG in this case is to describe the operation sequence required for the 'delete string' command and its relation to other aspects of the task language, not to illuminate the nature of the mapping from external task to internal task.

Our position is in close agreement with Moran (1983), in that we see the need for a psychological mapping from external to internal tasks as well as the acquisition of task language semantics and syntax. This view agrees with our claim that simple-tasks are a psychological construct.

Simple-tasks, then, are equivalent entities in human computer interaction to operators in the classical problem space view of problem solving (Newell and Simon, 1972). It is instructive to explore this connection.

One obvious difference between human–computer interaction and the kind of puzzles studied by problem-solving theorists is the need for a task language to map the operators onto action sequences. The psychological implications of this mapping are the central concern of the TAG model. To address this issue we have found it necessary to depart from the treatment of operators in the puzzle-solving literature. Puzzle-solving operators are more or less atomic entities, whose use is determined by preconditions and postconditions. The relationship of one operator to another is not explicitly represented, except with regard to roles on solution paths (e.g. the preconditions of one operator may become the goal state which prompts application of a second). In contrast, TAG treats simple-task operators as semantic concepts which are organized into mental categories.

To describe learning effects in problem-solving domains, it is necessary to allow operators to be chunked into macro-operators (e.g. Chase and Simon, 1973). We regard simple-tasks to be dynamic in a similar way. For the novice user, simple-tasks are, roughly, all those tasks for which there is a distinct command or operation in the task language (and which have been learned). It is this level of analysis that we have found to be most useful in assessing the learnability of task language designs. For the more advanced user, several simple tasks may have been composed to form more complex tasks that can nevertheless be performed without a problem-solving effort.

5.2   Tasks as concepts

We hypothesize that simple-tasks are mentally represented as concepts. The thrust of this suggestion is that the internal structure of tasks and the intensional relations among tasks are both of major importance in the user's mental representation of task languages.

There exists in the literature a lively debate about the mental representation of concepts (Smith and Medin, 1981). Are concepts represented by sets of defining features, as the classical view maintains (Bruner *et al.*, 1956; Katz, 1972), or as schematic prototypes (e.g. Rosch and Mervis, 1975), or even as networks of exemplars (e.g. Medin and Schaffer, 1978)? So lively is the debate and so difficult the issues that they have led some commentators to conjecture that many important tensions will never be resolved (Armstrong *et al.*, 1983). The safest general view of concepts would appear to be a permissive one: all of these representational forms exist, but they are used for different purposes. By taking this stance, one is able to offer a theory of certain aspects of conceptual performance without being necessarily committed to a unitary view of concepts. This is exactly the approach taken by Tversky (1977) in his theory of similarity computations. Following Tversky, TAG utilizes feature-set representations of task concepts, and of lexical command names, without insisting that other representations are redundant or that the debate in the linguistics literature (e.g. Lyons, 1977; Miller and Johnson-Laird, 1976) is dead.

In view of the importance of featural descriptions of concepts in TAG, it is well to be clear exactly what is meant by a feature. The term is being used in exact accord with the conventions of semantic theory — anything that can take a value with respect to a term. (See Rosenberg (1982) for a rigorous mathematical treatment.)

As in mainstream semantics, the features and components that are specified in a TAG description should have psychological validity, in that they are important for the categorization of the task world. Unfortunately, again just as in semantics, there is nothing that analysts can do to ensure this ideal, except to rely on their intuition.

5.3   Feature-tagged rule schemas

With regard to their role in the rewrite rules, it may be helpful to view features as strongly typed variables, for which the entire range of values is defined by an *n*-tuple, usually small. The assignment of values to features in TAG rule schemas is therefore parallel to the assignment of values to variables in advanced production system architectures, and indeed sometimes serves similar purposes, such as the capturing of certain kinds of organization. However, the strong typing of features, and the fact that they play an important role not only in the rule-schemas but also in the categorization of task concepts and of the action world, does mean that rule-schemas are heavily constained compared with generalized production rules and often make quite different predictions.

The use of semantic features in syntactic rules is a major break from the devices employed by linguists' theories of syntax, most of which stress the role of syntactic features. The break reflects the simplicity of the syntactic structures of task languages relative to natural language. Syntactic features are simply not needed to describe the regularities compactly, but semantic features are needed to express important characteristics of the mental representation of even such simple syntax.

A similar device is employed in the 'semantic grammars' used by Burton (1976) to implement natural language dialogues in intelligent computer-assisted instruction and in 'attribute grammars' originated by Knuth (1968) as a means of specifying the 'semantics of context-free languages'.

Attribute grammars supply a corresponding semantic rule for every rewrite rule, specifying the attributes of the left-hand side non-terminal in terms of the attributes of the right-hand side, or some already meaningful symbol (e.g. a number). This technique allows the specification of a language's intensional semantics. Our convention of associating values to attributes consistently throughout a rule is a very limited version of this idea. The limitation represents an important constraint: that the componential semantics of an interactive command can be derived in a simple additive fashion from the command's constituents. Further research is required to investigate the validity and implications of this constraint; it may prove advantageous in the long term to provide separate semantic rules in the analysis.

5.4   The competence hypothesis and formal power

In identifying and defining the class of simple-tasks we hope to clarify that important distinction between the user's knowledge of the task language and the goal-driven problem solver (unspecified but constrained by the TAG model) which interprets that knowledge. The separation distinguishes this work from other attempts at formal modelling in human–computer interaction (Card *et al.*, 1983; Kieras and Polson, 1985) but dovetails with current thinking in computational linguistics, where it is dubbed the competence hypothesis: 'a reasonable model of language use will incorporate, as a basic component, the generative grammar that expresses the speaker–hearer's knowledge of the language' (Chomsky, 1965, p. 9, quoted in Bresnan and Kaplan, 1983).

The competence hypothesis affords us a crucial advantage by enabling a model of the user's knowledge with a tightly specified and very limited formal power, despite its large expressive power. Previous attempts at modelling human–computer interaction have not been able to offer this degree of restraint, instead offering systems of unspecified and unclear, but worryingly powerful, capabilities.

The benefits of restricting the formal power of computational models may not be immediately apparent. After all, both production systems and semantic networks have unlimited computational power, yet are regarded as successful models by many. We do not want to suggest that unrestricted power necessarily removes empirical content. Consideration of strong equivalence (as opposed to mere duplication of input/output pairs) disallows such a simple argument (see Pylyshyn, 1980, 1984); production systems may accurately predict the time complexity of different mental operations. Nevertheless, the formal power of meta-languages is a particularly important flavour of theoretical parsimony. For if a meta-language is to prove useful as a theory, it must be applied to a large number of different language constructs (in our case, different task languages). Yet the more powerful the meta-language, the greater the choice of grammatical descriptions of any given construction — the degrees-of-freedom problem we discussed above. As Pylyshyn (1980) put it: 'the more constrained a notation or architecture, the greater the explanatory power of resulting models. It [the architecture or meta-language] provides a principled rationale for why the model [the grammar] takes one particular form, as opposed to other logically possible ones' (p. 126).

In our work on TAG we have only managed to go part way to this ideal, and so we have adopted 'style rules' such as minimizing the number of simple-task rule schemas to constrain possible descriptions further. TAG itself is a highly constrained meta-language (as we have seen, it only has context-free power); we believe that it is constrained according to psychologically plausible mechanisms.

6.   TAG DEVELOPMENTS AND EXTENSIONS

Payne and Green (1986, p. 125) expressed the following prediction about TAG (omitted from this reprinting): 'We fully expect that the TAG notation will need to be developed and extended to tackle more diverse issues than we have yet been able to consider'. We were right: since the first presentation of TAGs (Payne, 1984), several human–computer interaction projects, at different sites, have extended TAG, or its core ideas, to attack new problems, and to overcome limitations in the original specification.

We will begin this review of developments with the work that is closest to the original, limited target of the TAG model: work that attempts to explicate the notion of user interface consistency.

6.1   Conceptual consistency

Kellogg (1987) offers a framework for the consideration of consistency which broadens the scope of our analysis in the Introduction. Perhaps Kellogg's most important contention is that there is an important level of consistency that does not appear to be addressable with the apparatus of TAGs. This observation is borne out by the work of Green and Schiele (in press), who attempted to use TAG to derive a characterization of the Apple Macintosh 'style'. Although TAG can readily illustrate the universal nature of operations such as pointing, clicking and dragging, Green and Schiele argue that it does not get to the heart of the consistency of Macintosh applications. This 'conceptual consistency' has no simple definition of the kind we offered for simpler aspects above. However, we share the strong intuition that it is psychologically real, and of great importance in user interface design. The notion is perhaps best conveyed by the following description: conceptual consistency is a property of user interfaces that exhibit a coherent underlying device model.

We do not pretend that this is a definition, because the key explanatory concept of a device model itself needs definitional work. In the empirical work to date, a useful distinction is that between 'how it works' knowledge and 'how to work it' knowledge (Kieras and Bovair, 1984; Halasz and Moran, 1983). 'Device model' has been coined to label the former type of knowledge. However, as one thrust of the empirical work has been to show that device models affect procedural knowledge, it is clear that this convenient separation is a psychological simplification: to really explicate device models not only do we need a theory of how they are represented, but also this theory must be intimately interwoven with a theory of 'how to work it' knowledge (Payne *et al.*, 1989).

TAG offers a limited theory of 'how to work it' knowledge. Can it be extended to throw light on device models, and so on conceptual consistency? We know of two attempts to do this. The first, by one of us (Payne, 1987, 1989; Payne *et al.*, 1989), posits a new model to play a role alongside TAG in a more complete theory of user knowledge. The second, by Tauber (1988), attempts to extend (quite radically) the TAG notation, so that conceptual issues come within its purview.

Both of these developments are marshalled around a single observation, due initially to Moran (1983): devices are a conceptual world, containing objects and interrelations. Users must come to understand this device-internal conceptual world and, in particular, how it maps onto the external world of tasks. Moran attempted to understand this cognitive problem by using an external–internal task mapping analysis technique (ETIT).

The approach taken by Payne and colleagues is similar to Moran's, but differs in one major respect. Payne (1987) argues that what users have to map from one domain to another is not a set of tasks but a problem space. Although the user' goals are defined as states in an external state space (the goal space), operations apply only to the internal state space (the device space). So users need to construct this device space and map it onto the goal space. Payne (1987) calls this the yoked state space hypothesis.

By specifying the objects in the device space and the goal space, and the mapping between them, Payne argues that complexity issues can be highlighted. String-based screen editors are relatively simple, because although the user needs to construct a new device space object (the string) this object maps onto all the main objects in the goal space. Once the way of dealing with sentences has been mastered, paragraph operations are instantly inferrable. Yoked state spaces offer a formal definition of the term 'device model', and hence of conceptual consistency.

Whereas the yoked state space model of conceptual consistency emphasizes the mapping between device space and goal space, Tauber's approach concentrates on giving a formal, complete description of the device space, by specifying what he calls a user's virtual machine (Tauber, 1988). Tauber uses Jackendoff's formal theory of the language of thought (Jackendoff, 1983) to reformulate TAG. The resulting ETAG (extended TAG) specifies not only the simple tasks and their mapping onto actions, but the conceptual objects which the simple tasks manipulate, and their interrelations. Jackendoff's theory is too elaborate to present meaningfully in the space available, so we will only be able to give a flavour of Tauber's enterprise. A key principle is that objects and events can be specified as combinations of primitive concepts (in a way that parallels Schank's (1975) well-known theory of conceptual dependency).

To give a simplified example, the text-editing operation of copying an object from the text to the buffer is specified as an EVENT, with a name COPY_TO_CB. The event is described as the GOING of a DUPLICATE of some OBJECT:x (a variable) of type STRING, WORD or RULER, TO a place ON(CB) (see Fig. 3.7 for a full denotation of this EVENT). Any system that uses combinations and compositions of primitive functions in this way can expose interrelationships between the entities. So COPY_TO _TEXT will move the same OBJECT types TO a different location; this relationship can be extracted formally.

Tauber's approach clearly sacrifices much of the simplicity of TAG, but the hope is that, by tackling conceptual structuring head on, interface descriptions can be produced which expose the subtle parameters of conceptual consistency.

Task Dictionary, Entry 1.

name:
  [EVENT=COPY_TO_CB],

conceptual description:
  [event.GO([OBJECT=DUPLICATE([OBJECT:*x])],
    [path.TO([place.ON([OBJECT=CB])])])].

where-clause:
  [OBJECT:*x]=ONE-OF{[STRING],[WORD],[RULER]}
  AND
  [state.BE([OBJECT:*x],
    place.ON-REGION.[OBJECT:*x]([OBJECT=TEXT])])],

attributed symbol:
  T1   [OBJECT=ONE-OF{[STRING],[WORD],[RULER]}],

comments:
  "copy an object from the text to the clipboard."

Fig. 3.7 — Fragment from an ETAG description of MacWrite (Tauber, 1988).

Another of Tauber's declared aims is to expose the extent to which the conceptual structure of the device is supported by the display. This is clearly an important issue, and one which the straightforward TAG model does not begin to address. As Green *et al.* (1988) point out, as far as TAG descriptions are concerned, the display can be turned off. Users are not so tolerant.

6.2   Display-based competence
In fact, there is evidence that users of menu-based systems are more heavily reliant on the display than we might imagine. Mayes *et al.* (1988) have shown that experienced MacWrite users cannot recall the menu structure of the interface, even though they can happily navigate it in the service of tasks. It seems that competence is critically dependent on display cues.

Howes and Payne (in press) have shown how a simple extension to TAG can begin to address this aspect of display-based competence. By allowing rewrite schemas to be augmented with 'display_item' functions it is possible to specify task–action mappings which are critically dependent on features of the display. Furthermore, by allowing the display_item function access to the semantic features of the current task, consistency in the task–display relationship can be captured by higher-level rules, in a way that closely parallels TAG's treatment of syntactic consistency of semantic–syntactic alignment.

6.3   From interface evaluation to interface extension
TAG was invented to evaluate the consistency of task languages from design specifications. However, as a cognitive model of user competence it clearly exhibits another potential, to inform the development of instructional materials of various kinds. Furthermore, as a formal, programmable model (see below) it might be incorporated into on-line interface extensions.

A good example of user-interface extension utilizing TAG-based structures is the work of Hoppe (1988, in press). Hoppe points out that, although 'task' is a fundamental notion in human–computer interaction, tasks are not explicitly represented anywhere in the device. To change this, Hoppe develops the attribute grammar approach of TAG to define formally the mapping from user action sequences to tasks. This mapping is implemented in a Prolog program, which can parse user inputs into task descriptions. Such a parser can be contrasted with a standard interaction language parser which parses input sequences syntactically (to check for errors) and translates them into system state changes, without reference to tasks. Of course, the standard parser will still be needed in a working system, because the user's input must be dealt with whether it conforms with a task–action mapping or not. However, Hoppe's system provides a way of extending the system that might be used, for example, to provide task-related on-line help. Furthermore, the same system can be used to generate action sequences from task descriptions, a facility that may be used in intelligent tutoring systems.

6.4 Towards performance models

TAG is a competence model and, as such, can make psychological predictions about learnability, but not about the dynamics of performance. However, like all competence models, it necessarily constrains performance models, and might be extended to address some important performance issues.

Hoppe's (1988) task-oriented parser, running 'in reverse' as a generator, can in some ways be considered as a performance model that shares assumptions with TAG, although, given that it was not designed for this purpose, it is not clear what its psychological implications are. Green (1988) has developed a purpose-built performance model based on TAG, also implemented as a Prolog program. It was originally developed with the aim of verifying TAG descriptions of large systems, but other possibilities turned up, allowing performance metrics and 'what-if' questions to be explored. (It is well known that executable specifications have certain advantages over non-executable ones, and it seems that executable formalizations also have advantages.)

One possibility is to explore 'mental effort'; for instance, the number of rules used in deriving an action sequence can readily be counted, and be summed over a repertoire of basic tasks. This gives a simple but possibly useful index for an interface, although it should be interpreted with great circumspection, because even if people's knowledge of an interface language can be at least partly described by a TAG there is no necessary guarantee that their processing is even loosely related to that grammatical structure. To make the logic clearer, consider English speakers. Their knowledge of English can be partly described by a grammar, but when they listen they use semantic cues, prosodic cues, and pragmatic expectations to cut down the need for strictly syntactic parsing; thus the grammar, a competence model, is not a very good predictor of performance.

Another possibility is to use the executable TAG representation to help to predict trouble spots, places where people make frequent mistakes. The class of 'description errors' (Norman, 1983) turned out particularly easy to handle. Description errors are slips like putting salt in your tea instead of sugar, or deleting a word instead of a character, which in TAG terms can be regarded as making a mistake about a single feature. Since a simple-task is defined by a vector of feature values, all the 'off-by-one' action sequences can be quickly obtained by systematically changing the value of one feature and running the interpreter to see what actions it produced. The relative likelihood of these slips depends on the discriminability of the features: putting salt in your tea instead of sugar is perhaps more likely than pouring the hot water into the sugar basin rather than the teapot, but to the TAG interpreter they would have equal status. Given the relevant information, however, a profile of likely slips could be generated, and in principle it would be possible to compare these predictions against a corpus of slips from an actual system. It should also be possible to predict 'capture errors' by searching among rules for common subsequences, although this has not been investigated. Mode errors, on the other hand, are not readily predictable by examining a TAG representation (although this weakness may be addressed by task-side-effect rules introduced by Howes and Payne (in press)).

7. GENERAL DISCUSSION

7.1 TAG as task analysis?

The title of this volume suggests that this chapter is a contribution to the discipline of task analysis. We believe that this becomes accurate only when it is appreciated that the meaning of 'task analysis' has extended beyond its traditional confines. In particular, TAG is a kind of analysis which is highly device dependent, and which seeks to uncover the cognitive structure of tasks, and the methods for accomplishing them. (Furthermore, by deliberately limiting itself to 'simple-tasks', TAG fails to address issues of composition of methods that are at the heart of much task analysis, in human–computer interaction and elsewhere.) In contrast, much task analysis attempts to be partly device independent, and to uncover the logical, or the practical, structure of tasks. Tasks have a logical structure, in as far as certain subtasks are dependent on the status (e.g. completion) of others. Logical structures are independent of the human operator, but of course constrain behaviour. (Some theorists have argued that logical task analysis is a prerequisite for psychological theorizing, e.g. Marr, 1982.) The behavioural, or practical, structure of tasks describes the ways that human operators achieve them, which may be influenced by organizational norms, as well as by operator psychology. The cognitive structure of a task is a structure of information processing performed by the operator. Cognitive task analysis makes a heavier theoretical commitment than logical or practical task analysis. These distinctions suggest a two-dimensional framework, into which differing approaches to task analysis, including those in this volume, may be placed. There are several other salient dimensions of task analysis for human–computer interaction, including the grain of analysis (cf. Card *et al.,*

1983) and the degree of formalization of the product. However, for our current purposes, a simple, two-dimensional map will suffice. This is illustrated, with just a couple of examples, in Fig. 3.8.

	Relationship with technology	Device-independent . . . . Device-dependent	
Determinant of structure			
Logic		Shepherd (Ch 1) Carey *et al.* (Ch 2) Walsh (Ch 6)	N/A
Practice		N/A	"Motion Study" e.g. Gilbreth (1911)
		Job Components Inventory* Banks *et al.* (1983)	
Cognition		TAKD (Diaper & Johnson, 1989)	Johnson (Ch 5) Diaper (Ch 4)
			TAG (Ch 3)

* Although JCI specifically lists the tools of a job, its analysis is too coarse grained to depend critically on device design, hence it occupies an intermediate position on the technological dependence dimension.

Fig. 3.8 — Task analysis techniques may aim to expose the logical, the practical or the cognitive structure of tasks. In general, logical structures will constrain practice, and practice will constrain cognition. Task analysis also varies according to its dependence on the particular technology. When task analysis is to be used for design it may be appropriate to target logical task structures that apply independently of specific devices.

We introduce this framework here, not only to place TAG in the context of other efforts in this volume, but because the framework exposes a current debate in human–computer interaction: are cognitive models (or, in our new terms, cognitive, device-dependent task analyses) a Good Thing? Cognitive models, like TAG, are targetted on the evaluation of usability issues. The attempted advance over prototype testing is that evaluations can be made from design specifications, prior to implementation. Some recent commentators on human–computer interaction have proposed a different role for psychological theory — as 'a mother of invention' (Landauer, 1987; see also Carroll, 1989). In this role, cognitive analysts do not have to wait for interface designs to evaluate; their job is to prompt the invention of new ideas.

Despite the obvious ambition of this approach, there do exist some successful exemplars. The suggested methodology for invention is to use a device-independent mode of task analysis to analyse problems associated with the task per se, and to target devices at eliminating these problems (e.g. Furnas *et al.*, 1987). The 'problems' do not need to be deeply cognitive. Organizational or social practices, or the informational logic of the task, may each provide their own constraints, so that non-cognitive task analyses may be used to promote usable systems.

However, as Carroll and Campbell (1988) point out, such a linear path is an idealization, as is the idea of pure device-independent task analysis. Instead, designs will need to be iterated through a task–artifact cycle. In such a scheme, it becomes less clear that cognitive models of device use can be dispensed with, In fact, we are convinced that they cannot.

What is even less clear, however, is that human–computer interaction needs global all–encompassing cognitive theories. The work we have reviewed above explores the limits of TAG as a theory. We noted that some workers have extended the TAG notation to address new problems. However, of course, this extension has severe limits. There are many aspects of device use that TAG is simply not equipped to address. One approach to this dilemma is the standard scientific approach — to seek a division of issues into natural, theoretically meaningful subissues, and to attempt to provide coordinated, consistent theories that address the separate subissues, with an overarching theoretical framework to provide the necessary integration. Payne's (1987) work on the yoked state space hypothesis seeks to develop such an approach, using Newell's (1981) problem space hypothesis as the overarching frame. Green (1987) suggests a different approach, tailored to the practical needs of human–computer interaction. We shall conclude by discussing this idea.

7.2   An explicit framework of limited theories

Perhaps we should not try to expand the scope of our theories, but instead seek principled limitations? In its initial conception TAG was deliberately targetted to one specific user interface issue. Green (1987) has suggested that human–computer interaction might be served by limited theories that address specific requirements. In this way the problems that theories address need not reflect a 'carving of nature at her joints' at all — instead the division into limited theories depends on a decomposition of human–computer interaction design into separate design critera. For each criterion, a different theory may be appropriate and, as long as each theory does its job, we do not need to worry about cognitive or scientific compatibility between theories. Limited theories can then be linked into a requirement structure, which exposes the interrelationship between design criteria (Green, 1987). Fig. 3.9

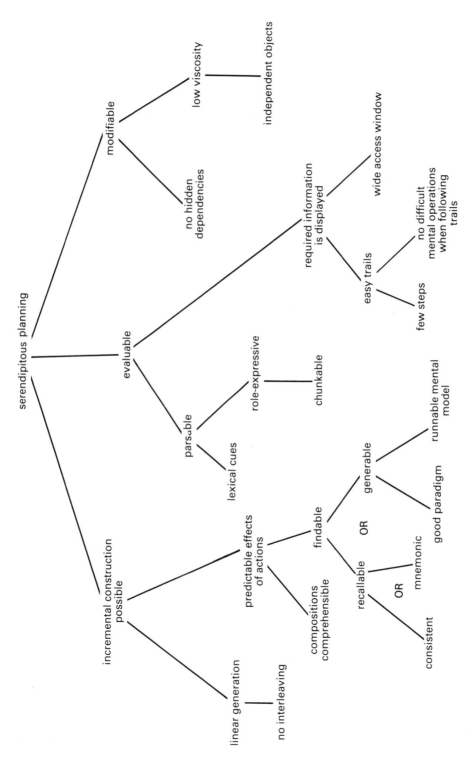

Fig. 3.9 — A 'requirement structure' for concepts in HCI. Lower items are requirements for higher ones, e.g. 'incremental construction' requires linear generation. To achieve 'serendipitous planning', the preferred mode of planning for design tasks, all components are required. The diagram can also be read as showing the purpose of an HCI concept, e.g. the purpose of a 'runnable mental model' is to allow easy generation of actions. No HCI theory is to be quizzed outside its indentified purpose.

shows a putative requirement structure for designs that fosters opportunistic planning.

Fig. 3.9 should be read thus. 'To achieve "serendipitous" (opportunistic) planning, the user must be able to work incrementally, to evaluate each incremental change, and to modify the structure. To work incrementally, the user must be able to attack goals linearly (rather than simultaneously) and to predit effects of actions. To predict effects of actions, the user must be able to comprehend the outcome of multiple actions (compositions), and to find the actions appropriate for a given goal. To find appropriate actions, the user must be able *either* to recall them *or* to generate them de novo. To recall them, the user must be able *either* to deduce them from configural properties, e.g. consistency, *or* to invoke a mnemonic.' TAG describes *only* how the consistency requirement may be met. Other HCl models (e.g. work on mental models) describe how other requirements may be met.

Whether a requirement structure — design criteria approach or a traditional scientific theory building approach will prove better for human–computer interaction in the long run is an open question. We feel sure that human–computer interaction needs psychological theories, and that unified psychological theories that answer all designer's questions will not be forthcoming. Fig. 3.9 shows how small a part TAG is envisaged as playing in one possible picture of a human–computer interaction science base, and though the picture may change the limited quality of the role will not.

ACKNOWLEDGEMENT

Stephen Payne's work on developments of TAG has been funded by Alvey/ SERC grant GR/D 60355, a collaborative project with British Telecommunication plc.

4

Task Analysis for Knowledge Descriptions (TAKD): the method and an example

Dan Diaper
Department of Computer Science, University of Liverpool

1. INTRODUCTION

Task analysis for knowledge descriptions (TAKD) was first developed as part of a national syllabus development project for young trainees in information technology (Johnson *et al.,* 1984; Diaper and Johnson, 1989). TAKD's role was to analyse the data from the observation of relevant tasks and to redescribe them all within a single, consistent representational form that specified the general information technology knowledge that trainees needed to possess. TAKD, as it currently exists, consists of a method that generates a hierarchical description of tasks and a Knowledge Representation grammar (KRG). The KRG allows a level of the hierarchy, and its superordinate levels, to be written in a sentence form. It was claimed that while the KRG form may not map on to a real psychology of people (i.e. it lacks psychological validity), the hierarchical structure used by TAKD is compatible with a psychological model and that this isomorphism allows the prediction of human behaviour. TAKD has since been applied to a range of applications and for several different purposes within the area of Human–Computer Interaction (HCI).

As with many other task analysis methods, TAKD has never been fully described and documented. Thus applying TAKD, at present, requires more of a craft skill than an engineering one. This chapter aims to redress this by outlining the steps needed when using TAKD. This description takes, as its starting point, observational data from tasks (see Chapter 7). Before this, a brief discussion of TAKD's range of application is provided. TAKD is illustrated using a worked example involving the annotation of documents with the goal of producing a specification for a hypertext system to support collaborative writing. As with any relatively new methodology, TAKD has not yet been applied to an exhaustive range of exemplar tasks in HCI and the author is continuing to extend its range of utility. Thus this chapter contains a discussion of TAKD's current limitations and some suggestions for its further extension are proposed. However, even in its current instantiation, TAKD is at least as powerful as alternative task analysis methods for many HCI purposes and is already better documented with respect to its method of application than some of these (e.g. Diaper, 1988a).

2. APPLICATIONS AND PURPOSES

TAKD has been used in a number of applications following its development for syllabus design and for purposes unconnected with training. Johnson (1985), for example, used it to model 'the identification and description of a series of messaging tasks. The purpose of this analysis was to identify user requirements and to form the basis from which a new interface for an extended electronic mail system could be designed.' However, Johnson uses a KRG that is rather more complex than the one originally developed and described in this chapter. He has since developed TAKD into a different form of task analysis (see Chapter 5).

It is important to appreciate the difference between applications and purposes. The former refers to the domain to which task analysis is applied, whereas the latter is the reason why task analysis was used. The range of applications of TAKD and its possible purposes are described below.

2.1 Applications

HCI applications of TAKD so far investigated have included mail systems, both by Johnson and by the present author, expert system interfaces, annotation of documents and collaborative writing. In addition, Diaper (1987, 1988b, 1989a) has suggested that TAKD is suitable as a knowledge elicitation and analysis tool for knowledge-based systems development, an application of task analysis also advocated by Wilson (1987, 1989). Most of the applications investigated by the author have involved tasks performed without the aid of a computer, but ones which might be automated. There are two reasons for this. First, a large number of tasks analysed using TAKD for syllabus design involved tasks where a person operated some computer equipment (e.g. word processors, databases, a CNC lathe, etc.) and thus it is known that TAKD can be used to analyse such tasks. Second, and rather more trivially perhaps, the author has been involved with teaching TAKD to second-year undergraduate psychology students, many of whom are not knowledgeable about computers. Thus the applications investigated, with the exception of the expert system example, have not involved computer usage. However, in all cases the purpose of using TAKD was computer orientated. Less trivially, however, that TAKD can be taught and used by non-experts allows a powerful claim to be made as to its relative simplicity and to its coherence and completeness as a method. These non-computer applications have all involved cognitive tasks where there are very few tools. This is in contrast to the non-computer tasks analysed for syllabus creation, which tended to be heavily tool based, as most of these involved the construction or testing of digital circuitry.

Thus it is known that TAKD can be applied to a wide range of tasks that involve computers directly in the tasks and also to tasks that are not currently carried out with the aid of a computer. Furthermore, in this latter set of tasks TAKD is not restricted to tasks which have a large tool-based component to them.

2.2   Purposes

As already mentioned, the original purpose of TAKD was to provide a description of the knowledge that young trainees needed to possess to be able to perform suitable information technology tasks. While the use of task analysis for training specification is its most traditional purpose (e.g. Annett *et al.*, 1972, and Chapters 1 and 2), it is not the central purpose of task analysis in HCI. Task analysis can be used at two very obvious and distinct stages in the computer system development life-cycle. First, it can be used to describe tasks as part of producing a requirements specification. Second, it can be used for evaluation purposes once a computer system or prototype has been built. While, from a theoretical viewpoint, the latter use of task analysis is the less interesting of the two, it is vital, and is still underused, in system development and, as argued in Chapter 7, is to be greatly preferred to relying on only the verbal comments of people about a computer system. In these evaluative uses, task analysis is, of course, apparently competing with other evaluations of user performance. One view, not necessarily to be encouraged, is that all measures of user behaviour are a form of task analysis. TAKD cannot be used in this way and the author suggests that in general the term task analysis should be restricted to cases where many behaviours are being described or measured, rather than evaluations that are like psychology experiments and take just a few, simple measures such as times or errors.

For many involved in HCI there is an interest in incorporating good HCI, both good human and organizational factors, at the earliest stages of the design of computer systems and preferably before any firm decisions are made about either hardware or software. This is in contrast to using HCI as a damage limitation exercise, after computer system development, to make a computer usable and in some cases even useful. However, once the major design decisions have been made then the effectiveness of HCI is severely reduced as the scope for substantial modifications of system functionality is limited. Those interested in applying HCI to the earliest stages of design are consequently interested in the complete computer system as well as its users and operating environment, both physical and social, and not merely in the design of the user–computer interface. Thus HCI is involved in complex, complete systems, in the systems theory sense (e.g. Open Systems Group, 1972), in such applications. Task analysis provides a major tool for the analysis of tasks that are currently carried out manually, or with a computer system that is to be replaced, and should provide a major input to the requirements specification of the system to be designed or modified.

The example of TAKD described in this chapter focuses on a noncomputerized task which could be supported by a change in technology. When used for early requirements specification, methods such as TAKD need to identify the relevant tasks and personnel and to provide an output that is in a form suitable for the other people involved in the design process who are not HCI or task analysis experts. Walsh (Chapter 6) discusses in more detail this problem and proposes the use of a JSD notation to bridge the gap between task analysis and system requirements specification. This chapter's proposals with respect to TAKD are somewhat different from those of Walsh, however, who in part solves the problem by concentrating on the user interface specification. TAKD, in contrast to Walsh, concentrates on the complete system, which includes the computer, its direct end users, the other personnel who are affected by the new system (indirect end users — e.g. Diaper, 1987), and on the client organization that pays for the system. Thus in the early requirements specification usage of TAKD, the user–computer interface is only a minor aspect of the system, albeit an important one. Furthermore, there is an assumption that if systems are well designed then the cost of interface development, which may now be 50% of the total cost of a modern system, will be reduced because the system, rather than the interface, will support both the tasks and the style of input and output that users require. This is an argument for increasing the transparency (e.g. Hayes-Roth *et al.*, 1983) of a system, though it must be recognized that complete transparency cannot be achievable given the difference between human and machine cognition (e.g. Diaper, 1984, 1989a).

One of the first and most critical decisions facing those using task analysis in early system design is to identify clearly the purpose of the system to be designed. This is critical because it needs to be recognized that task analysis, including the observational components described in Chapter 7, is an expensive exercise both for the analyst and often for the client organization. However, one of the main uses of TAKD is to identify and perhaps to limit the desirable scope of a system to be designed and thus the early specification of the purpose of a system needs to be stated in a broad manner. However, even when TAKD is being used in such scoping exercises to investigate whether it will be profitable to proceed with system development, it is not the case that TAKD can be used without some specification of the reason for doing it. Furthermore, a purpose such as 'to improve an office's efficiency' is so broad and the range of tasks so extensive that while it would not prevent applying TAKD it would be generally too expensive an approach to employ. Changing the purpose to 'to improve an office's efficiency by introducing computer systems' provides a very major restriction on the purpose as many office tasks which are critical to efficiency are not computerizable. Such a purpose would still leave many potential tasks requiring analysis and in general a purpose needs to be specified in more modest terms (e.g. to improve an office's efficiency by introducing computer systems that will improve inter-office communication, or integrate records, or support document preparation, etc.). How such specifications are formulated is beyond the scope of this chapter.

3.   THE TAKD METHODOLOGY

At the heart of TAKD's methodology lies the building of a Task Descriptive Hierarchy (TDH). This is the aspect of TAKD that has been least well documented. The reason for this is that building the TDH involves the task analyst's making a range of subjective decisions of varying extension and consequence that are often difficult because inductive, as well as deductive, logic is involved. TAKD as an analytical method is not alone in fudging descriptions involving induction simply because induction, unlike deduction, is not a well-understood process either philosophically or heuristically. A first attempt at a set of TDH heuristics has been published (Diaper, 1988a) and these are elaborated below in section 3.2. The input to TAKD is described in section 3.1. Section 3.3 then describes how a high-level, generic description is produced and represented in a KRG format.

3.1   Input to TAKD

As already mentioned, the notion of a level is critical to an understanding of TAKD. TAKD takes as its input one or more descriptions of low-level entities from task observation (Chapter 7). This level of input is the lowest employed within TAKD and it is important that it is at a sufficiently low level that all critical information for subsequent purposes is represented. At the current point in TAKD's development there have generally been two types of low-level entity lists: specific objects and specific actions. The need for a third type of low-level input that has not yet been fully explored, but is argued for later in this chapter (section 3.5), is that of specific sequences. The nature of this input, which must be used in a slightly different way from specific actions and specific objects, will not be described in this section. However, the heuristics governing specific sequence data are similar to those for specific actions and objects.

While in most cases both a specific action and a specific object list will need to be constructed, there are cases where only one of these will be necessary. Such cases arise when there are very few relevant actions or objects. In an example involving the evaluation of an expert system, a specific action list was not warranted because the number of actions of interest were restricted to either a couple of key strokes or the reading of a form and the latter was not a relevant component of the task with respect to the purpose of analysis. Similarly, the worked example described in this chapter also concentrates on specific objects. In contrast, in a study involving authoring, either individually or collaboratively, there was no need for a specific object list as the only relevant physical objects involved were pen and paper, and the actual text written, it was decided, was better captured in the behaviours associated with its production (Rogers, 1989).

3.1.1   Specific objects

The specific object list contains all the objects that are relevant to the performance of a task, or set of tasks. The definition of an object is somewhat problematical in that a specific object may be a part of a larger object. For example, for some purposes a computer's QWERTY keyboard may be treated as a single specific object, whereas for others it may be necessary to identify individual keys (e.g. the return or input key) or groups of keys (e.g. cursor control keys) as specific objects. Furthermore, for some parts of a task it may be appropriate to describe an obvious, complete object (e.g. a floppy disk) but in other parts within the task it may be necessary to identify a particular part of such an object only (e.g. a floppy disk's write protection notch). This, however, is not a major problem with TAKD and it is not even necessary to state explicitly the sub-relationships and super-relationships between an object and its parts as this, where relevant, will be dealt with automatically by the TDH. That such relationships are not always relevant lies in the fact that specific objects may be treated in semantically different ways in different parts of the task. To stay with the floppy disk example, a floppy disk may be treated in two different ways. First, it may be an information storage device and, as such, is treated as a single specific object to which typical disk operations such as READ, WRITE, DELETE, etc. are performed. Second, it can be a physical object which may have physical behaviours directed towards its parts, such as covering the write protection notch, or placing it within its protective envelope. While the real-world object (floppy disk) is the same in both instances, its semantics within the task are different and thus it is treated as two different specific objects (or a set of objects), one informational and one physical, and it is advantageous to separate such usage.

A second problem, while generally straightforward, which deserves at least cursory recognition is the identification of objects which are irrelevant to the purpose of analysis. Irrelevant does not, however, necessarily mean unimportant, but rather that the task performer does not generate any specific actions towards irrelevent objects. To take a trivial example, the desk on which a computer sits is in many cases irrelevant to task performance other than that a surface of suitable height and extent is required. In such cases the desk would not be listed as a specific object. There are, of course, cases where even for a desk this is not the case, as for example when the purpose of the analysis is at least in part interested in the physical ergonomics and biomechanics associated with task performance, say for work station design, or where the desk does have actions directed towards it, for example, when used as a layout device for note cards, piles of paper, etc., and where its physical properties may constrain the task.

Task observation as described in Chapter 7, produces an activity list that describes how a task is carried out. The specific object list is simply a list of every relevant object extracted from this list. Cases where the analyst is in doubt as to whether to include an object in the list, or whether to count two similar objects as the same or different, must be resolved by applying a conservative heuristic. This heuristic proposes that, if in doubt, include it separately. Redundancy in this list, that is, where objects need not have been included or where the same object is represented more than once, can be easily handled subsequently. In contrast, omissions from the list are disastrous, or at least very expensive, as the most important property required is that the specific object list is complete. Completeness refers to the inclusion of all relevant objects and there are likely to be major problems with constructing the TDH if this criterion is not met and which may require the entire analysis to be repeated from scratch with a complete specific object list.

While applying the above conservative heuristic is essential for ensuring completeness of the specific object list, it needs to be recognized that there is a cost to including irrelevant or redundant specific objects in a list. The costs ensue from an unnecessarily long list of specific objects which are harder to manipulate and use in the TDH building exercise. Thus the level of description used for the specific objects is critical and there is a secondary heuristic which needs to be employed that operates against the conservative one described above. This heuristic states that specific objects should be described at the highest level possible consistent with their subsequent, intended use. For example, if across a range of tasks using different computers there is no intended evaluation of the layout of the different keyboards, then specific keys should not be listed as specific objects but simply characterized as being a computer keyboard. In the original development of TAKD to produce an IT training syllabus it was decided that the latter specific object 'keyboard' was sufficient for the purpose. Clearly, and as stressed in Chapter 7, it is crucial for the analyst to be very clear as to the purposes of the analysis before starting the TAKD analysis exercise.

3.1.2   Specific actions

Specific actions, like specific objects, are first constructed as a list in TAKD. Specific actions are the behaviours performed by a person that are directed towards specific objects. It is important to note that in all applications of TAKD already investigated, and probably always with HCI applications, that actions are carried out by people and not by objects such as computers or their software. The same heuristics, both the conservative and highest level possible ones, are applied to the activity list data from task observation. In general, where both specific action and specific object lists are being constructed, then the specific object list tends to be much longer than that for specific actions. Generally, there are surprisingly few different specific actions that people carry out in computing tasks. In most such tasks, similar actions are repeated on different specific objects.

The two lists of specific actions and specific objects may be constructed simultaneously, though it is often easier to finalize the specific action list after fully constructing the specific object list. However, the specific actions are much more difficult to identify, particularly if the task observation did not involve video recording. The reason for this difficulty lies in the difficulty of observing a range of perceptual, as opposed to motor, acts. Even with video recording it is rare that the task performer's direction of gaze is captured. While head movements may indicate gross changes of attention, say between a hard copy document and a visual display unit (VDU), it is unlikely that there will be data as to where a task performer is looking on a VDU. Thus in many HCI tasks involving computers there may be relatively long periods of apparent inactivity, lasting from a few seconds to, occasionally, several minutes. The use of a post-task walkthrough technique (Chapter 7) can provide an invaluable guide to identifying many actions that do not contain a motor component, provided that the task observer is sufficiently astute to ask the appropriate probe questions during the walkthrough. Perhaps the one major advantage of concurrent protocols recorded during task performance is that they allow the task performer to say what they are doing in such periods and often the performers will point at the object to which they are attending. However, as discussed in Chapter 7, concurrent protocols interfere with task performance as the task tends to be carried out more slowly, a quantitative difference, and perhaps differently, either more or less carefully, for example, a qualitative difference.

Even where data on direction of gaze and/or concurrent or post-task protocols are available, it is still often the case that the task analyst will need to infer some of the task performer's perceptual acts. In many cases such inferences are reasonably straightforward in that a perceptual act is logically necessary. However, it is crucial that the analyst is honest with herself or himself and recognizes the inferential nature of the 'observation' and does not attempt to overspecify the unobserved. Thus the need for inference tends to produce specific actions that are more general (i.e. at a higher level) than those of specific objects which is partly why specific action lists tend to be shorter than specific object ones.

A reasonably straightforward inferred set of perceptual activities might be those involved with correcting a typing mistake in a word-processing task. The typing mistake needs to be recognized by the task performer as a mistake and its spatial location noted. The cursor will need visually locating and, after moving it, it is necessary that the error and cursor are perceived to be appropriately positioned. However, there are usually many alternative routes by which a cursor can be moved to a target location and the reasons for the performer's choosing one, rather than another, are generally impossible to infer. Thus, even in this simple case, the logically necessary perceptual actions cannot be too precisely specified.

There are perceptual acts which are much more difficult to analyse, however. One class are those of which the task performer is entirely unaware and these may only come to the attention of the task analyst when an error occurs. For example, in a task where a highly expert word processor operator was performing a file save operation to a floppy disk drive, the expert detected that the operation would fail from the sound the disk drive made and was already taking corrective action, to change drives, before the error message was displayed on the VDU. The problem is that in such cases it is only when an error occurs that the action of checking the sound the disk drive makes becomes apparent yet, logically, the task performer must be checking this at least most times the disk drive is used. However, the task performer is unaware of doing this so it will not be reported in either a concurrent or a post-task walkthrough protocol and the task analyst is faced with the problem of whether to assign this perceptual act to every disk operation or not. In general the analyst is probably best not inferring that such specific actions always take place and this issue often only needs to be seriously addressed when statistical data about behavioural frequencies are required. Such examples, however, do illustrate the value of observing performance that is not error free and the analyst should, perhaps, pay particular attention to errors. In general it is not that task experts do not make mistakes during task performance, but rather that they know imme-diately how to correct errors which they can detect very promptly. Thus, in the example above, the task performer knew that the disk surface he was attempting to save on was full and that after reading from that surface he had forgotten to change to a disk surface with sufficient space.

3.1.3 Specific action and specific object lists
The output from the first stage of analysis from TAKD will generally be the two lists of specific actions and specific objects. For many purposes it is also often helpful to assign frequencies of occurrence to each member of the lists as a crude measure of their importance, though, of course, there are very infrequent specific actions which if not carried out will cause the task to be impossible to perform. The specific action and object lists are a represen-tation of the task, an acquisition representation in Long's terminology (e.g. Long, 1986, 1989), but as a representation the lists are incomplete. What has been lost from the activity list data in constructing the lists is information about the sequence of actions and also the relationship between specific actions, what the task performer does, and the specific objects, the entities on which the performer operaters. The next stage in TAKD involves constructing the TDH and the relationship between specific actions and their specific objects is reinstated during this stage.

3.2 Constructing a TDH
Perhaps the main purpose underlying the attempt to place on a more formal basis the process by which a TDH is built is to allow the range of subjective decisions that the analyst must make to be explicit. This has the advantage of informing the analyst when such decisions are made and allows different versions of the hierarchy, or parts of it, to be explored. The author has never managed to build a TDH in a single pass but has always had to resort to a number of versions which have undergone extensive revision. At present TDHs have generally been built using a word processor so that parts of the hierarchy can be copied, moved and easily modified, though there is a need to develop a dedicated software tool that would aid what is a cognitively difficult and time-consuming task.

3.2.1 Properties of a TDH
This section describes the properties that a TDH must possess if it is to provide a successful redescription of a task or set of tasks at a higher, more general level. The TDH should provide a multitude of potentially different levels of description from which one can be extracted for subsequent use.

A TDH must first be a true hierarchy, rather than a network, such that all lower levels can be redescribed as higher ones without cross-linkages or loops. Levels in the hierarchy may be omitted and portions of the hierarchy may be repeated. There are three types of relationship which could be used, mutually exclusively, at any level. First there is the logical XOR relationship which specifies that a specific object, for example, can be redescribed as either one type of higher-level entity or another. This is the most common type of within-level relationship. Secondly, there is a logical AND relationship which allows several properties to be possessed at a particular level. This AND relationship is usually used at the very highest levels of the TDH. Thirdly, there is a logical OR relationship where there may be more than one property possessed at a level but, unlike the AND relationship, more than one property is not necessary. It is important to note that for a legal example represented in a TDH none of these logical relationships can be a Boolean zero (i.e. XOR implies one and only one option; AND implies all options; and OR is an optional AND with a minimum of one option selected). The general form of the representation is similar to the systemic grammar networks of Johnson (1987, 1989), Halliday (1978) and Bliss *et al.* (1983). Critically, the TDH developed must allow every specific action and/ or specific object to be redescribed by only a single unique route through the hierarchy.

Fig. 4.1 takes a dummy example from Johnson (1989) to demonstrate the main properties of a TDH in as simple a manner as possible. Johnson's example is about classifying news-stand publications. The conventions adopted in the TDH and used throughout this chapter are as follows: the hierarchy is read from left to right with the highest level on the left; nodes at the same level are spatially located under each other; XOR relationships are characterized by a vertical line '|', OR relationships by a brace '{', and AND by a slash '/'.

The TDH in Fig. 4.1 illustrates most of the typical properties of these hierarchies. Example publications, specific objects, are represented on the right and all can be described at the highest level as news-stand publications. Specific actions are not included as the TDH characterizes the publications rather than describing what a person might do with them (e.g. buy one as a news-stand customer, or order copies if a news-stand vendor). The high-level AND relationship between status and format is a necessary relationship in that all publications must be assigned both a status and a format. In contrast, the lower-level OR relationship between colour and monochrome pictures is an optional relationship in that any specific object must possess one of these properties but could possess both. The requirement of the TDH to be a true hierarchy requires the repetition of the colour–monochrome picture nodes and the readership nodes (general, women, men, children) and it is often helpful initially to include these exhaustively and only to delete nodes to which no specific objects are ever assigned once the TDH is completed. Indeed, it is often an empirical fact of considerable interest to identify logically plausible nodes that have no specific objects attached to them. However, it is not always necessary to be exhaustive and the XOR relationship between daily, weekly or monthly is not carried over as it is already known that there are no monthly newspapers and no daily maga-

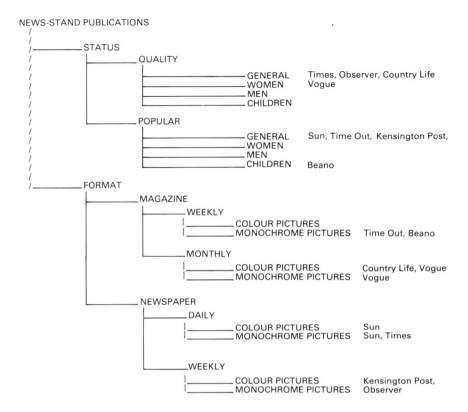

NEWS-STAND PUBLICATIONS

Fig. 4.1 — A simple TDH allowing the specification of news-stand publications (after Johnson, 1989). The *Times* and *Observer* are serious newspapers, the *Sun* is a popular tabloid and the *Kensington Post* is a local London newspaper. *Country Life* and *Vogue* are specialist, glossy magazines, *Time Out* is a London events listing magazine and the *Beano* is a children's cartoon comic.

zines. If this turned out to be incorrect then the appropriate monthly or daily nodes could be added along with the necessary repetition of all the associated lower-level nodes. The readership nodes have been established as XOR relationships and this is a decision made by the analyst on the basis of improving the clarity of the representation. An alternative would have been to use an OR and to have three nodes (women, men and children) so that the general node could be represented by women AND men. A level has been missed out in the status part of the hierarchy so that the readership and picture sections of the hierarchy are aligned. This alignment is not normally done until after the hierarchy is complete.

A TDH generally deals with specific objects, rather than specific actions, except in cases where only specific actions are analysed. In all the cases so far investigatated where both were analysed, relatively few specific actions were found and it has been possible simply to identify appropriate higher-level, generic actions without employing a TDH. The strategy adopted in the syllabus design work was to construct a separate TDH associated with each generic action because different actions may be associated with a different range of objects to which the action is directed. This strategy allows each TDH to maintain the three simple logical relationships between nodes described above. In general, such TDHs, where different, have been closely related to each other. The main difference tends to be the number of AND relationship nodes at the highest levels.

3.3   Building a TDH
Whereas the previous section described the properties required of a TDH, this section describes the practical method that needs to be carried out actually to construct a TDH. It thus describes the heuristics that need to be employed and offers advice, based on the experience of constructing TDHs, that the author has found to be useful. In general it is necessary to apply the heuristics; the other advice describes a style of working that the author has found useful but may not suit everyone else who in future wishes to use TAKD.

One such piece of advice, for example, is that it has been found both to be easier and to produce a better TDH if it is worked on collaboratively, though this is not necessarily the quickest way of working. The reason for advocating collaborative work is that the construction of a TDH involves the analyst in making a large number of subjective decisions and for success these need to be made explicit. Working with at least one other person facilitates making such decision explicit as the dialogue, both discussion and argument, helps to elicit the rationale behind many such decisions.

3.3.1   The first vintage TDH
This section outlines how the specific action and specific object lists contribute to building a TDH and is an elaboration of the description provided by Diaper (1988a). The first point is that it is not possible to build a TDH in an entirely inductive, data-driven manner starting with just the low-level specifications from the specific action and specific object lists. It is essential that the analyst is highly familiar with the specific action and object lists and has a clear specification of the purpose for which TAKD and its TDH is being used. The first step is to construct a very high-level description that will describe all the specific actions and specific objects. The heuristic to employ that allows this is that the highest-level description is so general that, by itself, it is immediately recognized to be too high for any useful analytical purpose. Thus in the news-stand publication example (Fig. 4.1) the highest-level description of all the specific objects (publications) was specified as 'news-stand publications'. Even this is not trivial since it immediately excludes many publications that are only available by subscription. The purpose of this highest-level description is to allow the analyst to use a deductive logic and to make decisions at the early stages of analysis as to what are the important high-level nodes. Thus in the news-stand publication example it was decided that all such publications could be assigned the

properties of 'status' AND 'quality' and it could be readily confirmed that all the exemplar publications (specific objects) could be so categorized. The general principle underlying TDH construction involves working in both a bottom-up (inductive) and a top-down (deductive) fashion simultaneously and to work towards the specification of the nodes at the hierarchy's intermediate levels. Johnson (1989), in a similar exercise using the same example, starts with the following two pairs of nodes: quality and popular (status); and magazine and newspaper (format). She recognizes that these nodes can be arranged hierarchically in a number of different ways. For example, status could be at a higher level than format (Fig. 4.2), or vice versa (Fig. 4.3), as opposed to placing them, as in Fig. 4.1, at the same level and relating then with a logical AND. Implicit in this hierarchical ordering of levels, and crucially for TAKD, is the notion that distinctions made at a higher level are more important than those at the lower levels of the hierarchy.

Fig. 4.2.

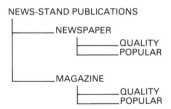

Fig. 4.3.

It is not, of course, the case that any one of the three hierarchies in Figs 4.1, 4.2 and 4.3 is either correct or incorrect, but rather that the analyst must make a subjective decision as to which is more suited to the purpose of carrying out the analysis. Whereas neither Johnson or this author has specified the purpose of the TDH in Fig. 4.1, the simple TDH in Fig. 4.2 may be the more suitable for characterizing the display of news-stand publications from a purchaser's point of view. Thus a purchaser may, for example, only wish to consider quality publications and would therefore have a preference for a display that groups magazines and newspapers of a similar status together and thus eliminate searching publications of an undesirable status. In contrast, Fig. 4.3 might be more suitable from a vendor's point of view as the shelf space required for magazines and newspapers is usually very different. Other nodes represented in Fig. 4.1 might be more important to the vendor, for example the frequency of publication, which might be placed at a very high level to support the vendor's need to remove and replace publications that are out of date, particularly if a sale-or-return contract is in operation. There are, of course, possible nodes that may be extremely important for the vendor that have not been specified in Fig. 1. For example, it may be the case that the crucial difference between publications is not their status, format or frequency but their publisher or distributor. Such information must have been elicited by task observation, including using interviews, before starting to construct the TDH so that the purpose and potential high-level nodes are clearly and completely specified.

Once the analyst has determined the very high-level specification of the TDH then the rest of the hierarchy can be constructed. The goal is to generate a hierarchy which has the property that every low-level specific object or specific action can be described by a single unique route through the TDH. An important heuristic that needs to be followed if the TDH is to be useful is that each node in the hierarchy should have only a small number of immediately lower-level nodes linked to it. This means that the analyst should work towards building a TDH which is deep (i.e. has many levels) rather than shallow. If the heuristic is not followed then a shallow, flattened hierarchy is produced which will lack analytical power for two reasons. First, if there is insufficient depth then there will be little opportunity for redescription of the task observation data at a useful level. To take the extreme case in the context of the news-stand publications example, a TDH of two levels, 'news-stand publications' and 'the publications' (e.g. *The Times, The Sun, Vogue*), allows no such redescription. Secondly, the very act of making the subjective decisions about what the levels should be, and what is their ordering, is the very process by which the analyst comes to understand the data. In general, each node at a level should have between two and four, and certainly no more than six, lower-level nodes linked to it. The cost of increasing the depth of the TDH is an expansion of breadth at the lower levels because of the need to repeat sections of the hierarchy under different higher level nodes, for example the repetition of audience (general, women, men, children) and pictures (colour, monochrome) in Fig. 4.1. There must be a least two lower-level nodes to each higher-level node as if there is only one then the same information is being represented at more than one level in the TDH. It is in such cases that levels can be omitted from the hierarchy when they are aligned, as for example between quality and the four audience nodes in Fig. 4.1.

As already mentioned, the analyst cannot expect to construct a TDH perfectly in a single pass. One useful way of working is to start by building a relatively shallow hierarchy and then to expand it in depth. An advantage to this approach is that it allows the analyst to check that the criterion is met that every specific object is describable by a single unique route through the hierarchy. This is much easier to ensure when the TDH is relatively shallow. The analyst will necessarily have to refer continuously to the low-level, specific entity lists to ensure that this criterion is met.

The analyst must also be preparared to alter radically whole sections of the hierarchy and even to reorder nodes and levels as the TDH is developed. One of the advantages, however, of deciding on the very highest levels at the early stages of the analysis is that such restructuring then tends to occur at the intermediate levels and is thus easier to handle. It is for this reason that these highest levels are generally too high to be ultimately useful, which is why they may be fixed permanently as the analysis progresses.

Once a first vintage, after Bacon (Hesse, 1964), TDH has been constructed it is a generally useful approach to take individual specific actions or specific objects and to elaborate the TDH by fully working out their route through the TDH. Successively choosing radically different specific entities facilitates the elaboration and increasing depth of the TDH. After a number of such exercises it is usually necessary for the analyst to examine the complete hierarchy and to replicate the new sections developed where they are also logically necessary in parts of the hierarchy which have not been part of the route of the exemplar specific entities already examined. Following this approach leads to the generation of a more complete TDH and the generation of levels and nodes which are logically possible but for which no specific entities have been observed. This has important consequences for the evaluation of the TDH and allows the possibility of testing the completeness of the original set of tasks observed by directing the analyst to examining new tasks that may have these new elements in them.

Finally, the analyst will reach a point where she or he feels that the hierarchy is complete and is likely to meet the criterion that every specific entity can be described. The next stage of the analysis involves proving that this criterion has been met and is described in the next section.

However, before moving on to the development and use of a KRG to redescribe specific entities it is worth pointing out that the names given to nodes in the TDH are irrelevant and could be replaced by arbitrary labels. However, the use of meaningful labels serves as a very useful mnemonic for the analyst. As such, it does not matter what the analyst chooses to call a node, or that node labels may be repeated with different meanings at different levels in the TDH, provided that the analyst is clear on the intended meaning. Documentation of node labels, however, is crucial if the TDH, or any part of it, is to be made public. It is wise advice, but difficult to follow, for the analyst to make notes on the semantics of the nodes and their labels at the time the decisions are made during TDH construction. The author has several times found it difficult to reconstruct the rationale for particular node distinctions and the order of levels in a *post hoc* manner.

3.3.2   The KRG

TAKD's KRG provides a means of describing the route of each task step's specific objects through the TDH. The end product of this stage of TAKD is a list of KRG sentences, one for each route through the hierarchy. It is at this stage that the analyst returns to the original task observation data that will be represented as a series of task steps which will include specific actions and objects, or descriptions that can be re-represented as these specific entities.

Experience suggests that this stage is most easily achieved as a two-step process. Each task step, using the task step numbers, is assigned to the appropriate low-level nodes of the TDH. When complete, the data will look like those represented in Fig. 4.1 but with the task step numbers replacing the news-stand publications. (Note that the example represented in Fig. 4.1 is not a true task analysis in that it merely describes news-stand publications, rather than describing tasks directed to the publications so that there are no task steps. However, the principle can be demonstrated using this example provided that the reader is prepared to substitute task steps such as 'insert a floppy disk into a disk drive' for news-stand publications such as *'The Times'.*)

Following this assignment, each task step, or publication in the Fig. 4.1 example, can now be redescribed as a KRG sentence. There is no analytical component to this step in TAKD as the KRG merely provides a redescription of the previous step of assigning the task steps to the TDH. However, the KRG does provide a convenient and analytically powerful tool for the subsequent stages of TAKD. The conventions used in the TDH are similar in the KRG. The KRG does possess a grammar, though not one that is similar to English grammar. A KRG sentence usually consists of a single generic action which operates on one or more generic object phrases (GOPs). GOPs are defined by the AND relationships in the TDH and so are represented in KRG sentences between slashes ('/.../'). The components of each GOP are represented as nested brackets, either parentheses ('(...)') for XOR relationships or braces ('{ ... }') for OR relationships.

The following four KRG sentences (albeit without generic actions) redescribe the four newspapers represented in Fig. 4.1.

K1.   *The Times*
NEWS-STAND PUBLICATIONS/STATUS(QUALITY ((GENERAL)))/FORMAT(NEWSPAPER(DAILY{MONOCHROME PICTURES}))/

K2.   *The Observer*
NEWS-STAND PUBLICATIONS/STATUS(QUALITY ((GENERAL)))/FORMAT(NEWSPAPER(WEEKLY{MONOCH-ROME PICTURES}))/

K3.   *The Sun*
NEWS-STAND PUBLICATIONS/STATUS(POPULAR
((GENERAL)))/FORMAT(NEWSPAPER(DAILY{MONOCHROME
PICTURES}{COLOUR PICTURES}))/

K4.   *The Kensington Post*
NEWS-STAND PUBLICATIONS/STATUS(POPULAR
((GENERAL)))/FORMAT(NEWSPAPER(WEEKLY{MONOCH-
ROME PICTURES}))/

The same four KRG sentences are easier to read for those unfamiliar with
the KRG notation if the GOPs are separated on different lines. Thus:

K1.   *The Times*
NEWS-STAND PUBLICATIONS
            /STATUS(QUALITY((GENERAL)))/
            /FORMAT(NEWSPAPER(DAILY{MONOCHROME
              PICTURES}))/

K2.   *The Observer*
NEWS-STAND PUBLICATIONS
            /STATUS(QUALITY((GENERAL)))/
            /FORMAT(NEWSPAPER(WEEKLY{MONO-
              CHROME PICTURES}))/

K3.   *The Sun*
NEWS-STAND PUBLICATIONS
            /STATUS-POPULAR((GENERAL)))/
            /FORMAT(NEWSPAPER(DAILY{MONOCHROME
              PICTURES}{COLOUR PICTURES}))/

K4.   *The Kensington Post*
NEWS-STAND PUBLICATIONS
            /STATUS(POPULAR((GENERAL)))/
            /FORMAT(NEWSPAPER(WEEKLY{MONO-
              CHROME PICTURES}))/

3.3.3   *Generic KRG representations*
In the news-stand publication example, none of the publications has exactly
the same KRG sentence attached to them as any other. This is less likely to
be the case where there are many more KRG sentences produced and thus
the 'full' KRG sentences identify task steps (or publications) that are the
same. Obviously the same KRG sentence does not need to be written out in
full each time. The analyst can check the TDH at this stage as if two task
steps which s/he considers to be very different have identical KRG sentence
descriptions then this implies that the TDH is inadequate and probably
requires additional categories to be added. However, such problematic
occurrences tend to be rare if the TDH has been thoroughly constructed.

One of the major purposes of TAKD is that it allows the identification of
general similarity between task steps. The process of generification involves

the re-representation of task steps at a more general or higher level of description. Generification is a simple process and involves the removal of the lower levels of the TDH. In effect one slices or cuts through the TDH at a useful level somewhere between the very highest and lowest levels. Several such cuts may be tried depending on the purpose of the analysis. In the syllabus design work (Diaper and Johnson, 1989) two different sets of generic KRG sentences were generated. The higher-level one provided just over 20 KRG sentences and provided a specification for a two-week, introductory IT course. The lower-level set of KRG sentences, over 200 of them, provided a more detailed specification for a one-year training programme.

The four nespapers KRG sentences listed above could thus be first redescribed as:

K1'.   *The Times*
NEWS-STAND   PUBLICATIONS/STATUS(QUALITY)/FORMAT-
(NEWSPAPER(DAILY))/

K2'.   *The Observer*
NEWS-STAND   PUBLICATIONS/STATUS(QUALITY)/FORMAT-
(NEWSPAPER(WEEKLY))/

K3'.   *The Sun*
NEWS-STAND   PUBLICATIONS/STATUS(POPULAR)/FORMAT-
(NEWSPAPER(DAILY))/

K4'.   *The Kensington Post*
NEWS-STAND   PUBLICATIONS/STATUS(POPULAR)/FORMAT-
(NEWSPAPER(WEEKLY))/

However, this adds no additional categorical information as all of these publications still require different, generic KRG sentences to describe them. The implication is that the lower levels of descriptions that have been eliminated in these generic K' KRGs did not differentiate between the target publications. A similar finding occurs in the worked example (section 4.4). A second, still higher-level, cut through the TDH is, however, informative about the similarity between these four publications:

K1".   *The Times* and *The Observer*
NEWS-STAND   PUBLICATIONS/STATUS(QUALITY)/FORMAT-
(NEWSPAPER)/

K2".   *The Sun* and *The Kensington Post*
NEWS-STAND   PUBLICATIONS/STATUS(POPULAR)/FORMAT-
(NEWSPAPER)/

At this level the other news-stand publications listed in Fig. 4.1 can also be redescribed:

K3".   *Vogue* and *Country Life*
NEWS-STAND   PUBLICATIONS/STATUS(QUALITY)/FORMAT-
(MAGAZINE)/

K4″.   *Time Out* and *The Beano*
NEWS-STAND PUBLICATIONS/STATUS(POPULAR)/FORMAT-
(MAGAZINE)/

Thus the eight publications can be categorized at this level of description into the four types characterized by the four K″ KRG sentences above. Of course, in an example like this there is no great practical utility to such descriptions. The real utility of TAKD's generification process lies when there are hundreds or even thousands of KRG sentences which need to be reduced to a manageable and meaningful set.

3.3.4   *KRG sentence analysis*
Many of the applications of TAKD have used the list of generic KRG sentences from one or more tasks as the primary product of the analysis. In the syllabus design work the KRG sentences were listed in terms of their frequency of occurrence across tasks and this, along with a great deal of explanatory documentation, constituted the syllabus. A similar use of KRG frequency of occurrence data is described in the worked example.

Generic KRG sentences are intended to inform the analyst as to what are the common classes of activity associated with a task. Thus, in designing a computer system and its interface it is reasonable to expect that frequently occurring activities should specify the primary functionality of a system and that the users are supported by the human–computer interface so that they can access such functionality easily but also safely (e.g. Diaper, 1989b). If the functionality of the system is well specified and implemented then the common activities should be 'simple' in the sense of Kay's maxim that 'simple things should be simple; complex things should be possible' (Smith *et al.*, 1982), although as Smith *et al.* point out in describing the design of the Xerox Star system, 'it was sometimes necessary to make common things simple at the expense of uncommon things being harder'. TAKD provides a well-structured, empirically driven, analytical method for identifying such commonalities and thus is well suited to this role in the early stages of computer system design.

When TAKD is used during prototyping or for improving an existing computer system then it can be used in an evaluative role. In this role the frequency of occurrence of KRG sentences needs to be compared with the amount of effort needed to achieve the desired end. To take one example, with many large computer operating systems there are a very large number of possible commands, often with many possible options or parameters, not all of which are sensibly defaulted for a particular class of task in a particular organization. Users, however, usually use only a very small subset of the command set. Draper (1984) found that with UNIX, of the 570 commands available only 394 were used by the 94 users studied over an 8 month period and that the modal number of commands used by individual users was between 40 and 60 commands. TAKD provides a description of users' task performance that is more sophisticated than that which could be obtained from looking at mere command usage alone, for example, and can thus inform the evaluator and designer of where unreasonable user effort is involved in using the system.

The crucial aspect of KRG sentence analysis is the understanding of generic KRG sentences. What is usually of interest to the analyst is not the minor variations between task steps but the general requirements of a set of tasks. If the generic KRG sentences cannot be interpreted by the analyst directly then the simplest method is to list under each generic KRG sentence the set of full KRG sentences and/or the prose descriptions of the task steps from which each was derived. How the analyst uses generic KRG sentences depends on the purpose of carrying out the analysis. The worked example demonstrates one use of generic KRG sentences for the purpose of identifying system requirements, though, for different purposes, different uses of the generic KRGs may be required.

At present, TAKD is not prescriptive about the use of its products and the method is not alone at being weak at bridging the gulf that exists between user-centred task descriptions and computer-centred system design specifications (e.g. Diaper, 1989c). There is no doubt that further work needs to be done on both how TAKD's products are applied and how this gulf between user- and computer-centred representations can be bridged. This issue is further discussed in section 5.2.

3.3.5   KRG sequence analysis

The following analysis method has not been fully investigated within the examples of TAKD known to the author. This is more by chance than by design, but the following analysis seems an obvious extension of the use of KRG sentences for computer system design and evaluation. The task steps originally observed can obviously be re-represented by KRG sentences. Both within and across tasks the repetition of sequences of KRG sentences can then be analysed. It is likely that unless the generic KRG sentences are of a very high level then there will be a number of similar sequences of KRG sentences. This is the same type of difference that occurs with similar but slightly different low-level KRG sentences. The same type of solution could also be applied, that is, similar sequences could be represented by a sequence representation grammar (SRG) which, like the KRG, would recognize a number of logical relationships between KRG sentences, particularly KRG sentences that are optional in a sequence. In effect, the SRG would provide a sentence-like representation of a flow diagram that describes the common sequences of the users' behaviours. The advantage of a sentence representation is that it will be open to a similar generification process to that used on the KRG sentences.

The purpose of an SRG will be to identify to computer system designers potential macros that might be supplied for users. These macros might be fairly sophisticated so that they themselves will take options or parameters when invoked by the user and will probably need in some cases to supply confirmation prompts so that the users are aware of the consequences of complex sequences of commands which might be unsafe if wrongly used. Programming such macros may be beyond the ability of many users who are merely experienced at running applications programs and thus there is a potential need for the professional programmer either to supply them ready made or to provide tools that makes such macros easy to generate.

For example, a few years ago when text editing large documents on a microcomputer, the author regularly issued a series of commands to the disk operating system to save the current file once editing had finished. While the command 'save ⟨filename⟩' alone would be sufficient this was not used because it was very easy to mistype the filename and to overwrite the wrong file, particularly when many related filenames differed by only a single character. Thus each file saved had to be unlocked, saved and then locked again. In fact, the sequence of behaviour was rather more complicated but, having lost files from not following the procedure, the author placed a premium on file integrity above the effort involved. The actual sequence of behaviours, with several possible minor variations, was:

(1) check file name in command display
(2) unlock named file
(3) display file directory
(4) check unlocked file matches the command display file name
(5) save file
(6) lock the named file
(7) display file directory
(8) check all files are locked

With this sequence, if a typing error was made at any point then the user could recover the error without loss. Thus if the wrong file was unlocked at (2) then it was checked at (3). If at (5) the wrong filename was typed then an error message was displayed if overwriting of a locked file was attempted, or if at (8) there existed an unlocked file which indicated that the old file had not been replaced by the new one which would still be unlocked. Typing errors at (6) were of minor consequence as an error message was displayed if locking was attempted on a non-existent file, or if there remained one or two unlocked files at (8) depending on whether there was also an error at (5). Fairly obviously this sequence could be considerably reduced in terms of user effort without loss of safety if the designers had anticipated the real problems users might have in saving one of a series of files with very similar names. Furthermore, there were a number of very similar, minor variations of this sequence. For example, saving the next file in a sequence of files with related names required the user to remember that the filename in (1) was the name of the previous file and not the current one. Of course, more modern systems that support version management have been designed to overcome this problem.

3.4   TAKD method summary

Before presenting an example of how TAKD can be used, this section lists the major steps involved in TAKD. It should be noted, however, that there is a range of possible variations around this general scheme.

Step 1   From the observational data of task steps list all the specific objects and specific actions (note that the application and purpose for carrying out the analysis must already have been established).

Step 2   Construct the highest-level description of the task, representing it in a generic KRG format.

Step 3   Construct the first vintage TDH using example-specific objects and specific or generic actions, if appropriate.

Step 4   Construct the final TDH by assigning specific objects to the lowest-level nodes of the TDH.

Step 5   Calculate the frequency of occurrence of specific objects at all the nodes in the TDH.

Step 6   Redescribe each observed task step in the KRG sentence format.

Step 7   Generate generic KRG sentences by removing the lower-level node descriptions after aligning the TDH's levels so that the number of different generic KRG sentences is a suitable and manageable set.

Step 8   Calculate the frequency of generic KRG sentences.

Step 9   Interpret the generic KRG sentences with respect to the task domain of interest.

Step 10   Repeat step 6 with the generic KRG sentences.

Step 11   Extract repetitions of sequences of generic KRG sentences and represent these as an SRG and finally a generic SRG.

Step 11 is incomplete and only relevant where an analysis is intended of sequences of behaviour. They have only been dealt with superficially in this chapter (section 3.3.5).

4.   A WORKED EXAMPLE OF TAKD

This section describes an example of TAKD's application in HCI. The example demonstrates how TAKD may be used in the early stages of design to establish how people perform a task using traditional pen and paper media. It is intended that this analysis will feed into the requirements specification for a major system development programme. The basic work was carried out by second-year undergraduate students of psychology at Liverpool Polytechnic as part of their degree programme and with the help of the MUCH (Multiple Users Creating Hyperdocuments) research group at Liverpool University.

4.1   Supporting annotation in collaborative writing

In many areas of commerce, industry and academia it is becoming increasingly common for documents to be written by a number of authors. At present most text-processing facilities are designed for a single author, with notable, but rare, exceptions such as COLAB (Stefik *et al.*, 1983). The

MUCH research group is involved in developing a variety of tools to support the production of documents written collaboratively and most of the work centres on using a hypertext system to support such activities.

4.1.1   Introduction

The study used in this chapter to exemplify the application of TAKD involves an initial investigation of collaborative authoring involving the annotation of draft documents. This study arose out of the author's experience with starting the new international journal *Interacting with Computers: the Interdisciplinary Journal of Human–Computer Interaction* (IwC). The original General Editorial and Management Board (GEMB) of IwC consisted of about a dozen people who all communicated by electronic mail so that face-to-face meetings were rare. A number of substantial documents needed writing to establish the goals, procedures and so forth of IwC. The intended mechanism for such document creation was that there would be a primary author who would produce a first draft. This draft was then sent via electronic mail to all GEMB members to comment on. Comments were returned by electronic mail and the primary author then synthesized these and produced another draft. This cycle was repeated until at least most members of the GEMB were satisfied with the document. The author has used this method reasonably successfully for writing journal papers (e.g. Barlow *et al.,* 1989) so that, with only a small number of collaborating authors who knew each other, but were not all in the same country, it was possible to produce eight drafts within about three weeks. However, in the case of IwC with many more collaborators the system was less successful.

The advantage of using electronic mail lies in its speed and reliability compared with physical, paper-based mail systems as, not only do all collaborators obtain each draft at approximately the same time, but by using a single mailbox which distributes mail to everyone all the comments on a draft are also seen by everyone. Reliability is improved as the generator of a document, comment or message has this returned indicating that it successfully arrived at the central mailbox and was distributed. Occasional mailer failures to individuals can usually be detected by the receiving individuals from the content of subsequent comments. The system has worked reasonably well for more than two years as a means of holding a continuous committee meeting.

With large documents, however, there were two major problems. First was the problem of version control. Comments were sometimes sent on a version of a draft document that had already been superseded and in some cases this was not simply due to electronic mail 'crossing in the post', but reflected the time it took some of the collaborators to reply to earlier mail and to keep up to date with current mail. The second, and more serious problem, which the study below addresses, was the actual problem of annotating comments on to a draft document.

Given the international nature of the GEMB and the current state of electronic mail systems only simple, unformatted ASCII text may be reliably sent because the GEMB members use a wide variety of computer systems for editing and sending–receiving electronic mail. Problems arise when a co-author wishes to annotate a draft document heavily. This is crucial, particularly in the later stages of document production where there is a concern with minor, but important, aspects of style, grammar and so forth which cannot be neatly encapsulated in a general, new message but really needs marking directly onto the draft document. With two or three co-authors modifying a document there may not be a major problem because the annotator can merely edit the text and send it on the understanding that the other collaborators then use this revised version. With many simultaneous annotators making revisions which need to be synthesized by the primary author this route is not possible. The primary author needs to see from each contributing co-author the original version of the draft document and the suggested changes (annotations) must be marked or highlighted in some way. While there were a number of different styles adopted by GEMB members, in general what was done was that an annotator would load the draft document into their text-processing system and at each point where an annotation was required the appropriate section of text would be marked and then recopied so as to include the suggested change. A number of highlighting conventions needed to be adopted, particularly where deletions or substitutions were suggested. This method, while satisfactory in principle, turned out to be very clumsy in practice. It was very time consuming for the annotator and an annotated draft could quite easily become double the length of the original. To take a very simple example, the substitution of a word requires that the line or section needs to be copied and the highlighted word marked. For example, from the above line,

take a very simple example, the *substitution* of a word requires that the

take a very simple example, the *replacement* of a word requires that the

and with multiple annotations this can become very complex:

draft could quite easily become ** double the length of the original. *To take a very simple* example, the *substitution* of *a word* requires that the

draft could quite easily become *more than* double the length of the original. *For* example, the *multiple modification* of *text within a block* requires that the

Compared with marking annotations on a paper version this technique is clumsy and the job of the primary author is made more difficult by the variations of style used by the different collaborators and the different solutions suggested for the same problematic piece of text. For collaborators within the same country the electronic mail system was sometimes abandoned and annotated copies of drafts were sent physically or by facsimile to the primary author, with the consequence of excluding the other GEMB members. Even this was not particularly satisfactory as each collaborator tended to reformat the document when printing from their mail system so that the general visual cues, and even the line lengths, were not the same for different collaborators' contributions. The annotation-synthesizing role of the primary author was thus made considerably more difficult, and the synthesis alone, without these additional problems, was itself intellectually demanding.

The MUCH group was already committed to a major investigation of computer-assisted collaborative authoring environments and one of the perceived requirements of such systems is a need to support the sort of annotation task described above. They had already decided that a hypertext system would be required and the basic idea would be that sections of text could be highlighted and that annotations would be made in separate windows that the primary author, and the co-authors, could access by selecting the highlighted sections of text. Such a system would allow meta-annotation, that is, comments about suggested changes, and the job of both the co-authors and the primary author would be made easier by having only a single version of the document and common access to all suggested changes.

While the anecdotal description of the annotation problem described in the IwC example identifies the sort of problems that such a system needs to address, it fails to specify in detail what is required of such a system. Importantly, a first goal should be that using a collaborative authoring environment of this sort should ideally be at least as easy as annotating hard copy. However, even if this goal is not fully achieved, there might still be advantages to the system if it allowed distributive working via electronic mail, although this, of course, would require all collaborators to have access to the same collaborative authoring software on their own computers. Very little work has been done on the annotative task in collaborative authoring, though it is a very common task. As an initial, pilot investigation it was decided to analyse how document annotation was carried out using pen and paper. The task analysis of such tasks is intended to identify the sorts of features that need to be supported in a computerized annotation system and to identify further their relative importance. The study described below is only a pilot study but its products can be used to support further task analyses which, because the TDH has already been produced, can be carried out relatively quickly.

4.1.2   Method
The study involves taking a video recording of a subject performing an annotation task on a document. The video records only the document and the subject's hands. Immediately after completing the annotating task each subject then produced a walkthrough protocol (see Chapter 7). The walkthrough involved focusing the video camera on the television screen where the original video was displayed. Either the subject or the experimenter stopped and started the original video as the subject described what they had been doing. Where necessary the experimenter prompted the subject for comments.

4.1.2.1   Subjects

Three right-handed subjects were used: a professor of computer science
(S1); a computer science Ph.D. student (S2); and the author (S3), at that
time a senior lecturer in psychology. Subjects S1 and S3 were extremely
familiar with the sort of annotation task used in the study and the student
was not unfamiliar with such tasks.

4.1.2.2   Materials

Three different documents were used in the study, one for each subject.
These were as follows for subjects 1 to 3 respectively: D1, a book chapter
draft; D2, a paper submitted to an international conference; D3, a paper
submitted to IwC. The subjects had not previously read the document they
annotated.

4.1.2.3   Equipment

The study used a tripod-mounted automatic video camera, two VHS video
recorders and a television set. The video camera allowed a time stamp to be
visibly placed onto the video recording. In the annotation task the camera
was placed to the left of the small desk at which the subjects sat and was
mounted high on the tripod. The image recorded by the camera consisted of
only the document and a small amount of surrounding desk and when
displayed the paper appeared rotated 90° anticlockwise (i.e. with the top of
the document to the left of the display). The image quality was sufficient that
words appeared as blocks and annotations could be seen but these were not
legible from the video recording alone. All analysis that involved using the
video recordings was therefore done with a hard copy of the annotated
document. In the walkthrough part of the task the camera was moved
behind the subject and the television showing the original video of the task
was recorded from above the subjects head.

4.1.2.4   Procedure

All three subjects were familiar with the purpose of the study and thus no
great degree of explanation about the task was required. Before starting,
subjects made themselves comfortable at the desk while keeping the
document within the marks on the desk and their left hand out of camera's
view. During the annotation task subjects worked at their own pace and
were asked to point with the pen to what they were reading during the task.
The Ph.D. student (document D2) was asked to finish gracefully after 9
minutes, the other two documents were fully annotated in 12 minutes (D1)
and 34 minutes (D3). These differences are principally due to the different
lengths of the document, rather than to any great difference in the subjects'
rates of work. Having finished the annotation task the subjects took a brief
rest while the camera was moved and they then performed the walkthrough.

4.1.2.5   Analysis strategy

The study was analysed as part of a student exercise. The analysis was
carried out by six groups of students with 3–6 members per group. The

longest recording (D3) was divided into four approximately equal sections and thus each student group analysed a different portion of video tape. The student groups met about once a week when analyses were coordinated by the author.

For the students, the purpose of the exercise was to learn about observational studies and how systematic methods such as TAKD could be used on observational data. The purpose with respect to the collaborative authoring environment has already been described (section 4.1.1). The emphasis on the analysis reported in this chapter is on how a TDH was constructed and on the range of subjective decisions that the analysts needed to make. However, the number of versions of the TDH that were developed during the analysis are both too many and too large for inclusion in this chapter and so only the final version of the TDH is presented (Fig. 4.7). The TDH and the lists of KRG sentences were stored and manipulated on a word processor. This software is not ideal and the chapter finishes by making some suggestions as to software that could be designed to make the analysis both easier and less prone to error. As much as half the analysis time following the representation of the annotating behaviour as KRG sentences (about 60 hours) was occupied with correcting errors. Most of these would not have occurred if better software had been available.

4.2 Task observation

Working in small groups, the students started the task observation exercise by watching both the original and walkthrough video recordings of their part of the task. The principle observational exercise was then carried out on the original recording and the walkthrough was only occasionally used to help to disambiguate what a subject was doing in the task. What was produced by the observers was a prose description of each piece of annotation behaviour. After some practice and discussion between the student groups there appeared a general consensus about what should be observed and how it would be recorded. The aim of this exercise was to record the behaviours in sufficient detail so that the video record would not be required in subsequent analyses. As noted in Chapter 7, analysis of video recordings is time consuming and best done only once per tape. Fig. 4.4 shows the first page of document D3 and with the annotations included and numbered (the numbering was done at the same time as the prose descriptions were written). The prose descriptions are shown in Fig. 4.5.

It should be noted that these descriptions of the annotation behaviour have already involved a considerable number of decisions about what is not recorded. Most obviously, there is no record of the reading rate, pauses and so forth as indicated by the subject pointing at the text. Browsing, however, though not in evidence on page 1, was recorded in a similar form to that used in Fig. 4.5. Browsing behaviour was defined as any time when the subject stopped reading linearly and jumped either forwards or backwards in the text, either within or across pages and without making any annotation. Thus there was a browsing behaviour between behaviours A1 and A2 and between behaviours A3 and A2 but these are not recorded as browsing

Collaborative Writing

of Documents and Hyperdocuments

why not hypertext?

2

Roy Rada[*], Barbara Keith[+],

Marc Burgoine[*], Steven George[*], Vrinda Gholkar[*], David Reid[*]

Department of Computer Science[*]
Univeristy of Liverpool
Liverpool L69 3BX, England

Department of English[+]
North Cheshire College
Warrington WA2 0DB, England

4

Abstract

1

style?

A good writer understands his audience. Collaborative writing allows authors to also act as readers and thus to create documents which an audience is more likely to appreciate. We are studying the conditions under which computers can support the collaborative writing process. Simple computer editors can play a valuable role in group writing, if the authors have good channels of communication and a common purpose. In one of our experiments, secondary school students that were unable to produce a sophisticated document independently were able to produce a quality document through a group process.

3

Hyperdocuments (also known as hypertext) differ from traditional documents in that many links among parts of the document are made explicit. We hypothesized that collaborative writing would work particularly well with hyperdocuments because the links among the various writers' ideas could be more easily explored. In our experiences with graduate students at two universities, this hypothesize has *not* been supported. We suspect that our lack of understanding as to how these links should be created and what they mean is behind the difficulty in collaborative writing with hyperdocuments.

5

X

October 2, 1988

Fig. 4.4 — The first page of document D3.

A1.   Highlight a word (circle), a link to the margin and a general comment about all the
      document (1 word and the symbol '?').
A2.   A link from the text to a question (3 words and the symbol '?').
A3.   Highlight a phrase (underline 5 words).
A4.   A long arrow within the page from behaviour 3 to behaviour 2.
A5.   Highlight part of a word (circle 4 characters) and place an 'x' in the margin.

Fig. 4.5 — The prose description of the annotation behaviour in D3 on the first page.
Note: for the sake of readability these descriptions have been slightly tidied from
their original form but no information has been either added or deleted.

because annotations were made. Approximately a quarter of all recorded
behaviours were explicit browsing behaviours without concomitant annotating behaviour.

4.3   Task analysis

The prose description produced from the video tapes of the tasks was the
observational input that was used for all the subsequent stages of TAKD. It
was decided at the beginning of the analysis phase that concentration would
focus on specific objects rather than the actions of the subjects. In fact, it was
clear from looking at the prose descriptions that it was possible to encompass
all the subjects' actions by the two generic actions of 'mark text (i.e. make an
annotation) and 'browse'. A more detailed analysis of the specific actions
would have been possible but it was decided that, because the actions
involved in performing a pen and paper task are heavily dependent on this
technology, and because there was the confounding, irrelevant pointing
behaviour, a detailed analysis of the actions was not compatible with the
purposes of the study which was to provide data for a computerized system
to support document annotation.

4.3.1   The specific object list

This first stage in TAKD's analysis was admittedly not carried out fully for
all three tasks. Instead, a specific object list was produced from a sample of
the first five pages of document D3. This was used in discussions with the
student groups of observers to agree on what was to be observed and
recorded in the prose descriptions. While the resulting specific object list
was thus incomplete, the style of recording used in the prose descriptions
was such that by the end of the observational stage the complete specific
object list was recorded within the prose descriptions and the later analysis
stages ensured that all the specific objects were included in the resulting
TDH. The specific object list from the example from page 1 of D3 (Fig. 4.5)
is represented in Fig. 4.6.

4.3.2   The highest-level generic object description

A considerable number of organizing principles were now suggested by the
researchers of how the specific object list could be categorized into more
generic descriptions. This is the stage which requires the TAKD analyst to
be insightful and creative. This stage is crucial as it drives the subsequent

circle annotation in the document
word in the document
link to the margin
general comment
one word annotation in the margin
'?' annotation in the margin
three word annotation in the margin
underline annotation in the document
phrase in the document
long arrow annotation in the margin
word part in the document
'x' annotation in the margin

Fig. 4.6 — Specific object list derived from the prose descriptions listed in Fig. 4.5

production of the TDH, along with the specific object list. It is difficult to produce a heuristic, or even advice, for how to do this vital stage because it is so strongly determined by the nature and purpose of the application. From the specific object list there were clearly two separable spaces being used for annotating behaviour:

(i) in the document itself; and
(ii) in the margins of the document.

In addition there were links that in some cases tied an annotation in the document's text to annotations in the margins. After a number of attempts it was decided that an annotation could be defined as always having, at least implicitly, three components to it. These components were:

(i) a section of the document to which an annotation referred (the source);
(ii) a link to an annotation (a link); and
(iii) the annotation itself (the destination).

This high-level description of annotations was partly determined by the purpose of the study in that it is obvious that in a hypertext annotating system, as with any word-processor-like technology, it will be necessary to mark text in a document and then to link it to an annotation.

There were two sources of doubt and discussion that were aired while constructing this scheme. First, there were a number of cases where the marking of the text was itself the annotation. Behaviour 5 in Fig. 4.4 is an example of this in that the circling of a spelling mistake is itself the annotation, even though there is an 'x' in the margin, and an implicit link from the circled characters to the mark in the margin. The 'x' was a convention used by the subject to draw attention to a minor annotation in the text (this was explained by the subject in the walkthrough). Similar examples are common proof-readers' marks such as a twiddle separating two characters in a word to indicate that the characters are printed in the wrong order or the '^' character to insert space between words or letters.

Second, there was a distinction between annotations that were specific to a local section of text as opposed to those that were general to part or all of the document. There are two aspects to this point. In some cases an annotation marks one example of an issue that the annotating subject is suggesting needs to be dealt with throughout the document. In other cases the problem is that an annotation is common to a very large section of text in the document. The former of these is exemplified by behaviour A1 in Fig. 4.5 where the use of the word 'we' and the annotation 'style?' is intended (again explained in the walkthrough) to suggest that the document's authors should change this grammatical style throughout the document (note: the annotating subject has assumed that other examples of 'we' (two in the second paragraph of page 1 alone), and also that related syntactical constructions such as 'our', should be changed). The latter point is not illustrated on page 1 but occurred on the next page which contained only a 'Table of contents' to which the subject had written 'Probably not required' on the top of the page and obviously this annotation refers to the whole page. In this case there is a potential difficulty in marking a whole page of text if a hypertext system were used which, for example, marked text by the common convention of reversing foreground and background colours.

After working through a number of such examples, however, it was still agreed that annotations would be described as having the three parts described above. This decision was strongly influenced by the purpose of the study and a consideration of the necessary requirements and limitations of a computerized system. Had the purpose of the study been different, say, for example, to produce a standardized form of doing annotations with pen and paper, then it is likely that a very different high-level description of the behaviours would have been produced.

Thus the highest-level description of annotating behaviour can be written in a KRG form such as:

MARK TEXT/source/link/destination/

where 'MARK TEXT' is the single generic action of interest and where 'source', 'link' and 'destination' are the highest-level GOPs. 'source' is used as the term that denotes what is marked or highlighted. This term is used because there are cases in the tasks where what is marked is not a section of the document's text but an earlier annotation. Such cases may be thought of as meta-annotations (i.e. annotations about annotations) and where perhaps the simplest example is the annotation 'stet' to indicate that a suggested annotation should be ignored. Similarly the term 'destination' is used because there are cases where a subsequent annotation is linked to a previous one. The long arrow link in behaviour A4 (Fig. 4.4) back to the earlier annotation behaviour A2 is an example of this.

4.3.3   Constructing the first TDH
Having generated both the list of specific objects and the highest-level nodes of a potential TDH, TAKD now requires that these highest and lowest levels are linked by the intermediate levels of a TDH. The heuristics and advice about this have already been discussed in section 3.3.1. As this study was carried out as a class exercise amongst a number of groups of students the approach adopted was that sections of the TDH were developed using specific examples provided by the students. This was done using an overhead

projector in the classroom and taking each example and working separately on the three GOPs of the TDH of source, link and destination. Often several examples were worked on simultaneously so that the subjective decisions made in building the TDH could be checked against what appeared to be 'difficult' examples for the TDH's current form. After a class session the author then took the overhead foils and synthesized these into the current version of the TDH using a word processor. In carrying out the word processing the logical repetition that might be required in the final form of the TDH was inserted even though no examples had yet been found at the current state of analysis. The word-processed forms of the TDH were distributed to the students so that before the class the following week they could analyse more of their own examples and identify where the growing TDH needed to be extended or modified.

Fig. 4.7 shows the final TDH developed. The annotations from the first page of document D3 are numbered in bold on the right-hand side. The prose description of annotation A4 (the long arrow) has been incorporated as part of annotation A3 because it provides the link to the destination (annotation A2). The conventions described earlier (section 3.3.1) are used to represent the different logical relationships at the different levels of the hierarchy. Some of the lowest-level nodes are empty because they were felt to be logically possible nodes. However, not all the necessary nodes are included even in this TDH as this would be likely to double the size of the TDH, making it unwieldy. Many of the node names should be self-explanatory, but some definitions are required to explain the rationale of this example TDH. The structures of the three AND sections (GOPs) are described below.

At the highest level under source is the distinction between whether an annotation contains explicit highlighting on the relevant part of the document. When explicit highlighting occurs there are four types recorded: circling; horizontally marking; vertically marking; and a category of 'other', which deals with unusual cases not covered by the first three. Circling and horizontal marking are separated at this relatively high level because it became apparent during the analysis that there was a tendency to use circling to mark relatively short sections of text, particularly single words or parts of words, whereas a set of rather different annotations, particularly underlining, were used to mark more than one word (phrases). Similarly, still larger sections on the document tended to be marked by a vertical line in the margin. The consequences of these different highlighting styles are discussed later with respect to a possible hypertext implementation of a system for annotation.

Under each of these types of highlighting style in the TDH, the distinction is made between highlighting text or figures which are part of the original document and highlighting annotations, usually for the purpose of meta-annotation. It was decided to keep these three distinctions of text, figures and annotations at the same level in the hierarchy, although an equally plausible alternative would have been to have two levels of document versus annotation and then have had a level under document of text

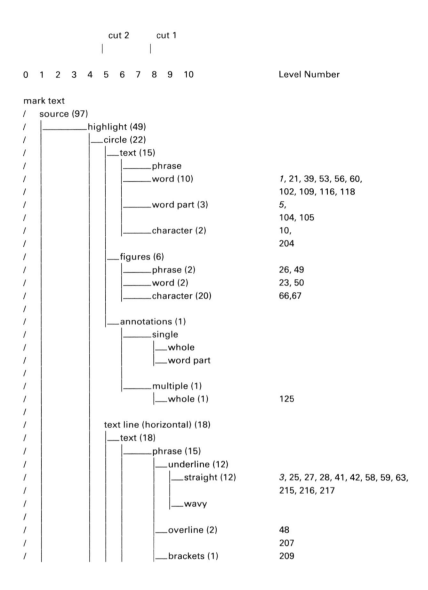

Fig. 4.7 — The completed TDH. Numbers on the right indicate the annotation behaviours for the three tasks (task D1, between 100 and 200; task D2, above 200; task D3, less than 100). The numbers in parentheses represent the frequencies of the annotating behaviours (note: in the destination below level 4 these frequencies do not sum to those above level 4 because of the repetition of KRG sentence numbers caused by the logical OR relationship). The numbers in italic show the annotation behaviours for page 1 of document D3. The TDH has been aligned and cuts 1 and 2 are indicated at the top of each page and occur between levels 4 and 5 and between levels 7 and 8 respectively.

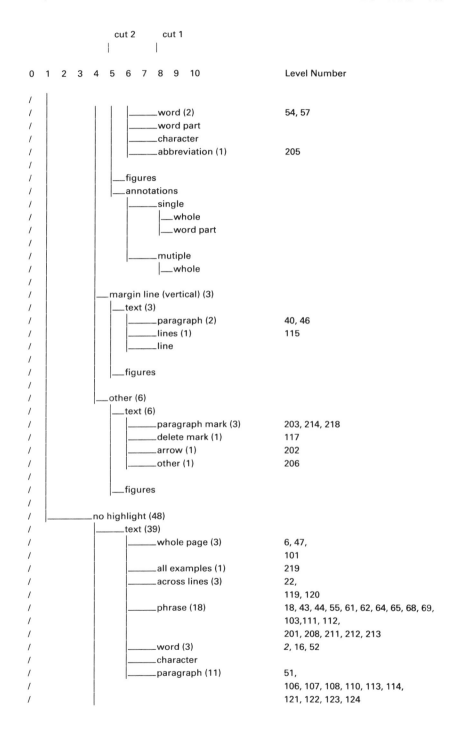

cut 2   cut 1

0 1 2 3 4 5 6 7 8 9 10   Level Number

```
/  |
/  |              |_____word (2)                   54, 57
/  |              |_____word part
/  |              |_____character
/  |              |_____abbreviation (1)           205
/  |
/  |         |___figures
/  |         |___annotations
/  |              |_____single
/  |              |   |__whole
/  |              |   |__word part
/  |              |
/  |              |_____mutiple
/  |                  |__whole
/  |
/  |    |___margin line (vertical) (3)
/  |    |   |__text (3)
/  |    |        |_____paragraph (2)               40, 46
/  |    |        |_____lines (1)                   115
/  |    |        |_____line
/  |    |
/  |    |   |__figures
/  |    |
/  |    |__other (6)
/  |    |   |__text (6)
/  |    |        |_____paragraph mark (3)          203, 214, 218
/  |    |        |_____delete mark (1)             117
/  |    |        |_____arrow (1)                   202
/  |    |        |_____other (1)                   206
/  |    |
/  |    |   |__figures
/  |    |
/  |    |_____no highlight (48)
/  |            |_____text (39)
/  |                 |_____whole page (3)          6, 47,
/  |                 |                             101
/  |                 |_____all examples (1)        219
/  |                 |_____across lines (3)        22,
/  |                 |                             119, 120
/  |                 |_____phrase (18)             18, 43, 44, 55, 61, 62, 64, 65, 68, 69,
/  |                 |                             103,111, 112,
/  |                 |                             201, 208, 211, 212, 213
/  |                 |_____word (3)                2, 16, 52
/  |                 |_____character
/  |                 |_____paragraph (11)          51,
/  |                                               106, 107, 108, 110, 113, 114,
/  |                                               121, 122, 123, 124
```

Fig. 4.7 — (continued)

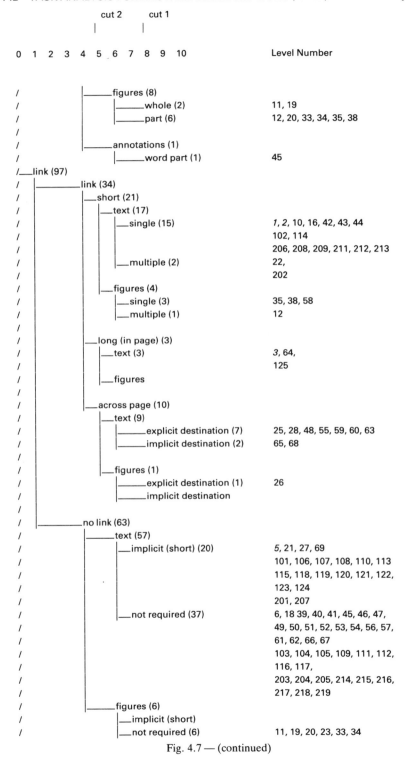

Fig. 4.7 — (continued)

```
                    cut 2        cut 1
                      |            |

 0   1   2   3   4   5   6   7   8   9   10                  Level Number


/___destination (97)
  |___private (3)
  |   |___local (3)
  |       |___annotation (3)
  |           |___comment (3)
  |               |___text (3)
  |                   |_____phrase (3)              27, 60,
  |                                                    208
  |___public (94)
        general (23)
          annotation (21)
          {    comment (18)
          {    |___text (18)
          {    |       |_____phrases (9)            2, 18, 47, 61, 62, 64, 65, 68,
          {    |       |                               219
          {    |       |_____words (9)              1, 57,
          {    |                                       102, 119, 120,
          {    |                                       201, 211, 212, 213
          {    |___figures
          {    |       |_____phrases
          {    |       |_____words
          {─ symbols (11)
          {    |___text (7)
          {    |       |_____question mark (2)       1, 2,
          {    |       |_____punctuation (5)         10, 47,
          {    |       |                                103, 111, 112
          {    |       |_____other (4)
          {    |               |___paragraph mark
          {    |               |___delete mark
          {    |               |___"&" (1)              62
          {    |               |___"=>" (2)             64, 65
          {    |               |___"—" (1)              68
          {    |
          {    |___figures
          {    |       |_____question mark
          {    |       |_____punctuation
          {    |       |_____other
          {    |
          {─ emphasis (3)
          {    |___text (3)
          {    |       |_____underline (1)           62
          {    |       |_____double underline (2)    10, 57
          {    |
          {    |___figures
          {    |       |_____underline
          {    |       |_____double underline
          {
```

Fig. 4.7 — (continued)

```
                    cut2        cut1
                     |           |

    0   1  2  3  4  5  6  7  8  9  10                    Level Number


                    |  |  {
                    |  |  {__ abbreviations (4)
                    |  |     |__text (4)
                    |  |     |    |_____abbreviations (4)        10, 62, 64, 65
                    |  |     |    |_____acronyms
                    |  |     |
                    |  |     |__figures
                    |  |          |_____abbreviations
                    |  |          |_____acronyms
                    |  |
                    |  |__no annotation (2)
                    |        |_____text (2)
                    |        |    |_____to annotation (1)        3
                    |        |    |_____no annotation (1)        105
                    |        |
                    |        |_____figures
                    |             |__to annotation
                    |             |__no annotation
                    |
                    |__local (71)
                         |__annotation (58)
                         |  {__ comments (47)
                         {  |    |__text (35)
                         {  |    |    |_____phrases (12)          6, 40, 41, 43, 44, 46, 49, 51,
                         {  |    |    |                              55, 58, 59, 63
                         {  |    |    |_____words (22)            10, 21, 22, 28, 42, 52
                         {  |    |    |                              101, 106, 107, 109, 110, 113,
                         {  |    |    |                              114, 118, 121, 122, 123, 124,
                         {  |    |    |                              125
                         {  |    |    |                              202, 206, 209
                         {  |    |    |_____word part (1)         45
                         {  |    |
                         {  |    |__figures (12)
                         {  |         |_____phrases (2)           19, 38
                         {  |         |_____words (7)             11, 20, 26, 33, 35, 53, 56
                         {  |         |_____character (3)         66, 67, 69
                         {  |
                         {__ symbols (32)
                         {  |__text (25)
                         {  |    |_____question mark (13)         6, 16, 18, 21, 28, 42,
                         {  |    |                                  51, 52, 55, 56, 58, 59,
                         {  |    |                                  207
                         {  |    |_____punctuation (1)            19
                         {  |    |_____other (11)
                         {  |         |__paragraph mark (3)          203, 214, 218
                         {  |         |__delete mark
                         {  |         |__"×" (1)                     5
                         {  |         |__other "psy" (3)             22, 28, 59
                         {  |         |__"*"                         25, 44, 58
                         {  |         |__"/" (1)                     52
```

Fig. 4.7 — (continued)

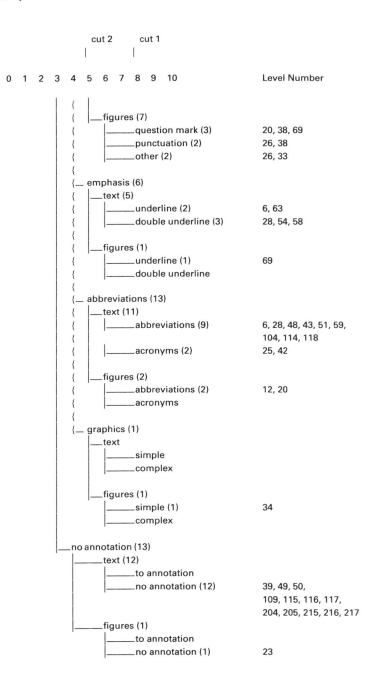

                cut 2   cut 1
                  | |

    0   1   2   3   4   5   6   7   8   9   10   Level Number

                        { |
                        { |___figures (7)
                        { |_____question mark (3)   20, 38, 69
                        { |_____punctuation (2)   26, 38
                        { |_____other (2)   26, 33
                        {
                        {__ emphasis (6)
                        { |___text (5)
                        { |_____underline (2)   6, 63
                        { |_____double underline (3)   28, 54, 58
                        {
                        { |___figures (1)
                        { |_____underline (1)   69
                        { |_____double underline
                        {
                        {__ abbreviations (13)
                        { |___text (11)
                        { |_____abbreviations (9)   6, 28, 48, 43, 51, 59,
                        {   104, 114, 118
                        { |_____acronyms (2)   25, 42
                        {
                        { |___figures (2)
                        { |_____abbreviations (2)   12, 20
                        { |_____acronyms
                        {
                        {__ graphics (1)
                            |___text
                                   |_____simple
                                   |_____complex

                            |___figures (1)
                                   |_____simple (1)   34
                                   |_____complex

                        |___no annotation (13)
                               |_____text (12)
                                      |_____to annotation
                                      |_____no annotation (12)   39, 49, 50,
                                                                     109, 115, 116, 117,
                                                                     204, 205, 215, 216, 217
                               |_____figures (1)
                                      |_____to annotation
                                      |_____no annotation (1)   23

Fig. 4.7 — (continued)

versus figures. It was considered important to distinguish highlighting text from figures as in a hypertext system it is likely that different highlighting conventions are likely to be needed because of the different manner in which most computers internally represent text from graphics. Furthermore, people may behave differently when annotating figures rather than text. The weak rationale for keeping these three distinctions at the same level in the TDH was also determined by considering the possible hypertext system as it is likely that highlighting annotations would also be differently represented within the system from highlighting on the original document. The annotation node is not included under the 'margin line' and 'other' nodes simply because it never occurred in the tasks and thus a little space is saved in Fig. 4.7.

The 'link' part of the TDH in Fig. 4.7 first identifies whether a link between the source and destination is made explicit or not. Where an explicit link is made there are three types of link: short, long (in page) and across page. Short links tend to be a brief line from a source to a margin whereas long links within the page are those such as the long arrow described by prose description A4 (Fig. 4.5). There is clearly a problem with paper-based systems of how links are made between different sheets of paper, though this is likely to be less of a problem for a hypertext system, provided that the complete document is available in the system. It is for this reason that the three explicit distinctions are represented at the same level in the TDH. The binary distinction between the 'link' and 'no link' nodes is represented at a higher level than the three explicit link types. An alternative would have been to represent both link and no link nodes at the same level on the grounds of the differences between pen and paper technology and a hypertext-based technology. In the case of pen and paper it is relatively easy for an annotator not to bother to use an explicit link between the source and destination as it is often obvious how these are related. With a hypertext system, however, it is likely that every annotation source will have to have a link within the system to its destination.

Under each of the link types the distinction is made between links from text and from figures for the reasons outlined. There were found to be occasions when multiple short links were used and thus this is an additional level under this node. As all the long links within a page were always from a single source this level has been omitted. Two types of across-page link were recorded: 'explicit destination' links stated precisely where on another page the relevant destination could be found (e.g. '*PTO page 3' and where there is a corresponding '*' on page 3); in contrast, 'implicit destination' links merely referred to some other page and often were contained in the annotation itself which might say something like 'see previous comments'. Under the 'no link' node, after making the text versus figures distinction it was clear that 'no links' were produced for one of two reasons. As discussed above, the links may be implicit and short where it is obvious how the source and destination are linked. There are also the cases where no link is required because the source and destination are the same, as in the case of using printers' marks in the text where such marks both highlight and inform.

These 'not required' links are likely to be a source of some difficulty in implementing a hypertext annotating system and are discussed later.

At the highest level of 'destination', which is the annotation itself, there is a binary distinction made between 'private' and 'public'. The former was rare, which is why the TDH has not been fully developed under this node. 'Private' here means that the annotation was made by the annotating subject for herself or himself and not for public use, say by a co-author. In task D3 the subject made the following two-part annotation 'is this conclusion enough here *check later for analysis' where the second part, following the '*', is a private annotation to the subject to remind him to check the point later, perhaps after going through the whole document. The rationale for making the private versus public distinction at a high level in the TDH again lies in the purpose of the analysis; such private annotations in a hypertext implementation would, after the task was finished, need to be removed and so should be represented differently from other annotations so that such removal is easy.

Under 'public' in the TDH there is a second binary distinction of 'general versus 'local'. The 'general' node, already mentioned, refers to annotations which apply to many instances and where only an example is annotated (as in annotation A1 in Fig. 4.5) or where the annotation refers to a large amount of, or the whole of, the document. 'Local', of course, refers to a comment that is specific to a single piece of highlighted text. Again it is the likely requirements for differing internal representations in a hypertext implementation that drive the rationale for this high-level distinction.

The nodes of the TDH under 'general' and 'local' are in essence the same with a few minor variations at the lowest levels only. A third binary distinction is then made at the next lower level between 'annotation' and 'no annotation' to represent the major difference between whether a comment is made or not. Annotation A3 (Fig. 4.5) is an example where the destination has no comment because it is another annotation. Where an annotation is made then there are four nodes under this level which are logical OR relationships. These four (comment, symbols, emphasis and abbreviations) reflect the textual or figural requirements of the destination part of the annotation: 'comment' refers to the textual component; 'symbols' to the wide range of both conventional keyboard and special symbols used; 'emphasis', usually underlining, is used to mark to readers the importance of a comment; and 'abbreviations' is used to words that are either shortened or written as acronyms. While the textual node's use is obvious, the other three are included to investigate the other requirements that a system might need to support. Thus a wider range of symbols may be desirable than those usually available on a QWERTY keyboard, some annotations may need to be seen as more important than others, and some abbreviations might be better supported for the reader if a hypertext implementation automatically generated them in their full form. Again under these nodes the distinction is made between 'text' and 'figure' for the reason specified above. Under the 'no annotation' node and under both 'text' and 'figures' is the distinction 'to annotation' versus 'no annotation'. The 'to annotation' cases are discussed above (annotation A3) and in most cases the 'no annotation' refers to instances where the subject did not feel it necessary to make a comment because it was made by the highlighting alone. Annotation 5 (Fig. 4.5) would have been an example of the latter had the annotating subject not placed an 'x' in the margin.

The four annotation behaviours marked in bold on Fig. 4.7 can be represented as KRG sentences that describe their path through the TDH. Thus:

Annotation 1.
MARK TEXT/source (highlight (text (circle (word)))) /link (short (text (single))) /destination (public (general (annotation {comment (text (word))} {symbols (text (question mark))})))/

Annotation 2.
MARK TEXT /source (no highlight (text (word))) /link (short (text (single))) /destination (public (general (annotation {comment (text (phrase))} {symbols (text (question mark))})))/

Annotation 3.
MARK TEXT /source (highlight (text line (text (phrase (underline (straight)))))) /link (long (text)) /destination (public (general (no annotation (text (to annotation)))))/

Annotation 5.
MARK TEXT /source (highlight (circle (text (word part)))) /link (no link (text (implicit))) /destination (public (local (annotation {symbols (text (other ("x"))})})))/

This representation is, of course, identical to that in Fig. 4.7 and involves merely a change of format. However, different analyses result from using the TDH itself compared with using the KRG format and the two analyses are dealt with in the following sections.

4.3.4   The low-level KRG analysis

Once all the annotation behaviours for all three tasks had been represented as low-level KRG sentences in the style of the four above then it is possible to calculate the number of KRG sentences and the number of different annotation behaviours (i.e. the total number of different KRG sentences). Table 4.1 gives these for the three tasks separately and across the three tasks. In fact, there is little difference between the total number of KRG sentences (97) and the number of different ones (75). This can be taken as a strong indication that the lowest level of the TDH used is sufficient for capturing the differences between annotations. Thus this analysis is a test of the adequacy of the TDH construction exercise. Furthermore, the KRG sentences generated were generally different for the three subjects as shown by the difference between the number of different KRG sentences when

Table 4.1 — The difference between the total number of KRG
sentences (i.e. number of annotating behaviours recorded) and the
number of different KRG sentences (i.e. number of different
annotating behaviours)

Task number	Number of KRG sentences	Number of different KRG sentences
D1	25	13
D1	18	11
D3	54	52
Combined tasks	97	75

tasks are combined (75) from the sum of the different KRG sentences from
each subject $(13+11+52=76)$. This indicates that at the lowest level the
three subjects adopted slightly different conventions of annotating.

4.3.5 Specific object frequency analysis

Once all the specific objects are each assigned to a low-level node in the
TDH then the frequency of occurrence of specific objects can itself be
informative. Fig. 4.7 shows the complete set of data for all three tasks. Each
annotation behaviour is numbered and the frequency of each node is
represented in parentheses after the node label. The presence of low-level
nodes with zero frequencies is itself often informative of what is not required
in a task. However, in this study no great weight is placed on such zero
frequencies as what is being described is a pilot study and there are
insufficient data for any strong conclusions to be drawn. Before making
strong recommendations for the design of a hypertext-based system to
support annotating it is imperative that further annotating tasks are
observed with a wider range of appropriate documents and with a larger and
perhaps more representative set of subjects. Ideally each document studied
should be annotated independently by several subjects. In particular, all the
annotations made on figures come from document D3 and this is clearly an
inadequate database.

With respect to the data on highlighting (i.e. the first GOP in the KRG),
it is of interest to note that there is a considerable difference in convention
between circling and marking text horizontally, usually by an underlining.
Of the 22 instances of circling, 10 of these (46%) involved circling a word and
15 (68%) involved circling a word or word part. More importantly, not one
instance was found of circling more than one word in the documents text. In
contrast, horizontal marking of text was principally involved with marking
phrases. Of the 18 instances recorded, 12 of these involved underlining
phrases (67%) and only 3 instances (11%) involved highlighting text of a

single word or word part. Thus in the paper-based annotating task it appears that the subjects use different conventions for highlighting words or word parts from highlighting two or more words. This could have consequences for the proposed hypertext system in that two different highlighting facilities might be provided. One might operate over many words, perhaps by marking the beginning and ending of word strings, and a separate facility could be used for marking individual words or word parts. Another option would be to provide a key to highlight complete words and which the hypertext-using annotator could simply hit repeatedly to mark each word in a phrase and a second key to mark word parts. Such a solution might speed up the annotator's task by supporting the different accuracies with which the cursor needs to be placed on target pieces of text. If the relative infrequency of highlighting sections of text or paragraphs (3%) is supported by further analyses then this might indicate that a block marking method may not have to be implemented or, if it is, that it might be one of the more effortful utilities provided by the system for the user.

The link data indicate that, of the 97 annotations, only 34 (35%) has an explicit link although 77 (79%) either possessed a link or did not require one (i.e. there were only 20 cases where an explicit link could have been drawn in by the annotating subjects and was not). From the analysis of the KRG sentences, discussed later, the cases where a link is not required (43 cases, 44%) are principally of two sorts: (i) where the annotation is a general one and not specific to a particular part of the document; and (ii) where the highlight and the annotation are the same, as in the use of printers' marks in the textual body of the documents.

The destination data (i.e. the annotations themselves) are informative about the size of the annotations and the range of symbols or objects that are not available on a standard QWERTY keyboard. Not surprisingly, general comments tended to be longer (9 cases of phrases (50%) rather than a just a few words (9 cases, 50%)) than those that were local to a part of the document (12 phrase cases (35%); 22 word cases (65%)). Combining the local and general annotations, the subjects mostly used symbols that are supported by standard keyboards but in addition used emphasis and abbreviations that the annotating hypertext system designer may wish to support. In the case of text alone there were 29 cases (50%) of such annotation elements, although these cases break down into a mixture of different types. For example, emphasizing annotations by underlining or by another means obviously requires a very different implementation from supporting or dealing with acronyms and abbreviations.

4.4   Generification
Generification is the term used in TAKD to represent the use of the TDH within TAKD to induce higher-level, more general KRG sentences. Once the TDH has been constructed the process is potentially automatic. However, in most cases there is ususally a subjective component involved. The process of generification involves the removal of the lower levels represented in the TDH and the KRG sentences. It is critical that the levels in the

TDH are aligned for this exercise to be carried out. While this alignment has already been carried out on Fig. 4.7, it is actually often easier to do this after the low-level analysis has been done. The reason for this is that the low-level frequency data described above can be highly informative as to which nodes have sufficient data (specific objects) attached to them so that they are better maintained at a higher level. Obviously such a *post hoc* element in the analysis needs to be treated with a little caution. Perhaps improperly, the private/public destinction has been ignored because of the very small amount of data collected such that the three cases under the private destination are not included in this analysis. Thus only 94 KRG sentences are analysed.

The list of KRG sentences is most easily used for this aspect of the analysis. Two generification attempts were tried and the levels at which lower-level TDH nodes were combined are indicated by the markers 'cut 1' and 'cut 2' in Fig. 4.7. Cut 1, which involved removing only the very lowest-level nodes, resulted in very little difference from the complete data and there was very little combination of similar generic KRG sentences so that the results were very similar to those of Table 4.1.

Cut 2, however, which is taken at a much higher level and thus does produce highly generic KRG sentences, provides a small, manageable and meaningful set of generic KRG sentences which are informative with respect to the purpose of the study. Cut 2 reduces the TDH to that shown in Fig. 4.8.

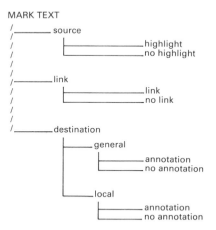

Fig. 4.8 — The generic TDH above cut 2. The data from the private part of the destination are ignored and the TDH appropriately restructured.

Using this generic TDH there are only 16 possible generic KRG sentences. Thus the original set of 75 KRG sentences has been reduced by 80%, which is a fairly typical reduction where a large number of different

KRG sentences are initially found (75 is not, actually, a particularly large set). At this level the 16 possible KRG sentences are shown in Table 4.2.

Table 4.2 — The 16 possible generic KRG sentences above cut 2 with their frequencies of occurrence tabulated on the right (to save space and for ease of reading the higher-level nodes of source, link and destination are not included)

highlight /link /general (annotation)/	3
highlight /link /general (no annotation)/	1
highlight /link /local (annotation)/	12
highlight /link /local (no annotation)/	0
highlight /no link /general (annotation)/	1
highlight /no link /general (no annotation)/	1
highlight /no link /local (annotation)/	16
highlight /no link /local (no annotation)/	13
no highlight /link /general (annotation)/	7
no highlight /link /general (no annotation)/	0
no highlight /link /local (annotation)/	9
no highlight /link /local (no annotation)/	0
no highlight /no link /general (annotation)/	10
no highlight /no link /general (no annotation)/	0
no highlight /no link /local (annotation)/	21
no highlight /no link /local (no annotation)/	0

These generic KRG sentences can be interpreted and fall into a number of meaningful classes and, because complete, a class of meaningless ones. There are four meaningless KRG sentences:

no highlight /link /general (no annotation)/	0
no highlight /link /local (no annotation)/	0
no highlight /no link /general (no annotation)/	0
no highlight /no link /local (no annotation)/	0

All four of these have neither a highlight nor an annotation and thus the first two are meaningless as a link must have at least one of these (see the comment below concerning annotation A3 in task D3 under class 1.1). The latter two do not even have a link so cannot be annotations. That their frequency of occurrence is zero merely indicates that a mistake has not been made in this part of the analysis.

There are two meaningful classes of generic KRG sentence with each of these classes being subdivided into two subclasses. The classes approximately divide on the difference between whether destinations are general or local. It should be stressed that this is an empirical result arising from an understanding of these generic KRG sentences.

Class 1.1

This subclass consists of generic KRG sentences that represent general comments that are either highlighted or linked, or both. The most common form of occurrence of these within the tasks is where a specific instance is highlighted and it needs generalizing for all or a major part of the document. The single occurrence of the 'highlight /link /general (no annotation)/' KRG sentence has already been exemplified. It is caused by annotations A3 and A4 (Figs 4.4 and 4.5) in task D3 where a phrase was underlined and a long, within-page link was made to an earlier annotation. Thus there was a destination but no annotation.

highlight /link /general (annotation)/	3
highlight /link /general (no annotation)/	1
highlight /no link /general (annotation)/	1
no highlight /link /general (annotation)/	7

The frequency of the total set of generic KRG sentences is 13%.

Class 1.2

The single generic KRG sentence in this subclass consists of a general comment that is not located in the document as it has no highlight and no link. Most frequently it is found when a very general comment is made; for example, in document D3 the annotator made a number of general comments about the document on the final page in a large blank area.

no highlight /no link /general (annotation)/	10

The frequency of the total set of generic KRG sentences is 11%.

Class 2.1

These generic KRG sentences represent the standard local annotation that may be highlighted or linked or both or neither. It should be noted that the 'highlight /no link /local (annotation)/' KRG sentence confounds two distinct types of annotation: (i) where there is a highlight and an annotation in the margin; and (ii) where a meaningful printers' mark is used, unlike in class 2.2, where similar annotations are idiosyncratic.

highlight /link /local (annotation)/	12
highlight /link /local (no annotation)/	0
highlight /no link /local (annotation)/	16
no highlight /link /local (annotation)/	9
no highlight /no link /local (annotation)/	21

The frequency of the total set of generic KRG sentences is 62%.

Class 2.2

The generic KRG sentences in this class represent the use of an idiosyncratic highlight such as underlining or circling which is used without further annotation. This can be contrasted with the use of standard printers' marks that serve as both highlighting and annotation within the body of the document (see class 2.1)

highlight /no link /local (no annotation)/   13
highlight /no link /general (no annotation)/   1

The frequency of the total set of generic KRG sentences is 15%.

4.5   Designing a hypertext system to support document annotation

The very act of carrying out the study has considerably clarified for the
MUCH research group the requirements of a hypertext-based document-
annotating system. For example, the highest-level KRG representation of
the three GOPs of source, link and destination was derived from the study
and was only poorly articulated prior to using TAKD, although admittedly
the full application of TAKD would not have been necessary to identify this
structuring of annotations. Perhaps one of the problems of convincing
designers to use task analysis is that after such analyses it is often easy to
claim that many of the results are self-evident and do not require the
considerable effort involved in using methods such as TAKD. In part this
problem is to do with the nature of human memory as it is often difficult to
remember one's previous state of ignorance in the light of subsequent
discoveries.

Apart from the general enlightenment derived from the effort involved
in using a systematic method such as TAKD there are, of course, a number
of results from the analysis which are specific to the purpose of carrying it out
and would be difficult to obtain by any other means. Many of the consequences for designing a hypertext system to support document annotaion
have already been mentioned in the previous sections and not all of these
will be repeated here, except as appropriate examples. The generic KRGs
above cut 2 indicate that only 77% of annotation are of a local nature
(summing the frequencies of class 2.1 and 2.2 generic KRGs) and thus the
system to be designed will have to support not only this obvious class of
annotation but also the more problematic annotations of a general nature,
which in the study constituted about a quarter of all annotating behaviour.
The local annotations are intended to be supported by the annotator's
highlighting a section of text on the source document and then opening a
window into which the highlighted section of text may be copied. This copy
can then be directly edited in the case of minor suggested changes or a
comment about it can then be made. The reader of such an annotated
document, for example the primary author, can then select the locally
highlighted parts of the document which will then display the annotation.
The linking between source document and annotation window is, of course,
automatically supported by the hypertext system. The reader should pre-
sumably be supported by the system so that if she or he agrees with a
suggested change by an annotator then this can be automatically inserted
into the source document from the annotation window without retyping.

There still remains a problem with multiple, simultaneous annotators as
it can be expected that ideally each will need to highlight the text in a
different manner. The number of highlighting conventions supportable by a
system is, however, seriously restricted, even with colour displays. This

issue has not been addressed in the present study which looked at only a single annotator and the current suggestions for system design are more suited to cases where annotations are done serially so that the current annotator or primary author can see all previous annotations on the same hyperdocument. With multiple, serial annotators, meta-annotation can be supported by treating an annotation window as a source document onto which highlights can be made and additional windows opened when such highlights are selected. This would be in addition to a facility to add further annotations to an existing annotation window.

The problem with supporting general annotations is twofold. First, the reader of an annotated hyperdocument needs to see the parts of the document that are highlighted. This is problematical for general annotations that involve large parts of the document as obviously such conventions as reversing foreground and background colours will be very clumsy if used over large sections of text. No doubt there are a number of possible solutions to this problem, but most of them require implementations that treat the highlighting of such annotations in a manner different from that used with local annotations. One possible solution would be to provide an iconic form of the document where the text itself might not be readable but which showed the document's structure and where this icon contained the highlighting. A different alternative would be for the reader to turn on or off highlighting of large sections of text so as to remove the confusion likely to be caused by a section of text containing both general and local highlighting. Systems such as Guide 2.0 (e.g. Brown, 1987) have already implemented similar solutions to this problem. Such solutions, and there are others, will require the reader to work on general and local annotations separately, although the option would remain to the reader either to deal with all general annotations and then with all the local ones, or to switch frequently between the two while revising the source hyperdocument.

The second class of problem with general annotations centres on the instances principally characterized in generic KRG class 1.1 where the annotator using pen and paper had highlighted only an example of a general class of suggested changes. There are two general styles of solution to this problem when considering the hypertext annotating system. Either the annotator can be supported by the system to search for the other instances and these can all be linked to a single annotation window, or the reader can be supported by such a search facility. Supporting both annotator and reader is not, however, excluded as an implementation option. The point has already been made (section 4.3.1) that searching for these other instances may be computationally non-trivial. In the case of annotating one instance of the word 'we' and suggesting that all other instances be changed, it would not be too difficult for the hypertext system to search for all other occurrences of this word and for the reader or annotator to confirm the validity of each instance offered by the system. However, even in this simple example, unless the system contains some intelligence, the use of related syntactical constructions, such as the use of 'our', will not be found. Where a phrase is involved the problem will often be very much more complex and with the current state of artificial intelligence it is unlikely that a commercially affordable system could be designed, if the problem can even be solved, even partially. That more than 10% of annotations are within this generic KRG class indicates that this problem is one that will be required sufficiently frequently by annotators or readers that it does need supporting on a hypertext annotating system.

As the current status of the worked example is only that of a pilot study it would be premature to make too much of the full KRG sentence data either with respect to logically possible KRG sentences defined by the TDH that were not found to occur (i.e. low-level nodes with zero frequencies of occurrence), or with respect to the relative infrequency of some KRG sentences or specific objects. Thus more data are required, for example, before it can be confidently stated that in general annotators can be adequately supported by the symbols normally found on computer QWERTY keyboards.

5.   DEVELOPING TAKD

This section is intended to identify where TAKD still requires further development. While TAKD has been widely used by the author in recent years for a range of applications and purposes it is still the case that it is a method, like many of the other task analysis methods described in this book, that is still under development. Many, if not all, the issues discussed below are currently being worked on. However, even in its current state, TAKD is able to provide a powerful analytical tool to system designers. It is hoped that the publication of this chapter will encourage others to use the method as the primary goal has been to describe TAKD in sufficient detail so that it can be used by people other than those who originally developed it.

5.1   Sequence Representation Grammars
SRGs have already been covered (section 3.3.5). There is, however, considerable work still to be done on the methods that need to be employed to generate an SRG from either full or generic KRG descriptions of task steps. The absence of these methods is a major, current weakness in TAKD and must be resolved in the near future. However, the development of an SRG representation is not expected to be particularly difficult as it is intended that the same style of representation and the same sort of methods used for identifying KRG sentences will be appropriate for developing SRGs.

5.2   Bridging the gulf between user- and system-centred representations
The general problem in HCI mentioned in both section 2 and section 3.3.4 is that there exists a problem of converting descriptions of user performance into specifications for the design of computer systems. Task analysis methods, including TAKD, generally provide descriptions that are user centred. The problem is to convert such descriptions into recommendations that can be followed by computer system designers who often have little HCI

expertise. Section 4.5 and some of the previous sections in the worked example provide illustrations of how the products of TAKD can be used in supplying computer system design recommendations. However, it has to be admitted that the translation from user- to system-centred representations both with TAKD and in HCI generally remains a craft skill which relies on the expertise and creativity of the analyst and HCI professional. The advantage to methods such as TAKD lies in the well-specified, structured description of user behaviour that is provided. In TAKD, the TDH and KRG representations provide a basis and an anchor which has the potential for the design of more formal methods of translating between the user- and system-centred perspectives. Structured system design methods (see Chapter 6) such as Jackson Structured Design (e.g. Cameron, 1983) or SSADM (e.g. Downs *et al.,* 1988) can provide the anchor in the system-centred domain and have the potential for identifying the points and representational forms into which the KRG representation can be translated. These points remain to be identified and the translation process needs both specification and empirical testing.

5.3   Software tools to support TAKD

The production of the TDH and KRG analyses in the worked example used a word processor and, as already commented on in section 4.1.2.5, this software is not ideal for supporting TAKD. What has not been described in detail in the worked example are the very large number of files that the author generated containing different versions of both the TDH and the full and generic KRGs. There was a major problem with errors caused by typing mistakes and omissions that had to be laboriously corrected when it was discovered that the number of KRG sentences did not match between the files, either because a specific object had been omitted or a KRG sentence had been inadvertently duplicated. Such errors could really only be detected when the frequency of occurrence data were found not to appropriately total the number of KRG sentences or the number of specific objects in a GOP.

What is required is a software tool that will allow the TAKD analyst to work on only a single representation. This tool needs to have two components to it. First an editor is required that will facilitate the construction of a TDH. This editor should be able to make it easy for the analyst to copy partial sections or the TDH so that particularly where the TDH involves OR relationships these can be fully specified even in the absence of observed examples. The editor should automatically insert the TDH notation that currently represents the AND, XOR and OR relationships by the use of '/', '|' and '{' respectively. The editor should also make the alignment of the levels in the TDH a simple matter for the analyst. All of these TDH construction functions are difficult on a standard word processor where the analyst can spend many hours trivially fighting the tabbing and other conventions of such systems rather than actually performing the TAKD analysis.

Once the TDH has been constructed and all the specific objects assigned to the low-level nodes then the TAKD software tool should automatically calculate the frequency of occurrence data associated with all the nodes in the TDH. Furthermore, it should be possible for the tool to detect many classes of error when these data are calculated. For example, where two GOPs do not contain OR-related nodes then if the TDH is complete then the frequency of occurrence data should have the same total associated with each GOP. KRG sentence generation from a TDH should be an automatic process, something that is clearly impossible with a word processor although it is not computationally difficult. Not only will this remove the most substantial source of errors in the current, manual method of performing a TAKD analysis, but again it should be possible for the TAKD tool to detect some errors of omission in the specific object assignment to the TDH where KRG sentences are found to be missing a GOP. Generic KRG sentence generation should, of course, also be a process carried out automatically by the tool.

The advantages of developing such a tool will thus free the TAKD analyst from much of the effort currently associated with using the method and allow her or him to concentrate on the difficult subjective decisions that require the application of human intelligence. Such a tool will also allow the analyst to test the consequences of making such decisions quickly and efficiently and so result in better and more useful TDHs.

A second advantage to developing such a tool is that it is likely to improve the marketability of TAKD and the standardization of its application. Sophisticated task analysis methods are still not widely used in systems development and this is probably in part due to the very difficulty of both understanding and applying task analysis. Removing much of the trivial effort from methods such as TAKD may thus encourage and educate those who should, but currently do not, use task analysis. Indeed, in the commercial and industrial sectors a package that contained both a tutorial and a software tool that ran on commonly available hardware is likely to be a much more attractive proposition than a mere textual description as contained in the chapters of this book.

6.   CONCLUSION

This rather lengthy chapter has attempted to present both the general principles that underlie TAKD and to illustrate these with a worked example. There is still a substantial amount of work that needs to be done on further formalizing the method and further applications for a wider range of purposes still need to be investigated. This chapter has tried to emphasize the importance of clearly identifying the purpose for which TAKD is being used and has suggested that unless this is done well then either the method cannot be used or the subjective decisions that must be made by the analyst will be inappropriate. Section 5 has tried to outline the current deficiencies with TAKD. The author's current strategy is to develop the TAKD software tool described in section 5.3 and to incorporate an SRG analysis component.

Such a tool should facilitate the mapping between the user-centred description of users' behaviour provided by TAKD and the system-centred description that is required by those who design, build and evaluate computer systems.

5

Supporting system design by analyzing current task knowledge

Peter Johnson
Department of Computer Science, Queen Mary and Westfield
College, University of London

1. INTRODUCTION

The knowledge that people have of the tasks that they can perform is an important subset of the total knowledge that they possess. This knowledge should be taken into account in the design and development of interactive software systems, since task knowledge forms a significant part of the total knowledge that the user will recruit when they attempt to use that software to perform tasks. Task knowledge structures (TKSs) represent the knowledge people possess about tasks they have previously learned and performed in a given domain. Task knowledge is assumed to include goals, plans, procedures, actions and objects. TKS theory makes assumptions about the representativeness (typicality) and centrality (importance) of particular aspects of task knowledge (Johnson *et al.*, 1988). A method has been developed for analyzing task knowledge called Knowledge Analysis of Tasks (KAT) (Johnson and Johnson 1989), which provides detailed descriptions of task knowledge and informs design decisions. This process of analysis produces a description of a person's or group of people's knowledge of tasks that are currently performed in the domain of interest. The application of the theory of TKSs and the analysis method of KAT to the design of interactive software systems can be facilitated by using this analysis in conjunction with conventional design practices (such as SSADM — structured systems analysis and design methodology) or as an information base in conjunction with *ad hoc* design practices such as rapid prototyping.

A family of models for applying the results of KAT to user interface design have also been considered (Johnson *et al.*, 1988; Waddington and Johnson, 1989), and are in the process of further development. Design decisions such as those concerning which parts of the general system will be supported by an application program and will influence the ease with which a user is able to carry out his/her desired tasks with the subsequent system. By expressing the proposed design in terms of user's tasks the effects of such decisions on the usability of the system in terms of its support of user tasks could be identified. Similar expressions of design in terms of user tasks could also be made as other design choices and decisions are being made, such as the dialogue structure, resulting in a family of task-oriented design models, each making visible how the system could be used to perform an identified task. Being task based, each model also describes the task knowledge that would be required by a user. The potential of task-oriented design models is considered further in this paper. This paper provides a detailed review of the TKS theory, the analysis and knowledge modelling approach and suggestions for the use of TKS in conjunction with current design practices.

2. TASK KNOWLEDGE IN HUMAN–COMPUTER INTERACTION

This section reviews alternative approaches to task analysis in the context of human computer interaction. Traditionally, task analysis has investigated what people do (either in terms of overt behaviours or in terms of psychological processes and structures) when they carry out one or more tasks. This involves collecting information about how people perform those tasks. Various approaches to task analysis have been developed, particularly in the context of Human–Computer interaction (HCI), probably the most often cited of which is the GOMS approach of Card *et al.* (1983). One central tenet of GOMS is that goals, operators, methods and selection rules constitute a user's cognitive knowledge structures and that these structures are processed by various information-processing systems (such as those assumed to operate while information is held in an active state in working memory). By extending the original ideas of Card *et al.* these four elements could be considered as the basic structural components of any task knowledge that a person might recruit to perform a task. In other words, we might suppose that people not only perform tasks, but also develop structures to represent the knowledge that the person recruits to perform a particular task. One assumption to be made is that people have goals, operators, methods and selection rules represented in memory and these constitute the structures of knowledge associated with task performance. These task knowledge structures are then assumed to be processed by various information-processing subsystems such as those proposed by Barnard (1987). Card *et al.* define a human information processor model that is an approximation of these psychological processors that are assumed to operate on some or all of these four elements. Kieras and Polson (1985) argue that production rules can be used to model goals, operators, methods and selection rules and that these production rules bear a close relationship to the way a person does (or would) structure their knowledge of the task. From this assumption Kieras and Polson then claim that counting these production rules provides an assessment of the degree of learning required to use the system, and the complexity of a user interface. In yet a further approach to modelling users and tasks in HCI the theory underlying Task–Action Grammars (TAGs), Payne and Green (1986, Chapter 3) also claim that people possess task knowledge structures and that this structuring of knowledge is captured by the rules of their grammar.

More recently, Johnson *et al.* (1988), Davies (1988), have proposed a theory of TKSs which assumes that, as people learn and perform tasks, they acquire (or, more correctly, develop) knowledge structures that are established from previous task experiences and applied to future task performances in a dynamic process.

2.1   Using and identifying task knowledge in system design and development

Various attempts have been made to show that models of task knowledge can be used to influence the design of software systems and to improve the usability of such systems (Moran, 1981; Reisner, 1981; Card *et al.*, 1983; Kieras and Polson, 1985; Payne and Green, 1986, Chapter 3) and this is the main concern of many chapters in this book. However, there is little evidence that any such task knowledge models have ever been used in any commercial or actual design and development projects other than in research settings, or that the use of such models does or could produce significant improvements in the usability of software (although Shepherd in Chapter 1 does describe some exceptions to this general case). There are many reasons why this is the case, not least of which is that the people developing these models are researchers with little or no opportunity to be involved in actual design and development projects. Often, little effort is made by the researchers to show how such models can or might be applied to existing design practice. Without any good case histories of the usage of such models in actual design projects or any identified mapping between the models and their use in design practice it is almost impossible to see how the models can be used in design practice. One aim of this paper is to suggest how TKS theory and KAT methods could be applied to current design and development practices and to describe some of the applications of this method that have occurred.

2.2   Transfer of knowledge between tasks

The process of the development and application of task knowledge structures is not fully understood. However, it is clear that people do acquire knowledge about tasks and subsequently transfer this knowledge to new or different tasks (sometimes successfully and sometimes inappropriately). Transfer of knowledge is of interest to the application of task analysis to HCI and it is a central and often implicit assumption of all the approaches mentioned in section 1. Usability and learnability are directly related to the amount of existing knowledge that the user is able to transfer from the existing tasks to the revised form of those tasks as they should optimally be performed using the designed software. Pollock (1988) has demonstrated that people who are required to learn to use a second word processor, after first having learned a different word processor, recruit and apply (sometimes inappropriately and sometimes with success) knowledge they have acquired about using the first word processor to the second. This long-established phenomenon, prevalent in training, is known as transfer of training. There is widespread evidence that in those cases where there is an appropriate transfer of existing knowledge from one task situation to a new or different task situation that there are considerable savings of training time to be made, in terms of the length of practice or instruction required to achieve a given level of task performance. Where it is possible for a person to employ an effective transfer of knowledge this can result in that person achieving a higher level of task performance sooner and with less training effort than otherwise would be the case. The concept of transfer of knowledge is often exploited in the context of HCI particularly where claims are made that a system is easy and efficient to use because it uses terms that are familiar to the user or because it uses a style of interaction that is 'natural' or 'familiar'. Most often these claims are vacuous, unfounded and in some cases untrue. Such claims about new computer or software systems are nothing more than sales slogans. However, they are based upon commendable aims, but for the designer to take into consideration what is easy or familiar to the user requires more than a trivial understanding of what the user already knows and how people transfer knowledge from one task context to a new or different task context.

To understand how people transfer knowledge between contexts it is necessary to consider (a) what knowledge is likely to be transferred, (b) what knowledge is appropriate to be transferred (and not appropriate to transfer), and (c) what facilitates such transfer. In terms of what knowledge is likely to be transferred Pollock (1988) and others before her have considered the distinctions between the transfer of specific knowledge such as the positions of keys, the names of commands and the sequences of actions and the transfer of more general knowledge such as the fact that all word processors have files which can be created, saved, deleted and changed (even though the names and appearances of these will be different from one word processor to the next, as will the way in which the user is required to use them interactively).

Knowledge, that is both general and specific to the task domain, can potentially be transferred. It seems likely that general knowledge can only be utilized in task performance through specific knowledge. If specific knowledge, appropriate to the new task context, is not available then specific knowledge from the existing task contexts may be inappropriately transferred. For example, in order to be able to send a mail item from one user to another on an electronic mail system the person wishing to send the mail item must (amongst other things) know that the command for sending the mail is 'send'. This is an instance of specific knowledge of a command name that is required in order to perform the task of sending mail in the context of a particular electronic mail system. The person performing the task may not have this specific knowledge (i.e. know the command name for sending mail is 'send') and yet they may know that the next appropriate action in the task is to send the mail and that some command is required. In such circumstances they may transfer specific knowledge that is appropriate to sending mail in another context such as in a paper-based internal mail system, where the outgoing mail tray is labelled 'post'. Consequently this person may enter the command 'post' when using the electronic mail system.

This is an example of specific knowledge being required but an inappropriate transfer of existing specific knowledge occurring. Note that not all general knowledge is appropriate to be transferred to a new task context and not all specific knowledge is inappropriate. Diaper and Johnson (1989) have considered the distinctions between the transfer of general and specific knowledge in the context of devising appropriate training material.

Facilitation of transfer is defined to include only those situations in which there is an explicit intention to enable existing knowledge to be recruited and/or generalized to a new or different situation. This excludes those cases where transfer of knowledge occurs but is not brought about by any intentional act. An intent to facilitate transfer might be realized in the development of a particular training programme. The inclusion of referents to existing knowledge in the new or different task contexts arising from the proposed or developed system, and the use of examples in the manual or help facilities to show where existing and new knowledge is assumed to be required. This obviously does not cover all the possible or actual ways in which transfer can be facilitated; that is not the intention of this paper. What is intended is to point out that transfer can be facilitated. This transfer can arise from a positive intention on the part of the user (person) and can be helped or facilitated by the support the design provides. However, the support for this transfer can only be provided after a specific identification of the knowledge assumed to be required for transfer, where and when this knowledge is currently used, under what conditions, and how it is likely to be used in the new or different context.

There is no simple relation between knowledge and its transfer. Each of the three aspects of transfer mentioned above concerning (a) what knowledge is likely to be transferred, (b) what knowledge is appropriate to be transferred (and not appropriate to transfer), and (c) what facilitates such transfer, should be seen as contributing factors which interact in a complex way. Predicting transfer requires all three factors to be considered. Some attempts to show how a consideration of users' existing knowledge or required knowledge can be identified and applied to improve the design of computer systems, and user interfaces in particular, have been made with some success. For example, Knowles (1988) carried out a detailed analysis of the required and transferred knowledge of tasks in the domain of pattern design in the fashion industry. Her analysis clearly identifies where the system designer of a CAD system for pattern design failed to support users' existing and (in some cases) crucial knowledge of the pattern design tasks, and in other cases introduced new knowledge requirements that were directly at odds with what the user currently knew and expected to find supported by the computer system.

3.   TASKS, TASK STRUCTURE AND TASK KNOWLEDGE

A task is an activity that is undertaken by one or more agents to bring about some change of state in a given domain. Agents can include people, animals, or machines. Tasks can be grouped together in many ways. One grouping of tasks is in terms of a role. An agent assuming a particular role (examples of roles are author, referee, editor) is expected to carry out the set of tasks associated with that role (for example, the role of editor might include tasks of identifying authors, identifying referees, integrating the manuscripts and submitting the complete set of manuscripts to the publisher). One higher-order grouping of both tasks and roles is a job. A job can be defined in terms of the set of roles that a person is expected to take on and the tasks that are associated with them. For example, the job of lecturer might include the roles of administrator, teacher, researcher.

Clearly all is not as clear cut as this appears to be. There are many areas in which it is difficult to categorize some task as being discretely within any role; also, the same task may be found to occur in several roles. Some roles can be jobs in some contexts (for example while teacher is a role in the lecturer job context, in another context teacher is a job); these contexts can be determined by organizations and institutions. A task can be more precisely identified and defined by taking account of the context in which it is found to occur. The definition of what constitutes a task is also discussed in Chapters 1 and 7.

3.1 Structure in tasks

Task activities do not occur independently of one another. Some groupings of task activities are quite probable while others, which might be logically or physically possible, are never found to occur together in reality. Some activities are carried out together, and cause, enable or are subsequent to other activities. Task activities are essentially units of behaviour plus properties of the environment (e.g. objects such as tools, and contexts).

Tasks would be 'unstructured' if all activities could be and were associated with equal probability with other activities. All possible activities do not co-occur with equal probability. The **knowledge** used to carry out tasks is assumed to be similarly structured to reflect the structuring observed in task performances. Garner (1974) has expressed similar ideas in describing how people represent physical objects based on the structure and relations of those objects observed in the real world.

All intentional human behaviour requires knowledge in some form and it follows that if behaviour is structured then this structuring is either determined by or at least reflected in the way that the task knowledge supporting those behaviours is itself structured. One way that activities may be structured is in terms of a plan which provides a feasible and acceptable structuring on the activities that collectively satisfy a goal or subgoal. Empirical evidence for the representation of plans in long-term memory can be found in work on programming tasks (Green *et al.*, 1987). Further evidence for structuring and planning comes from the work of Byrne (1977) on tasks in domains such as cookery and menu creation.

3.2 Task Knowledge Structures

A theoretical approach to task modelling has previously been described by Johnson *et al.* (1988). The theory holds that task knowledge is represented in a person's memory and can be described by a TKS which is activated during task execution. Contained within TKSs are goal-oriented and taxonomic substructures; goal-oriented substructures represent a person's knowledge about goals and enabling states, subgoals, plans and procedures. Taxonomic substructures represent knowledge about the properties of task objects and their associated actions. This is similar to the GOMS view (Card *et al.*, 1983). The goal-oriented substructure can be thought of as including something like the goals, methods and selection rules of the GOMS approach. However, the TKS theory makes no assumptions about the processors that operate on these structures. Consequently, TKS does not include the notion of specific operators, unlike the GOMS approach. TKS extends the knowledge structures considered by Card *et al.*(1983) by including what might otherwise be termed declarative knowledge about objects, their properties and the actions they can afford. This knowledge is represented in the taxonomic substructure and is excluded by the GOMS approach. Payne and Green (1986, Chapter 8) attempt to take partial account of this type of knowledge in the TAG approach through the notions of family resemblances and common knowledge. The former refers to the common properties shared between different rules of a TAG description and the latter refers to the required knowledge that is assumed to be already possessed by people performing those tasks.

TKSs are assumed to be acquired through learning and previous task performances and are dynamically represented in memory. This notion is akin to the theoretical position taken by Schank (1982) in assuming that knowledge of frequently occurring events is structured into meaningful units in memory. Empirical support for the assumption that people possess something akin to TKSs can be found in the work of Galambos (1986) who showed that people recognize and use structures of events, such as order, sequence and importance of activities within the event sequence, to understand, explain and make predictions about these events. Further support for the view that knowledge structures similar to those proposed in TKS are represented in long-term memory comes from the work on text comprehension by Graesser and Clark (1985) in which general knowledge structures were hypothesized whose function in story understanding was to relate goals to causal and enabling states, to identify plans for achieving goals and intermediate states and alternative solutions or paths.

TKS theory assumes that the knowledge a person has acquired during the learning and performance of a task is contained within a TKS and this is stored in memory. The TKS is then activated and processed in association with task performance.

3.3   Central and representative knowledge elements of a TKS

A TKS includes knowledge in both the goal-oriented and the taxonomic substructures which may differ in terms of its centrality and representativeness relative to other knowledge used in the task. The notion of representativeness is similar to that used by Rosch (1985) and colleagues (Rosch *et al.*,

1976) to describe the relations between objects in the world and their categorical representation in memory.

It is assumed that in TKS the taxonomic substructure includes knowledge about objects (both physical and informational) and their associated actions. Actual objects and actions may differ in how representative (or typical) they are with respect to the task. For example, a task such as making a cup of coffee may include a number of objects such as a drinking vessel and heating unit. A representative or typical drinking vessel might be a coffee cup while a percolator might be a typical heating unit; in contrast a bowl might be an atypical drinking vessel (although, in some cultures or contexts it might be less atypical). Representativeness is concerned with the instances and their relations to the class and is a matter of degree rather than an 'all or none' property and is culturally and contextually determined.

Centrality is different from representativeness and is concerned with critical points in the task at which success or failure is determined. The notion of centrality is also touched upon in Chapter 4 in Diaper's discussion between the frequency and importance of task elements. For example, in coffee making, if no coffee is present then that task cannot be completed until coffee is obtained or the task is changed. This makes coffee a central object to the task. Similarly, if no action of heating occurs then that task would fail to be completed (assuming that a hot cup of coffee was required). This makes heating a central action to the task. Empirical evidence for the notion of centrality in tasks can be found in Leddo and Abelson (1986) who showed that for tasks such as borrowing a book from a library there were certain segments which were central to the task in that they were critical points at which success or failure of the task could be determined. Furthermore, it is assumed that knowledge which is deemed to be central to the task is more likely recruited and transferred to similar tasks in differing contexts (i.e. when the task is being carried out using different technologies).

3.4 A theory of TKS

By considering the above features of tasks and knowledge we are able to offer the following theory of TKSs. A TKS is a summary representation of the different types of knowledge that have been acquired through learning and performing a given and associated task. These TKSs are recruited and further processed when the task is performed. A TKS is related to other TKSs by a number of different relations. One form of relation between TKSs is within and between role relations. A role can be defined by the collection of tasks that a person occupying that role performs.

Within role relations
One form of relation between TKSs is in terms of their association with a given role that a person may assume. Within a role each task to be performed will have a corresponding TKS. When a person takes on a particular role with a recognized set of tasks, that person must either acquire or already possess the relevant TKSs for that role, or abandon or redefine the role.

Between role relations
A second form of relation between TKSs is in terms of the similarity of tasks across different roles. A task may be part of the collection of tasks associated with more than one role. For example, a person may be required to carry out the task of 'arranging meetings' while assuming the role of 'chairperson', 'holiday maker', or 'business traveller'. In such cases it is possible that a common TKS can be assumed to exist comprising the task knowledge common to each role–task instance.

Other relations
Further relations between TKSs include temporal and experiential ones. A TKS may change over time and with the development of expertise. The former is primarily concerned with how TKSs may become elaborated or faded as time elapses and assumes some form of cognitive processor operating on the contents of a TKS. The latter is essentially a problem of learning and knowledge acquisition and assumes the existence of some form of cognitive processor(s) which functions to add and restructure TKSs as expertise is acquired.

3.5   The representation of knowledge in a TKS
Within each TKS different types of knowledge are represented. There are three components to a complete TKS model:

(1) a goal-oriented substructure;
(2) task procedures;
(3) a taxonomic substructure from the generic task actions and objects;

The goal structure identifies the goals and subgoals identified within the TKS and includes enabling and conditional states that must prevail if a goal or subgoal is to be achieved. The goal structure can be thought of as a plan for carrying out the task. For well-practised tasks or parts of tasks that are performed by a given person, a procedural structure will have developed. Procedural structures are different from goal structures in so much as that they are executable as a single unit. It is this atomic aspect of TKS procedures that gives rise to one of the differences between this psychologically realistic view of task knowledge and others, such as ATOM discussed in Chapter 6. There may be alternative procedures for achieving a particular goal or subgoal. Consequently there is also conditional and contextual knowledge associated with these procedures. The procedures rely on knowledge of objects and actions which when combined constitute a given procedural unit. Properties of objects are represented in a taxonomic substructure. The taxonomic substructure identifies object properties and attributes including the class membership, the procedures in which it is commonly used, its relation to other objects and actions, and some reference to the properties of representativeness and/or centrality associated with the object in a given task context.

The taxonomic substructure contains the category structure for the objects. The category structure is divided into superordinate, basic and subordinate category levels. These levels are not static so that between individual people at different levels of expertise what constitutes a superordinate, basic or subordinate object will vary. The basic level is the level at which a person identifies objects and represents their knowledge about the object. It is at this basic level that the object properties and features are defined.

4.   KNOWLEDGE ANALYSIS OF TASKS

To identify the knowledge in a particular TKS we have developed a method, Knowledge Analysis of Tasks (KAT) from existing techniques used in task analysis, experimental psychology and knowledge elicitation. This method has three distinct parts: (1) identifying knowledge; these are techniques for identifying and collecting data about the knowledge people utilize in performing tasks; (2) analysis of knowledge; these are techniques for identifying the representativeness and centrality of a particular task knowledge component and establishing generic task knowledge; (3) construction of a TKS model. A fuller account of the various techniques mentioned below can be found in Johnson and Johnson (1989).

4.1   Identifying task knowledge

This section is divided into two parts; the first part is concerned with general guidelines for task analysis. The final section is concerned with guidelines for using the techniques to identify task knowledge components in KAT.

4.1.1   General guidelines for task analysis

Task analysis involves obtaining different types of information about tasks from different sources using appropriate methods. Task analysis is an iterative process where the analyst is constantly seeking to identify new information, and to reject or validate existing information. These general rules of thumb are further qualified by four general guidelines:

  (i) identify the purpose of the analysis;
 (ii) repeatedly check the analysis with the task performer(s);
(iii) analyse more than one person and more than one instance of a task;
(iv) make use of more than one technique for gathering knowledge.

4.1.2   Identifying knowledge components in KAT

KAT is concerned with identifying a person's task knowledge in terms of the components of a TKS, namely actions and objects, and the structure of those objects, procedures, and the goal structures. The techniques listed here are described in full in Johnson and Johnson (1989) and are here classified according to which aspects of knowledge they most appropriately identify.

Identifying objects and actions
Identification of objects and their associated actions used in carrying out the task can be obtained from one or more of the following techniques:

(i) selecting objects and the actions associated with them from textbooks, a tutorial session or pilot study or by the analyst's carrying out the task;

(ii) questioning the task performer in a structured interview about the actions and objects, and then listing all the relevant nouns and verbs produced by the person in answering the questions;

(iii) asking the task performer to list all the objects they can think of which are involved in the task, and the actions carried out on them;

(iv) directly or indirectly observing the person carrying out the task, carefully noting what objects they manipulate and in what ways;

(v) noting all the objects and actions mentioned by the person in either concurrent or retrospective protocols.

Identifying procedural knowledge

Techniques are described for identifying a person's knowledge of the task procedures, and the conditions and contexts in which these procedures are appropriate.

(i) Ask about standard and non-standard procedures. Include questions of the sort 'what do you do if, for example, X goes wrong or fails?' and 'how do you achieve Y?'. Ask whether any particular context or conditions exist for carrying out some part of the task, how they are identified, why they are there and what they are. Also ask what indicates or identifies the start and end of each part of the task.

(ii) Protocols and observation. This involves identifying from ongoing actions and/or verbal statements the ending of one part of the task and the starting of another.

(iii) Sorting. This technique identifies the sequence of carrying out routine procedures and involves some form of presentation of known task procedures to people who then sort the procedures into an appropriate order for task execution. The results can then be verified with other task performers.

Identifying subgoals

The identification of goals and subgoals can be obtained by using one, some or all the following four techniques:

(i) Asking what are the goal and subgoals of the task.

(ii) Identifying from a textbook, instruction manual, or any other available written material which decomposes the task into goals and subgoals.

(iii) Asking or aiding the person to construct a tree diagram, flow chart, or other diagram of the connected goals and subgoals of the task, making a specific requirement that they label different parts of the task.

(iv) From carrying out observations, concurrent or retrospective protocols. When using observations a subgoal of the task may be identified by pauses and/or marked changes in the state and/or behaviour. In concurrent and retrospective protocols, it is important to make a note of such statements as 'now, I intend/want to . . .', etc.

Task observation and its associated protocol techniques are discussed in greater detail in Johnson and Johnson (1989) and also in Chapters 6 and 7.

This section has summarized various techniques for collecting task analysis data. Together these techniques form part of the KAT methodology. The next section is concerned with analysis of and generalizing from the collected data.

4.2   Analyzing task knowledge: identifying representative, central and generic properties of tasks

This section is concerned with identifying central, representative and generic properties of tasks within a given domain or across domains. Some task components are more representative or typical of a task than are other task components. Representativeness is concerned with the particular instance and can be likened to the notion of the best example of a class. Central task components are those which are necessary to successful task completion, without which the task goal will fail to be achieved.

Generic task knowledge is that knowledge which at some high level of abstraction is common across a number of task performers and task instances. The function of identifying generic task components is that it is one way that general and transferable knowledge might be identified (see Diaper and Johnson, 1989). It assumes that general knowledge is that knowledge which is common across technologies, across instances of similar tasks in the domain(s) and across task performers at a similar level of expertise.

4.2.1   Representativeness and centrality

Task knowledge can be structured in terms of its representativeness in and centrality to the task. Representativeness and centrality are technical terms and will not necessarily be understood by any or all task performers. Consequently, a more everyday (colloquial) description of these terms is needed for presentation to people, such as best example (representativeness) and important or necessary (centrality). Identifying task element representativeness and centrality can be achieved using one or more of the following methods:

  (i) *Representativeness*. Count the frequency of how many times a particular task component is referred to. It is assumed that the more representative components will be referred to most frequently. However, this may not always be the case.

 (ii) Representativeness and/or centrality. The analyst may use rating scales where the name of each task knowledge component is separately presented and people are asked to judge the relative representativeness, typicality or centrality of each component using an appropriate scale, for example, from 1 to 10.

(iii) *Representativeness and/or centrality*. Present each task component separately to one or more persons who are then required to sort these into an order of increasing representativeness and/or centrality to the task.

4.2.2   Generification

Generification is the process of identifying generic knowledge of actions, objects and procedures. It is a process which involves a synthesis across all analysed instances of tasks, people and technologies. It is one way that general and transferable knowledge might be identified. Diaper (Chapter 4) describes a similar method, but with some differences appropriate to TAKD.

Generic actions and objects

The following can be used to identify generic actions and objects.

(1) The analyst constructs two separate lists, one for the actions and one for the objects that have been manipulated, mentioned or referred to in some way by the task performer(s). These lists will contain disparate and often repetitive information from each task performer over one or a range of tasks.

(2) Reduce the lists constructed in (1) to comprehensive and non-repetitive lists with each action, object, etc. appearing once only.

(3) Choose generic actions and objects by the following methods:

(a) Assuming a critical value or threshold of frequency for an object or action. For example, it may be decided to treat an item as generic if it is referred to by two or more task performers. If this yields an unmanageable (i.e. too large) list of generic actions and objects then the threshold may be raised. Setting the threshold relies to some extent on the analyst's intuition and experience; however, the analyst can systematically experiment with different threshold values. Threshold setting is an iterative process. Both Shepherd (Chapter 1) and Diaper (Chapters 4 and 7) discuss the subjective nature of this aspect of task analysis. The setting of such thresholds is illustrated in Chapter 4 where a task descriptive hierarchy (TDH) may be 'cut' at different levels to produce generic descriptions at different levels. This approach (i.e. KAT method (a)) identifies an individual item as being generic but does not identify any of the instances to which that item relates. To identify generic items and any instances method (b) below is recommended.

(b) Grouping like terms. The comprehensive and non-repetitive lists contain all actions and objects involved in the task and these can then be grouped and labelled. This involves:

(i) The analyst relying on intuition and using an iterative procedure to associate a particular term with all other similar terms. Similarity is determined by attempting to re-express the original task description in terms of the alternative or target term. If the alternative term was 'adequate' then the two are said to be similar.

(ii) Grouping by independent judges. The analyst asks one or more judges to sort objects, actions etc. into groups with the instruction to 'group together the X (e.g. objects) that go together, or are the same kind of X (e.g. object)'. The results of each judge's sorting can then be correlated to identify the agreed, generic task components.

(iii) After the groupings have been produced, identity a generic label or term which might cover all the individual elements in a particular set. These labels then constitute the generic items.

(4) Validate the generic elements by listing all the individual actions, objects etc. separately from the generic labels. The task performers are then instructed to identify to which generic label each action or object etc. belongs. If the action or object is not adequately covered by a generic label then the task performer is free to supply an alternative group label.

Generic procedures and goal structures

Procedures and goal structures are considered together here. One obvious way in which procedures and goal structures differ from generic actions and generic objects is in terms of the number of alternative choices available to the person. For example, there may be a large number of objects and actions which have to be manipulated in performing a task. However, there are likely to be a smaller number of alternative procedures involved in carrying out a task depending on circumstantial constraints, and even fewer alternative goal structures. The procedure for identifying generic procedures and goal structures is different from that of the identification of generic actions and objects. To identify generic procedures and goal structures:

(1) Present all the procedures or goal structures for a given domain to one or more task performers and ask the task performer to judge whether the procedures or goal structures are in any way overlapping or common.

(2) Generic procedures are those which are identified as overlapping or common.

(3) Verify the identified component with a further group of task performers by asking whether these procedures or goal structures could be used in the tasks(s).

4.3 Constructing TKS models

A task model is a model of users' knowledge of a task. The aim of this approach to task analysis is to identify the structure, content and attributes of peoples' task knowledge in line with TKS theory. In this section the construction of a task knowledge structure model is described.

There are three components to a complete TKS model:

(1) a goal-oriented substructure;
(2) task procedures;
(3) a taxonomic substructure from the generic task actions and objects;

4.3.1   Goal-oriented substructure

A goal-oriented substructure can be represented by a network of structured subgoal nodes with direct sequences of activities which unfold over time, and eventually satisfy goal nodes. Goals and subgoals can be hierarchically, heterarchically and/or concurrently related to each other. Goals and subgoals can be represented by nodes with a variety of links between them. Links include contexts, enabling conditions, and causal conditions. A further group of nodes are states and consequences which can be used to identify existing or required states and resulting states associated with goals or subgoals.

The goal-oriented substructure accesses appropriate knowledge from the procedures and taxonomic substructure. Associated with subgoals are sets of procedures which have to be executed in order to achieve subgoals directly or indirectly. The achievement of a single subgoal may give rise to a further planning activity resulting in a further subgoal structure. Consquently, only some goals and/or subgoals will have procedures directly associated with them, but all goals and subgoals will have procedures associated with them either directly or indirectly through further subgoals.

4.3.2   Task procedures

Task procedures define the ordering of action–object combinations in the execution of a given subgoal. The procedure contains sequence, iteration, and other control information that affects the execution of a subgoal. Task procedures are collected together in a procedure set (rather like a macro procedure). Task procedures are executable behaviours and can be modelled by production rules, state diagrams, or other forms of expression such as frames (Johnson *et al.*, 1988; Keane and Johnson, 1987). Task procedures access the goal-oriented and the taxonomic substructures.

There may be a choice between a number of different strategies which are context-dependent competing sets of procedures. One set of procedures may be more appropriate than other sets of procedures. Procedure appropriateness will be affected by contextual information and the circumstances under which the task is to be executed. Procedures may differ in how central they are to the task as a whole such that a failure to execute the procedure will result in the task being unsuccessfully completed. Of course, the set of available procedures may influence the construction of a goal structure in some cases. This is because task behaviour may vary according to the alternative strategies that the person knows for performing the task and also may be affected by unpredicted changes occurring during task execution. In some cases the development of a particular goal structure will be constrained by existing procedures. Consequently, task behaviour is a combination of top-down and data-driven processes.

4.3.3   Taxonomic substructure

The taxonomic substructure represents knowledge about objects and the relationships between them. The taxonomic substructure has three levels of abstraction (see Rosch *et al.*, 1976) and is not a static hierarchy.

The top level of the taxonomic substructure is the superordinate task category. The basic level of the taxonomic substructure contains the objects that constitute the superordinate task category. The basic level task category represents knowledge about (i) in which task procedures a category member is used, (ii) which other task objects a category member is related to, and what that relationship is, i.e. whether the category member causes, enables, follows or is carried out in conjunction with other task objects, (iii) which actions are associated with a category member, (iv) what features or properties a category member possesses, (v) the usual circumstances under which a particular category member occurs, for example, whereabouts in the task the category member is manipulated, (vi) whether or not the object is central, and (vii) a pointer or reference to the most representative instance of that object.

The bottom level of the taxonomic substructure is the subordinate task category which contains a particular instance of the type of the object represented at the basic level.

4.3.4   Summary TKS

A TKS includes a summary of the different types of general and specific knowledge a person has acquired and is expected to use in performing a task and gives the task analyst the opportunity to label the knowledge s/he has identified. One purpose of the summary TKS is that links to other TKSs (i.e. knowledge required by other tasks) can be made. Through making such links, commonalities between task knowledge may be identified, such as those existing in, within and/or between role relations. The summary TKS identifies what the common properties of knowledge across a variety of tasks are.

5.   APPLYING TKS AND KAT IN HCI

Applying TKS and KAT to HCI assumes that good design makes optimum use of users' ability to transfer appropriate existing knowledge easily, without preventing the creation of new solutions or the application of improved technologies where these can be seen to be appropriate, desirable and bring about an improvement in users' efficiency.

5.1   Making design recommendations

The TKS model contains useful information that can be used to influence the design of a computer program. Consider the design of a computer-based messaging system to support the common task of 'arranging a meeting'. This is a task common to architects, managers, secretaries and other job roles. The manner in which the TKS model may influence design relies upon the overriding assumption that a computer system will be easier to use in the first instance if the users are able to transfer some of their existing task knowledge to the newly created environment. This assumption underpins the metaphorical use of such existing knowledge as 'desk tops' or 'forms', in which the system design attempts to retain some identifiable links with a user's assumed extant knowledge about real desk tops and paper-based forms (see also Chapter 1). However, it is clear that making metaphorical relations is only one mechanism by which transfer of extant knowledge might be facilitated; furthermore, the way that metaphorical relations might function is itself the subject of some debate. Not all aspects of a person's extant knowledge will be relevant or transferable to the new environment. For example, the knowledge of how to dial and use a telephone may have little relevance to supporting communication by a textual computer-based messaging system. Alternatively, the more general task knowledge a person utilizes in asking questions, making requests, or providing answers would be applicable to both the old and the new environments for communication and could be supported in the new environment. However, metaphorical relations, unlike TKSs, do not, themselves, identify general or any knowledge in detail. TKSs may be used in conjunction with metaphorical relations to identify in detail the task knowledge relevant to a particular metaphor. This would give more emphasis to identifying which aspects of knowledge the metaphor was helping the person to transfer. Metaphorical relations should be thought of as a mechanism for facilitating transfer rather than as a means of identifying what knowledge it is that could be transferred. In contrast, TKSs identify the knowledge that could be transferred and can suggest mechanisms for facilitating transfer.

The TKS model identifies the knowledge structures that people are assumed to access and construct when carrying out a task. Having constructed a TKS model the analyst has identified a number of important properties of users' task knowledge of benefit to the system designer. At the highest level the TKS summary shows the relations between tasks and roles. This information provides the designer with a view as to the different kinds of tasks that the system should support by virtue of common task–role properties, and which different roles might expect to have access to the same task functions and to those task functions which are specific to particular roles. Task–role information is also of use to designers who may be concerned with configuring a system to suit the needs of a particular organization, since it shows the task–role match of the organization.

The goal-oriented substructure identifies the goal structure, the plans people construct for achieving particular and subsequent subgoals and procedures they associate with a particular task. This information may be of interest to the designer in so much as it provides an overview of the goals that users attempt to achieve and the particular contexts in which specific procedures of behaviour might occur.

The procedures represented in the TKS provide a description of processes (i.e. sequence rather than psychological process) that task performers would expect to follow, and the particular conditions under which one process would be chosen over an alternative. This knowledge determines the sequence or ordering of procedures necessary for successful task execution. TKS provides the system designer with a view as to how people structure their task knowledge, their task behaviour and the context for such behaviour. It also allows the system designer to decide how the user will expect to make use of the objects and actions and identifies the most frequent or preferred procedure for achieving a subgoal and interaction scenarios. This information can be used by the designer to set up default modes of operation, for instance, in the dialogue design (Johnson *et al.*, 1988).

Finally, in the taxonomic substructure the representative objects within the domain and their features are defined. The work on object knowledge representation of Rosch and her colleagues (Rosch *et al.*, 1976) leads us to suggest that, if the designer chooses to support a task and to provide a visible representation of the objects and the actions that can be carried out on those objects, then the taxonomic substructure provides an informative and detailed description of the features a person will expect to associate with those objects. Additionally, the degree of representativeness of objects and an indication of their centrality provide the designer with a guide as to which objects are deemed to be typical and necessary for successful task completion. Overlooking both central and representative task elements in system and user interface design may have adverse consequences on the ultimate usability of the system.

5.2   Relating TKS and KAT to design practices

Design of software systems occurs in many different ways, resulting in a certain reluctance on the part of academics and industrialists alike to speak of an ideal design process. However, it is becoming increasingly clear that task analysis has a part to play in current and future design practices; see, for example, Sutcliffe (1988a), Rossen *et al.* (1988) and other chapters of this book.

This section briefly considers the contribution TKS and KAT might make to current design practices. However, no recommendations about the appropriateness of specific design methodologies, structured or otherwise, are made. Many current design methodologies and practices could usefully exploit KAT and TKS modelling.

A 'traditional' system development life-cycle may involve the following stages; first, a feasibility study may be carried out to establish whether it would be possible to build a computer to support users' tasks, and whether there is a market for such products. A requirements definition may also be prepared, plus general and detailed designs of the system. The system is designed to meet the requirements definition. The design is specified in the form of general and detailed designs which are prototyped and implemented. The prototype implementation is tested and the system subsequently released. Maintenance schedules and phases of updating are usually included from an early part of the development plan and come into effect when the product is released. The order in which these events occur can vary and not all events may occur in any actual design activity.

A scenario is envisaged where task knowledge identified by KAT could augment existing user requirements in a software design life-cycle. First, it is expected that user and task requirements would be taken into account in any feasibility study. This would therefore involve a small-scale task analysis. Using KAT at this stage identifies commonalities across tasks through within-role relations and also by the identification of generic task elements. At the requirements definition stage a full and more detailed task analysis may be carried out to add to the user requirements a more detailed identification of the users' goal structure, task procedures and objects and their structure in the domain. This would then enable the requirements specification document to include an identification of what knowledge it was expected that the users of the system would need or be able to transfer, to provide a basis for identifying how to facilitate this transfer and to identify where users would be expected to acquire new knowledge.

The above section considers how the KAT methodology might be incorporated into system design such that more usable systems might result. Task analysis is playing an increasing role in system design but is not universally applied (Bellotti, 1988). One way to apply task analysis techniques to design is to adopt a currently used design methodology into which the KAT methodology can be integrated. SSADM (e.g. Downs *et al.*, 1988) is one design methodology into which KAT might be integrated. Work is currently in progress at Queen Mary College in this area. Designers who are familiar with and have used SSADM to design systems have been interviewed at length. The results of these interviews are being used to identify where and in what form KAT and TKS models can be used in this particular design method. The main theme of Walsh (Chapter 6) is to show how task analysis can be used in conjunction with the Jackson structured design method. Carey *et al.* (Chapter 2) mention how hierarchical task analysis may not be suitable in such applications and that a TKS-based approach such as KAT might be better.

However, SSADM is only one design approach and the longer-term aim is to identify how some appreciation of the user's knowledge requirements (i.e. what knowledge it is assumed that the user can transfer and what they will have to acquire) is taken into account in design. This would not be restricted to formal design methods. The reasons why this is important are becoming increasingly clear. Most designers now accept and carry out in practice some assessment of the usability of the design. These usability assessments are most effective when they identify where there are errors and poor performances caused by a failure on the part of the user to understand, identify or know how to use the system to carry out the tasks that they desire. The aim of applying an analysis of user task knowledge to the process of system design (no matter how informal that process is) is to provide a means by which some account of this aspect of usability can be made during the design creation. At the very least it would provide a set of criteria by which these aspects of usability (e.g. understandability and learnability criteria are both related to what is assumed that the user already knows about tasks in the domain and what they need to know) could be assessed at evaluation.

If user task knowledge is taken into account the designer can more accurately identify and create appropriate mechanisms to facilitate the transfer of appropriate extant task knowledge to the newly created environment and as a result the system would be easier to use and learn. Furthermore, predictions could then be made as to where this transfer is likely to be difficult, where interference with users' extant knowledge is likely to occur and areas where training might be necessary.

6. EXPERIENCES OF USING KAT

One test of KAT and TKS theory is in the success of its application to design. Although KAT and TKS theory may be well founded, their application to design may require further research. At present we are in the process of establishing how these ideas can be successfully applied to design. This research is following a number of routes. One of those routes was described above, in which attempts are being made to identify how KAT and TKS can complement SSADM. Other routes being pursued are to use KAT and TKS in design ourselves and to develop training courses to teach designers and human factors experts about this analysis and the focus of modelling user knowledge, so that they can use it in design contexts.

Two levels of training courses have been developed and run which attempt to get across some of the ideas in KAT and TKS. The first level of training course is a six hour introduction to the approach in which practising designers and human factors experts are given an appreciation of why we think it is important to consider user task knowledge and then are taken through some simple analyses using some of the KAT techniques. The kinds of simplistic tasks we use in this course may not, and are not meant to, test the applicability of KAT to real design problems. Through feedback during and after the course we have been able to get some assessment of the extent to which the ideas in KAT and TKS are seen as being potentially useful to design practice. Feedback is systematically collected from the course and one use of this is to identify areas in which further research is required and where some degree of success has been achieved. The main pointers we have at present are that the approach is seen as being potentially beneficial and that the analysis techniques complement the existing forms of analysis that are undertaken in design, giving a higher profile to the needs of users. The area where we feel more research is required is into the synthesis of design creations from such analyses. It appears that it is not sufficient simply to identify what knowledge the user has and could transfer. In addition some attempt must be made to identify appropriate mechanisms for facilitating this transfer (for example, the selection of appropriate metaphors).

The second level of training course we have developed is an intensive three day course in the use of the various techniques of the KAT method and the generation of design solutions. The course was run as part of the commercial activities of the London HCI Centre. We have collected detailed feedback from this course and have again found that the ideas of including an analysis of users' current task knowledge into the analytical phases of design is well received and that the particular techniques of the KAT method are seen as being useful and complement existing analytical methods. One area of concern, however, is in the form in which the outputs from any analysis are then presented. Course attendees who were from human factors backgrounds do not want to have to learn some formal (or semiformal) notation or modelling language. Instead they would prefer to write natural language reports. In contrast designers on the course wanted to use formal and semiformal notations and modelling languages but would prefer to use those that they currently know (e.g. state transition diagrams or entity relationship diagrams). Since these are important issues we are currently researching what alternative forms the outputs from a KAT analysis could take that would best serve their purpose. Several criteria are emerging:

- The output should be understandable by potential users of the designed system.
- The output should contain details about what knowledge should and could be transferred.
- The output should be unambiguous and precise.
- The output should be capable of being incorporated within a requirements specification.

These need to be added to the requirements previously identified, that the analyses should lead into and make suggestions about the appropriate mechanisms facilitating transfer of knowledge.

A number of options for the outputs from a KAT to support its application to design are currently being considered: these include the use of story boards to design symbolically the mechanisms by which transfer of knowledge might be facilitated by the user interface; the use of existing formal and semiformal notations (such as entity–relation diagrams); the development of special-purpose notations (a psuedo-functional language based on frames is being developed by Waddington and Johnson (1989); the use of representational tools such as HyperCard to construct on-line dynamic forms of some of the above (e.g. using HyperCard to present flow diagrams (Edmondson and Johnson, 1989)). The solution is likely to be some amalgamation of the different forms of expression together with some methods of transforming the output from the KAT analysis into the appropriate form.

A KAT case history
A further testing of the KAT and TKS approach is in progress which involves using this approach ourselves as part of the activities of designing software systems. Two projects have been completed each directly involving us in the development of a software system. The first is a simple design of a computer rendition of the Rubik's cube puzzle. This is being undertaken as a teaching exercise to teach postgraduate students about the design and construction of user interfaces. The application area was chosen by them to satisfy a number of constraints including the timescale of the project, the

availability of the application domain to analysis, and the potential for graphical interaction.

A KAT analysis of the tasks involved in playing the Rubik's cube puzzle was undertaken. For those who may not know what this puzzle is, the aim is to get each of the six faces of a cube to be a single colour, where each face of the cube comprises nine separate cubes. These cubes within the main cube have different colours on each face. The person then has to twist and rotate each layer of the main cube until a colour match has been reached on each face.

It was decided to use two sources of data; the instruction book that explained strategies for solving the puzzle and people playing with an actual Rubik's cube. The book provided a basis for identifying the particular aims and objectives of playing with the cube and some understanding of the procedures that could be followed in completing the cube. This book was used to develop a background understanding prior to a more detailed analysis of people solving the puzzle using the actual cube.

Both concurrent and retrospective protocol analyses were carried out of people attempting to solve the original puzzle. A total of six people were separately analysed carrying out the various tasks required to solve the cube puzzle. Each person was required to first perform the task of solving the puzzle as many times as they were able in a ten minute period. They were required to speak outloud about what they were doing while they were performing the task. Each subject's performance was recorded on a video recorder with an accompanying audio track. Immediately after the ten minute interval each subject was then required to give a retrospective protocol in which they were asked to describe what they had done at the time they were solving the puzzle, and to use the cube to demonstrate what they were doing. This protocol was also recorded on the video and audio tapes.

These data were analysed to identify the goal structures and procedures and the taxonomic structure of objects in the doamin. The following higher-level goals were identified:

- complete top layer
- complete middle layer
- complete bottom layer

Lower-level goals associated with each of these higher-level goals were also identified; an example of the lower-level goals for the 'complete top layer' goal were

- complete top layer goal
- find the face which is already most complete
- form a cross on the target face with adjacent edgepieces matching the colours of adjacent faces
- put all four corner pieces into correct positions.

Procedures associated with these goals were identified together with the context in which they were used. For example, the procedure for finding a face which is already most complete was:

Find face(s) with most top-edgepieces matching the face
> — IF more than one face is like this THEN choose the face with the most edgepieces that have adjacent-edgepieces matching the adjacent-face.
> — IF more than one face has equal numbers of matching edgepieces THEN choose any of these faces.

The basic level objects included layer, face and edgepiece, amongst others. A typical instance of the face object was the target-face. An example of the task model produced from this analysis is shown in Fig. 5.1(a),(b) and (c).

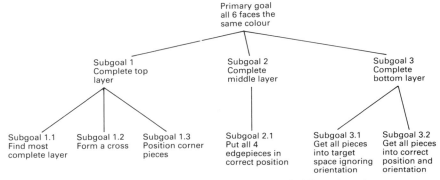

Fig. 5.1(a) — Goal-oriented substructure for Rubik's cube task.

Subgoal 1.1: Find the face which is most complete
(1) Find faces with the most top-edgepieces matching the face
  IF more than one face is like this THEN choose the face with the most edgepieces that have adjacent-edgepieces matching the adjacent-face
  IF more than one face has equal numbers of matching edgepieces THEN choose any one of these faces

Subgoal 1.2: Form a cross
Do while cross not formed:
  1.2.1 Locate an edgepiece and a position
  1.2.2 Move edgepiece into position
  1.2.1 Locate an edgepiece and a postion
    IF edgepiece is not located and the position is not located THEN rotate cube
    inspect faces with target-edgepieces=target-face
    for each candidate edgepiece identify adjacent-edgepiece
    identify position where target-position=target-edgepiece and adjacent-position=adjacent edgepiece
    choose edgepiece with least number of moves
    (2) ELSEIF edgepiece is not located and the position is not located THEN
      rotate cube
      find a vacant position in the cross
      identify target-position and adjacent position
      rotate cube
      identify edgepieces where adjacent-edgepiece=adjacent-position and target-edgepiece=target-position.

Fig. 5.1(b) — Some of the procedure knowledge used in the Rubik's cube task.

Superordinate category: RUBIK CUBE
Basic level category: FACE

Typical instance of FACE	TARGET-FACE
Centrality	HIGH
Part of	RUBIK CUBE
Related to objects	TOP-LAYER
	BOTTOM-LAYER
	MIDDLE-LAYER
	TARGET-EDGEPIECE
	ADJACENT-EDGEPIECE
	TOP-EDGEPIECE
	SQUARE
Actions associated	ROTATE
	CHOOSE
	INSPECT
Has features	COLOUR
Used in procedures	1.1, 1.2.1, 1.2.2, ...
In context subgoals	1, 1.1, 1.2, 1.3, 2, ...

Subordinate Category: TARGET-FACE, BOTTOM-FACE, TOP-FACE, ADJACENT-FACE

Fig. 5.1(c) — Some of the taxonomic substructure of the Rubik's cube task.

This shows part of a goal structure together with some of the procedures satisfying those goals and part of the taxonomic substructure identifying the objects and their properties.

From the descriptions of the knowledge associated with these tasks, several groups were required to design user interfaces to support these tasks. An example of one of the interface designs produced by Mark Magennis and Roger Kohli included the following features to support the user tasks. Here is an extract for their design specification:

'The top-face, identified in the task analysis as the most important is especially visible. . . .'
'Two types of rotation will be supported — rotating a specified layer by ninety degrees in one of two directions, clockwise and anticlockwise; rotating the whole cube by ninety degrees in one of three planes, parallel to the faces. . . .'

The top-face was identified as being a typical and central face since this was the one that the person most often concentrated on. Rotation was identified to be a central action with separate procedures for layer and whole-cube rotation.

One additional feature which this design team chose to include was an ability to present views of all six faces of the cube at any one time by using image projection of the otherwise hidden faces. This was done because it was identified that at times the person had rotated the cube to remind themselves of what the statuses of the other faces were. Since with a real solid cube it is impossible to see all six faces at one time without using some artificial aid (such as mirrors or a camera) this was felt to be a limitation of the technology of the cube and if overcome by having a generated display of all six faces this would then lessen the load on the person's memory.

Other design teams chose different solutions to these same problems, all of which were identified by the task analysis. The solutions were evaluated; the evaluations were designed from criteria developed from the task analysis and each design solution was compared against these criteria across all designs.

Further case studies of KAT

A second area of design application in which we are involved in conjunction with a software company is to develop graphical user interfaces to databases for CAD systems. In this context we have been augmenting requirements specifications by carrying out KAT analyses of user tasks in the area of design to which the system will be applied, and producing story-board designs of those parts of the user interface which we feel could and should facilitate the transfer of extant user task knowledge. This work is still in progress. However, the KAT analysis has been completed and the interface designs are now being generated. The KAT analysis involved collecting data from the existing specification document, interviews with the potential users of the system and demonstrations of different aspects of the various tasks involved in this domain. The whole analysis was limited in scope by the amount of time which had been devoted to the task analysis (a total of 15 days was set aside for the analysis and outline screen designs). This constrained the analysis by preventing us from coming into contact with a variety of task performers in various contexts. Instead we concentrated on an in-depth analysis of a single task performer. While this clearly limits the generality of the results of the analysis it was sufficient for us to be able to provide an initial user interface requirements specification and a prototype demonstration of aspects of the user interface which can then be used as a vehicle for validating the results of this analysis with other task performers.

7.   FUTURE DIRECTIONS

There are a variety of activities that are currently being pursued to develop and apply KAT and TKS theory to design practices. What looks to be a promising research topic is to identify the particular design decisions that KAT and TKS theory could influence. One type of design decision involves the scoping of the system; the KAT analysis could provide information about people's tasks that may contribute towards a more user-centred approach to scoping the system. Another type of design decision is concerned with deciding upon which parts of the domain to provide support for and which to leave unsupported. It is hoped that KAT and TKS could be of help here since an understanding of the dependencies between tasks and parts of tasks could provide criteria for deciding which aspects of the total system should be supported which are other than those concerned with the difficulty or cost of providing that support. Further input to design, and possibly the most significant, may come from the identification of where knowledge transfer can be best supported and encouraged and where training and extra help facilities are most likely to be required.

Support of the use of this analysis in the varied design contexts that exist can be encouraged by the development of tools to assist the analysis and modelling of user task knowledge. A number of tools have been proposed (Johnson and Johnson, 1989) and are currently being considered for further development. These tools might include data collection, data analysis, task modelling and the application of task models. Other chapters in this book (see Chapters 1, 2 and 4) also consider the use of tools (both software based and others) to support task analysis; however, none has yet been developed and tested in design use.

6

Analysis for Task Object Modelling (ATOM): towards a method of integrating task analysis with Jackson System Development for user interface software design

Paul Walsh†
STC Technology Ltd., Harlow

This chapter introduces a task analysis method called ATOM (Analysis for Task Object Modelling) that is intended to complement the Jackson system development (JSD) method. It is a structured method for user interface design that aims (a) to compensate for the failure of systems development methods to consider the user interface as part of the system development process, and (b) to deliver user interface specifications in a format that is timely and usable. The concepts used in the ATOM conceptual modelling language are objects, actions and relations. The procedure used in ATOM is described. It consists of three major stages, namely deriving user requirements, conceptual modelling and user interface specification. The chapter calls upon experiences in specifying a network manager workstation in order to illustrate and reinforce these points.

1. INTRODUCTION

This chapter is an introduction to a method called ATOM which facilitates user interface software development. ATOM is intended to be similar to structured methods for systems development, but different in the sense that it is concerned with the user interace. Examples of structured methods

† Most of the work that went into the composition of this chapter was carried out while the author was employed at the Ergonomics Unit, University College London. Grateful acknowledgement is made to Kee Yong Lim, John Long (both at the Ergonomics Unit) and Mary Carver (Michael Jackson Systems Ltd) who contributed significantly to the paper, and who will recognize their ideas throughout. The research was carried out for the Ministry of Defence (Royal Armaments Research and Development Establishment) under Contract number 2047/130 (RARDE). Views expressed in the chapter are those of the author and should not necessarily be attributed to the Ministry of Defence.

include SSADM (DeMarco, 1979), Jackson system development (JSD) (Jackson, 1983), and the Yourdon method (Yourdon and Constantine, 1978). Structured methods typically ignore the design of the user interface, even though most of the examples used to exemplify the methods are concerned with interactive systems. In addition, because these methods are intended to optimize the functionality of the system, the manner in which appropriate functionality is determined should be of greater importance. At the same time, an argument for using methods is that systems development is made easier and the resulting software made better through the application of a structured, rigorous approach. The purpose of ATOM is to provide a basis for specifying the user interface, while benefitting from a structured approach. Other chapters in this book (e.g. Johnson, Chapter 5; Shepherd, Chapter 1; Carey *et al.*, Chapter 2) also discuss the use of task analysis in structured methods, albeit more peripherally than in this chapter.

The present chapter is best regarded as a snapshot of ATOM at a particular stage in its development. ATOM is intended to be of assistance in the requirements capture and the user interface specification stages of the system development life-cycle. However, the current situation is that more detail can be presented concerning the contribution of ATOM to requirements capture than to user interface specification, and this is reflected in the chapter. ATOM is still in the process of being tested and refined through application to several real-life projects, and is therefore subject to modification. However, certain aspects are sufficiently static to warrant the initial reporting of the method.

The purpose of ATOM is to derive the basis for the HCI specification of the proposed system from a statement of user requirements, where 'specification' is taken to include both the functions that the system will be expected to fulfil plus a clear account of the system's appearance from the user's perspective. ATOM is user centred in the sense that it starts with the specification of the tasks that the user currently undertakes, identifies the subset suitable for embodiment in the proposed system, and proceeds to produce a design that is also easy to use. The ATOM method is not concerned with some aspects of design, however. These include the achievement of social or organizational goals through the development of an appropriate IT strategy, including the problems of implementing IT at an organizational level; and some features of interface appearance that are not amenable to analytical techniques, including aesthetic aspects of graphical interfaces. In addition, there are areas where it is expected that user testing would be recruited to supplement the method.

ATOM was designed to be a method that was compatible with other system development methods. In practice, this was achieved by considering issues that are deemed important in determining the utility of methods. These issues include (a) definition of a method, in order that ATOM can better emulate other methods, (b) the consideration of JSD, as an exemplar of structured methods, (c) the consideration of current approaches to user interface development and, in particular, the problems of timing and format that are associated with these approaches, and (d) the consideration of the system development life-cycle with particular reference to the positioning of user interface design. Each of these is considered separately.

1.1   Definition of a method
On the subject of what constitutes a method, Carver (1988) has written the following:

> *A method is more than a collection of techniques or a specification language or notation. It should specify what decisions are to be made, how to make them and the order in which they are to be made.*

Although the definition of a method is based on the tenet that it is more than a collection of tools and techniques, this does not of course preclude the fact that a method may include tools (including notations) and techniques. A method must include rules and recommendations for the use of such tools and techniques in order to progress the design from one discernible stage to the next. In addition, a method must help to focus attention on relevant issues at each stage (Potts *et al.*, 1986).

ATOM is a method for user interface development that is intended to satisfy the constraints imposed by the above definition. Therefore, it was developed by considering the concepts that should be utilized in specification in tandem with the procedures by which the specification should be obtained.

1.2   JSD and user interface design
Structured methods are general purpose in that they are applicable to the development of various types of applications. However, such methods generally ignore HCI aspects (Bubenko, 1986), and this problem is aggravated by failing to consult users during development. As ATOM was developed as part of a project that aimed to integrate human factors with the JSD method, the comments that follow are most directly applicable to JSD.

First, some background information on JSD may be helpful. According to Carver (1988), JSD is a method for specifying an implementing computer systems whose subject matter has a strong time dimension, e.g. real-time, data-processing and simulation systems. It consists of three major phases, which are called modelling, network, and implementation. In the modelling phase the analyst is concerned with building a model of the users' world (the 'real world'), taking into account the time ordering of events. The model is realized (via representation as JSD structure diagrams) as a set of sequential processes known as model processes. The functional requirements of the proposed system are specified in the network phase by constructing new processes which obtain information through their connections with the model processes. Finally, the implementation phase involves transforming the specification into programs more efficiently executable with the target hardware and software.

JSD has been demonstrated to be useful in system development, and this prompts the question whether it might not serve as a sufficient basis for the design of the human–computer interface. JSD, after all, relies on modelling the users' world rather than considerations of the analyst. It is also an operational method (Zave, 1982), and as such provides a basis for prototyping the proposed system, which will help the user to visualize the proposed system. On the other hand, there are certain deficiencies in the JSD method that compromises its suitability for such a purpose. In particular, the utility of JSD in requirements capture can be questioned. In fact, JSD is not intended to be a method for requirements analysis. Instead, JSD has a broader scope than most requirements methods, and hence JSD does not offer sufficient guidance to aid decisions about the entities that should be modelled (Finkelstein and Potts, 1985). In addition, the JSD guidelines for the manner in which actions, entities and functions are extracted from the description is too haphazard for large specifications. Finkelstein and Potts also argue that JSD tends to focus attention on individual parts of the system, and thus may occlude any overall view of the system that might have existed.

However, these objections are minor compared with the fact that no attention is paid to the design of the user–computer interface in the JSD method. This problem has been considered by the authors elsewhere (Walsh *et al.*, 1988, in press). They have proposed that expertise in HCI should be considered, for JSD purposes, as a form of specialist knowledge that is recruited to supplement the method. Such recruitment is not uncommon, and is obligatory when an aspect of the problem requires a solution that is not contained within the method. An example of recruitment might be the neccessity for database design, which is not supported by JSD, within a project that otherwise follows the JSD procedure. Walsh *et al.* (1988) also propose that task analysis can identify the problems, difficulties, procedures and knowledge of the target population of users, while the principles and notation used in JSD could be adopted to represent the product of this analysis. Finally, they identify instances during the system specification process (i.e. during the modelling and network phases) when human factors intervention is both necessary and desirable.

However, although task analysis is recommended to supplement the absence of a requirements capture method within JSD, there is no account in Walsh *et al.* as to which task analysis method, if any, would be best suited to this purpose. ATOM was developed to remedy this omission, that is to provide a method for the analysis of user requirements, which in turn acts as a basis for specifying the user interface, that is not incompatible with the specification obtained using JSD.

1.3   User interface design

In the HCI literature, user interface design is frequently seen as dependent upon the application of Task Analysis (TA) methods. Task analysis is used to study and provide a task description of an extant human–machine system, and to propose recommendations for design or modification that optimizes the system described, by projection from the task description. Some examples of TA methods includes Hierarchical Task Analysis (HTA) (Hodgkinson and Crawshaw, 1985; Shepherd, Chapter 1), TAKD (Johnson *et al.*, 1984; Diaper, 1988a; Diaper and Johnson, 1989; Diaper, Chapter 4), the user–device model (Kieras and Polson, 1985), Task Action Grammar (TAG) (Payne, 1985; Payne and Green, 1986, Chapter 3), and CTA (Barnard, 1987). Task analysis is therefore used as a generic title for a host of different methods and techniques, and there are many differences between individual TA methods. This section attempts to characterize extant TA methods along a set of dimensions. It can be read in parallel with Payne and Green (Chapter 3), who provide a graphical characterization of TA methods along the dimensions of 'device dependence' and 'logical–practical–cognitive'.

Some TA methods have their origins in non-automated work activities and, as Rasmussen (1988) points out, tend to be formulated in terms of a sequence of actions on the work objects. For this reason, TA methods may not focus on cognitive operations, in addition to these physical actions. It is generally considered that task descriptions for computer system development must include task knowledge in addition to task operations, and Johnson (Chapter 5), for example, provides a Task Knowledge Structures (TKS) theory as part of his KAT method. All the methods listed above, however, satisfy this requirement of focusing on cognitive as well as physical operations. Another difference between methods concerns the granularity of the task description that the method provides, i.e. whether it is a micro or a macro method (Harris and Brightman, 1985). A micro method is designed to focus on a single activity, such as text editing, and to provide a detailed, cognitive analysis of the knowledge employed. Macro methods, on the other hand, are concerned with all the activities carried out within a definable environment, such as an office. Such methods tend not to focus on cognitive operations, because of the constraints of scale. Similarly, some TA methods are able to represent unstructured tasks, while others can only cope with routine and well-structured activities. Unfortunately, many of the TA methods above are intended primarily for well-structured, micro activities.

Some TA methods are suitable for application early in the system development life-cycle, while others are best regarded as tools for 'late evaluation'. Examples of the former would be HTA and TAKD, while others such as TAG are examples of the latter. TA methods also differ on whether they model an 'ideal' user, or a typical one (Wilson *et al.*, 1986). TA methods differ in whether they are task driven or actor driven (Harris and Brightman, 1985). In a task-organization to accomplish certain objectives, while the actor-driven approach focuses on the goals, actions and difficulties of individuals. HTA, for example, is concerned primarily with a description of the hierarchy of procedures (or operations) that constitute the user's job. TAG, on the other hand, is intended as a tool for anticipating the errors that users might be expected to make.

Finally, TA methods differ enormously in the taxonomy of basic concepts that are used to represent tasks. In different methods, it is possible to find a description of tasks expressed in terms of one, some, or all of the following: objects, actions, roles, goals, procedures, functions, processes, forms, attributes, relations, predicates, rules, inputs/outputs, and transitions between states.

Although there is a variety of TA methods, and each method satisfies certain fundamental requirements for a user interface design method, it will be argued that none of the above methods is sufficient. This argument is based on the view that systems development exercises two additional requirements that are typically not contained, or are insufficiently considered, in the above methods. The first requirement concerns the problem of proceeding from the product of the method to an implemented design, where the purpose of TA methods in systems development is to support and enhance that mapping. All the chapters in this book address this issue of mapping methods to system development to a greater or lesser extent. There is also a requirement to support within-specification mapping, so that, for example, the analysis of a non-automated work system will map to the design for automation of (at least) parts of that system. The second requirement concerns the ability of a TA method to impact on design by virtue of its understanding of the system develoment process. It is suggested that the successful design and evaluation of user interfaces can only come about if the HCI analyst is aware of and follows a model of the system development life-cycle.

The failure of current TA methods to satisfy these requirements stems from the absence in those methods of the characteristics normally associated with structured analysis and design methods such as JSD. That is, TA methods should be concerned with the nature, method and order of decision making in the user interface design process. Furthermore, these decisions should be understood in relation to the general life-cycle model, for the reason that user interfaces do not exist in a vacuum. When, for example, pertinent decisions on issues such as functionality are taken by the software development team, the HCI analyst has to be in a position to contribute from the basis of the HCI analysis. A critical factor for the success of HCI in influencing the systems development process is therefore the **timing** of the HCI contribution. This issue will be explored further in section 1.4, which considers the positioning of user interface design in the system development life-cycle.

The other critical factor, apart from timing, is the **format** of the HCI contribution (Walsh et al., 1988). The specification of HCI aspect should be comparable with the system specification produced by systems analysis in terms of specificity and utility. Principles for the production of good software specifications (Balzer and Goldman, 1979) were considered in the development of ATOM. For example, a specification should separate issues concerned with the functionality of the proposed system from issues concerned with implementation, such that it is concerned with what is desired of the system rather than how it is to be achieved. In the HCI domain, a specification should contain an expression of the user's goals, which can be considered as expressions of what is desired. It is important that the expression of these goals begins at a high level, typically by analysing the goals of the organization rather than of an individual. This would mean, in HCI terms, that a goal such as 'edit a document' would be excessively narrow for this purpose. In ATOM, goals are not used as part of the conceptual modelling language, but are the basis for the user requirements specification.

It is also important that a process-oriented specification language is used. In other words, the 'what' nature of the specification should be a model of the desired behaviour in terms of functional responses to various stimuli from the environment. In some TA methods the emphasis has been the decomposition of task hierarchies rather than the description of procedures. In ATOM, procedural descriptions are an important part of the method, and are achieved by (a) analysing the principal objects of the system, and (b) identifying the major actions associated with each object. This is similar, for example, to TAKD's analysis of objects and actions (Chapter 4), although within TAKD 'actions' are more similar to 'actors' (discussed in section 2.1) in the ATOM method.

In addition, the specification must encompass the system of which the software is a component, i.e. it is only within the context of the entire system and the interaction among its parts that the behaviour of a specific component can be defined. For example, the system can be said to be composed of active and passive objects. The active objects, or agents, may initiate changes that produce further stimuli to which other agents may respond. Also, a specification must consider the environment in which the system operates, such that the environment is itself regarded as a system composed of interacting objects, both passive and active, of which the specified system is one agent. To ensure that these principles were satisfied, ATOM was developed in accordance with the conception of work offered by Dowell and Long (1988):

> *Work, as defined in the conception, occurs within, and is distributed by, organisations. The world in which work is performed is conceived as discrete objects. These are physical or abstract and are composed respectively of matter/energy and information/knowledge. Objects are characterised by their attributes. The same attribute(s) identify classes of objects and so also a hierarchy of classes. ... An attribute of an object is conceived as having a state which exhibits the potential for change.*

The system specification should be a cognitive model, that is, it must be a model of a system as perceived by the user community, rather than a design or implementation model. The main benefit of using a TA approach is to obtain a description, in user terms, of the extant system. There is an advantage in taking a TA approach, rather than a traditional requirements analysis approach, in that TA describes a cognitive model of the extant system rather than a model of a proposed system, which may not be easily envisaged by the users.

The specification must be operational, in that it must be capable of being used to test behaviours that are typical of the proposed implementation. If the specification is executable this principle can be satisfied. This is central to the assertion that the format of the HCI contribution is frequently incompatible with the remainder of the systems development enterprise, in that an HCI specification that cannot be readily operationalized will be at a disadvantage to the system specification that can. Because JSD is an operational method, targeting the product of ATOM to the requirements of that method will make the HCI specification more operationalizable. Of course, a specification is always a model of a situation in the environment, and, as such, may be operational but still incomplete, so it is important that it is tolerant of incompleteness and augmentable. A 'middle-out' design method, such as JSD, can handle this factor better than 'top-down' methods. Again, by targeting in JSD, ATOM avoids the dangers associated with a top-down, decompositional approach. Also, the specification must be constructed in a manner that anticipates the need to modify the system. By analysing the world in terms of objects, ATOM is expected to benefit from the advantages associated with the object-oriented approach, which include the maximization of modularity and re-usability.

In summary, ATOM differs from other TA methods in that it starts from an analysis of what makes system specifications more or less successful, and attempts to base itself upon those principles that have increased the utility of system specifications. One means by which it does this is by imitation of its target system development method, JSD. The fact that ATOM is targeted on an extant systems development method also differentiates it from other TA methods, which are not. The case for integrating the product of TA with other methods has been argued extensively in Walsh *et al.* (1988) and Sutcliffe (1988b).

1.4   The system development life-cycle

One of the principle arguments that is put forward in ATOM is that successful design and evaluation of user interfaces can only come about if the HCI analyst is aware of and follows a model of the system development life-cycle. Many life-cycle models have been proposed and contested in the literature, and it may be the case that no one model is adequate for all instances. Nonetheless, it is argued that individual enterprises, such as user interface development, should be constrained by a prototypical view of the development process. A life-cycle model, which reflects user interface development in the context of system development, using the JSD method, has been proposed. It is illustrated in Fig. 6.1.

The model attempts to portray the type of information that is required at different milestones in the system development process. Some of the terms will require clarification. The symbols X and Y refer to the extant and target systems respectively, where the target system is the system that is to be developed, and the extant system is a predecessor system that performs

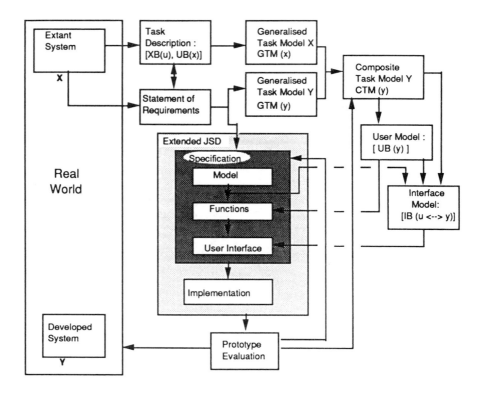

Fig. 6.1 — System development life-cycle model and integrated user interface design
activities.

some related task to achieve a similar set of goals or targets. These goals and
targets may have changed, and this typically constitutes the rationale for the
development of system Y. The arrows in the diagram represent design
activity processes, for example, transformation, decomposition or abstraction operations. U represents the user, and $UB(x)$ and $UB(y)$ denote the
user's behaviours on systems X and Y respectively. By contrast, $XB(u)$ and
$YB(u)$ denote the behaviour, with respect to the user, of systems X and Y
respectively. The terms $IB(u\leftrightarrow x)$ and $IB(u\leftrightarrow y)$ represent the behaviour of
user interface objects that are associated with the user's task as performed
on systems X and Y respectively. An example may be found in the domain of
withdrawing money from a bank. The user may use manned tellers (system
X) or automated tellers (system Y). The user interface objects may be a
withdrawal form, bank book and/or cheque card for system X; while for
system Y it may be the cash card and the PIN number. The behaviour of the
systems may be regarded as the task organization that is relevant to the
system, e.g. process the withdrawal form, check balance and/or signature
and issue cash. On the other hand, the user's task would include 'how to'
knowledge about using the user interface objects, such as withdrawal forms,

bank teller, etc. to effect a cash withdrawal. Correspondingly, the behaviour of the user and the user interface objects are described by the actions across the interface, or that which drive the interactions.

The term SR represents the client's statement of requirements, which typically consist of high-level information about the system and the implied user task on system Y. The terms GTM and CTM are generalized task models that are derived from the above-mentioned primitives, and may exhibit recombinant properties that are different from the properties of the primitives. This implies that desired recombinant properties have to be validated by evaluation and achieved through design iteration loops. Generally they are system independent, and describe the logic underlying the task to be performed with respect to the achievement of set goals. It follows that there will be a set R that comprises the remainder or discarded set of attributes of elements considered in the design.

Based on the life-cycle model represented in Fig. 6.1, the user interface design process is taken to consist of three stages, namely (1) requirements capture stage, (2) an initial design stage, which involves conceptual modelling and (3) a detailed design stage, which involves user interface specification. A fourth stage, called a prototyping stage, which may be iterative, could be considered, but it is beyond the scope of the present chapter. The requirements capture stage is primarily concerned with obtaining the SR, that is, the statement of requirements (section 3.1). The initial design stage (section 3.2) is concerned with deriving task descriptions of $XB(u)$ and $UB(x)$, the $GTM(x)$, the $GTM(y)$ and the $CTM(y)$. The detailed design stage is concerned with obtaining the $UB(y)$, the $IB(u{\leftrightarrow}y)$ and, ultimately, specifying the user interface (section 3.3). Finally, the prototyping stage would represent a means of validating the $CTM(y)$, which in turn may have consequences for the $UB(y)$, the $IB(u{\leftrightarrow}y)$ and, ultimately, the specification of the system (including the user interface).

2.   THE ATOM DESCRIPTION LANGUAGE

A description language is defined as a comprehensible medium for communicating information about the proposed system between those involved in its design. That means that the description language should be capable of supporting dialogue between designers with different responsibilites in the system project, between the designers and their peer group (for modifiability purposes), and, last but not least, between the designers and the client or users. The description language used in ATOM is intended to be a synthesis of concepts that have proved useful in three domains, namely knowledge engineering, object-oriented programming and requirements modelling. The juxtaposition of these three domains is not as unusual as it might first appear. Regoczei and Plantinga (1987), for example, have argued that systems analysis, software requirements definition, conceptual database design and knowledge engineering share the goal of acquiring the world knowledge of an informant who, depending on the situation, may be called an expert or a user. One of the reasons why knowledge acquisition is a bottleneck is that users 'change their minds', because 'any system development activity inevitably changes the environment out of which the need for the system arose' (McCraken and Jackson, 1982).

ATOM is predicated on the view (Borgida, 1985) that information systems are 'models' of the world that contain relevant information about the world, and that the world is populated by 'objects' that are interrelated through their 'attributes'. ATOM offers a means of analysis of this domain in terms of (a) *objects*, which consists of entities and actors, (b) *actions*, which are synonymous with events, and (c) *relations*. Most of these concepts have been used as the basis for semantic analysis of a conceptual domain in other methods. The purpose of the explanation offered in this paper will be primarily to highlight novelties in the application of these concepts.

2.1   Objects

Objects are a critical component of the ATOM description language, and this generally reflects the emphasis that has been placed on the object-oriented approach in current software engineering. Also, objects have been identified as one of the essential aspects of user interface composition, and the object-oriented approach is useful for user interface construction (Tesler, 1981; Schmucker, 1987). However, different object-oriented systems support different notions of objects (Bannerjee *et al.*, 1987), so the need remains to specify the sense in which the term is being used. One definition is that objects are like small programs for carrying out a specific operation, in that they contain data and procedures that operate only on the data in that program (Kaehler and Patterson, 1986). Each program is like a 'machine' that only knows how to do the task for which it was designed. As only the operations defined can manipulate the object, so the object is essentially the sum of its operations.

Based on the conception of work quoted earlier (Dowell and Long, 1988), objects are further classified in ATOM into concrete, or *designated*, objects, and abstract, or *non-designated*, objects. Some designated objects can be further classified as *actors*. The basis for the classification of designated objects is that some objects may be associated with 'proper names', while others may not. Objects that have proper names are described as designated objects (Martin, 1988). Objects that are designated may be human, in which case they are classified as actors. The concept of actors (or agents) is based on the definition that agents are objects that embody actions (Agha, 1986; Maibaum, 1987). The terms actors and agents are frequently used as synonyms for object and, while this may be a useful concept in object-oriented programming, it is not the sense of actor that is intended in ATOM. Actor objects must be involved in actions which require both personal identity and a human agentive role. For example, an actor is required in the statement 'John wants money', but not in 'faults stop machines'. The concept of actors is therefore a useful mechanism for the identification of functions that are associated with humans.

Non-designated objects differ from designated objects in that they are not physical objects and do not possess proper names, but are constructions that are created for the purpose of exposition. Non-designated objects are classified as either *simple* or *complex* (Lundberg, 1987). A complex non-designated object is described as a 'quasi-object', which exists only in terms of the atomic objects form which it is constructed. The two types of quasi-objects are *aggregate* and *collective* objects. An aggregate object is constructed from a number of objects for which a relationship holds. An example of an aggregate object is represented by the notation $\langle a, b \rangle$ in the following proposition: *year-of-marriage(1985,$\langle$jim, jane$\rangle$)*. A collective object is the construction of a number of objects which have a common property. An example of a collective object is represented by the notation $\{a, b\}$ in the following proposition: *staff-of (ABC, {jim, jane})*.

2.2 Actions

Actions are a second type of concept used in the ATOM description language. Action is commonly used in task description, in that the purpose of tasks is to produce intentional changes in the attribute state of an object (Dowell and Long, 1988). The performance of an action establishes a causal link between object states, and characteristics of causation also apply to actions. For example, actions typically involve an agent and a patient, where agents and patients can be either persons or objects. If the agent is human, they are presumed to have a goal, which is represented as a plan, that initiates some change of state in the patient. Carrying out such a plan constitutes an action in the sense that tasks suggest. Thus actions that are either not goal-directed or conscious as such to the agent would be ignored. A familiar action may be represented as a script (Schank and Abelson, 1977).

The identification of actions in requirements elicitation is necessary because, as Maibaum (1987) points out, the world of description at any instant is a state of information to which changes can occur, and these changes are the result of actions performed by agents.

The *designated state* of an object can be identified by examining the verb types that typify actions. In Martin (1988), three types of verb are identified, namely (a) *process* verbs, which involve change of some sort, e.g. 'becomes', 'dies', (b) *state* verbs, which refer to a continuous conditon, e.g. 'remains', 'waits', and (c) *action* verbs, which involve an action usally upon or to an object, e.g. 'kills', 'eats'. This allows us to consider process events, state events, and action events as three separate categories. Finally, an important 'action' involves an object sending a message to another object or itself.

2.3 Relations

A relation is an abstraction stating that objects from certain classes are associated in some way (Rumbaugh, 1987). The association is then given a name so that it can be a manipulated, for example, for the purpose of specification. In the entity–relationship model (Chen, 1976), an entity is a 'thing' that can be distinctively identified, and a relationship is an association between entities.

It is possible to derive a taxonomy of relation types. One example is the semantic network model proposed by Yasdi and Ziarko (1988), who classify attributes in terms of declaration, association, generalization, aggregation, equivalence, deduction and exception. Another relation type that is identified concerns temporal relations between objects or events (Ariav, 1986).

2.4 Comparison of ATOM and JSD

This section is devoted to exploring the similarities and differences between concepts as they are used in ATOM and in JSD. This is intended to aid readers who are familiar with the latter and who wish to understand the different uses of terminology.

The first point of comparison involves a consideration of how the concept of object compares with the concept of 'entity' employed in JSD. The criteria for entities in JSD are that they must perform or suffer actions in a significant time ordering, they must exist in the real world outside the system and they must be capable of being regarded as individual. If there is more than one instance, it must also be possible that they can be uniquely named. Objects will generally be subject to most of these constraints, except that there is no requirement for time ordering. However, because the nature of requirements capture is more general than the specification process that JSD supports, it is possible to relax the constraints during the first-pass analysis. The justification for this is that the constraints may not be satisfiable while the information available is incomplete, and it may be premature to reject objects that have not satisfied the constraints at this early stage.

In terms of the proposed life-cycle model, the identification of objects by requirements capture and entities by JSD modelling must ultimately be reconciled. That is, the eventual system specification, which includes the user interface specification, must refer to a common object list. It is not possible to perform this reconciliation until the interface model (see Fig. 6.1) has been developed. The timing of object reconciliation is therefore during the user interface specification phase.

The relationship between the concepts of action in ATOM and JSD is an important one. In JSD, a prerequiste for actions is that they can be usefully regarded as instantaneous, rather than extending over a period of time. Continuous activities must be decomposed to a number of discrete steps. Actions must also take place in the real world outside the system, and must not merely be an action of the system. However, an action must be an event that the computer system will need to know about (e.g. it may have to produce information about the event, or to initiate some activity as a result of it). The purpose of description, in JSD, is to support the functions that are to be provided by the system. Actions must also be atomic, in that they must not be decomposable into subactions. Because JSD is concerned with entity–action life histories, the constraints imposed upon actions have implications for entities also.

In ATOM, actions are bound only by the constraint that they are identified in association with a related object. The most notable difference is that actions that are outside the subject matter of the proposed system are considered to be relevant and hence identified. This dissimilar treatment of actions is the major difference between task anlaysis and JSD specification (Walsh *et al.*, 1988).

The treatment of relations in ATOM and JSD can also be contrasted. Firstly, it is worth noting that, in JSD, entities are modelled by a sequential process, and are different from the 'entities' found in the entity–relationship and other database models. Technically, JSD is not concerned with modelling entity relationships. However, part of the specification process in JSD is concerned with the identification of the attributes of actions, which are the data associated with the action. For example, in the specification of a library system, an attribute of the action 'register user' might be 'user-ID'. The main difference between JSD and ATOM is therefore more procedural than conceptual. The emphasis in ATOM is on static modelling, and relations are important as concepts that bind entities together. The identification of relations has implications for data capture, however, and the eventual reconciliation of the relations used in the interface model and in the entity attributes list is necessary. This is part of the user interface specification process in our life-cycle model.

3. THE ATOM PROCEDURE

The ATOM description language provides the basis for decomposing the domain of interest into objects, actions and relations, which can then be further subdivided according to the classification offered. In addition, ATOM offers a set of procedural guidelines by which the description language should be obtained, and, once obtained, how it may be manipulated to generate the user interface specification. The provision of such guidelines is in accord with Shepherd (Chapter 1), who suggests that rigid rules for carrying out task analysis are not desirable because they will be insufficiently context sensitive, and with Diaper (Chapters 4 and 7) who stresses the necessarily subjective element to both task observation and task analysis. In terms of the system development timescale, however, the product of such an enterprise would be obtained late in the development life-cycle. In order to minimize the problems that might accrue if the user interface design is separated from the main product development stream, a means for cross-referencing the HCI stream with the main system development stream has been proposed. ATOM therefore consists of three stages, each comprising a number of steps. The first stage is deriving user requirements, the second stage produces the conceptual model, and the third stage is user interface specification.

3.1 Deriving user requirements

The first step in ATOM involves interviewing people who can be characterized as experts for the domain of the prospective software. This assumes that certain preliminary activities have been carried out. For example, some idea of user requirements, albeit at a high level, will be necessary to obtain a preliminary scoping for the prospective system. This will be obtained from the organization that is commissioning the system, and it can be obtained by either the systems or HCI analysts. Another important activity is to decide what constitutes a domain expert. Interviews of the domain experts are semistructured in that there is usually an 'agenda' arising out of the preliminary discussions between the systems and HCI analysts, but interesting leads provided by the domain expert will be followed. Interviews should typically take place in the domain expert's place of work and be tape recorded using non-obtrusive equipment. It has been found that, during the initial interviews, the categories of questions should include the following: (a) organizational structure, including personnel issues and communications, (b) principal actors, focusing on the initiation, processing and delivery of work, (c) major activities, including popular and unpopular actions, (d) problem solving, with emphasis on the people and the methods that are used for troubleshooting, and (d) tools, including those that are currently used and those that are wished for. Johnson (Chapter 5) provides a more detailed list of data collection methods.

The second step involves transcription of the interviews to obtain what is called the basic text. Apart from separating utterances according to speakers, it has not been found useful to introduce too much detail to these transcripts. For example, speech pauses will yield less additional information to such question-and-answer interviews as they would to 'thinking-aloud' protocol analysis. The third step is called highlighting. The analyst goes through the transcription highlighting all relevant phrases (these are called 'assertions') uttered by the domain expert. This is hand crafted in that it is based on the analyst's judgement, but where necessary errs on the side of overinclusiveness. This is similar to TAKD's conservative heuristic used in constructing Task Descriptive Hierarchies (Chapter 4). The highlighted assertions are extracted, and the hierarchical relationship between sets of assertions is indicated by setting levels using a simple and typical indentation procedure. For each domain expert a separate file is maintained. The fourth step is outlining and categorization. The extracted assertions are exported to an outlining tool (e.g. LVT More™) where each top-level assertion is labelled consistently (e.g. 'security'). At this stage the assertions are only related to each other by topic area. Separate files are still maintained for each domain expert. The fifth step is synthesis. A composite file is constructed that consists of all assertion categories from all domain experts. This is sorted according to category. Each category is then sorted according to its subcategories. The result is a set of hierarchically organized categories pertaining to the subjects raised by domain experts.

Finally, step 6 involves producing a user requirements specification document. This is based entirely on the outline view derived in step 5. For each category, the proposed functions of the system are presented in a hierarchical fashion. This is a point when contact with the systems analyst is obligatory. The HCI understanding of the subject matter of the proposed system has been derived from the domain expert's elaboration of their systems. This is better than the systems analysis view alone, because it is based on experts' experiences. It will present a view of the expert's task in terms of the major 'activity blocks' that are involved. This document should recommend what HCI functionality is indicated by this analysis, with some ascription of the importance of each function. One reason for producing this function list is to cross-reference it to functions lists that are produced by other development streams so that possible functionality is not overlooked. In the specification activities that follow, it is necessary that both systems and HCI analysts make reference to a similar set of functions that the system will support. A user requirements specification document is therefore produced for distribution to the systems analysts.

These procedural guidelines can be clarified by recourse to an example case study that was carried out using ATOM. This was a project carried out for the Ministry of Defence, and involved specifying the HCI for a Network Manager Workstation. The purpose of the NMW was to allow a network manager to set up, control and monitor the Digital Data Network at the Ministry of Defence site. The particular DDN associated with the NMW had a distributed state configuration that consists of portswitches, network interface equipment, network manager equipment, and bridges.

The first part of the task of specifying the NMW was concerned with the deviation of a shared view of the functional requirements of the system. The project was initiated within the Ministry of Defence, and early contacts were between the clients, the systems analysis team and the HCI team. From these meetings, the systems analysis team were able to derive an outline view of the proposed system. This was supplemented by subsequent interviews and analysis of documentation provided by the hardware supplier. The principal goal of the systems analysts was to obtain a view of the proposed hardware, and the general requirement for the software, in order to proceed with the JSD method. The purpose of obtaining a view of the proposed hardware was to provide scope for the project, rather than a means of determining the functionality of the system. As a prerequisite to applying JSD, the systems analysts were interested in obtaining information about the entities and actions in the system's domain.

During this time, the HCI team was establishing contact with an organization that appeared to have a parallel system. The background to the interviews that were held at the two computer centres has already been presented, so we shall summarize by saying that the data were obtained from managers or members of network support teams or computer operators. Most of the examples that are used here were obtained from a manager and a member of a support team at two different sites. Also, considerable detail concerning the procedure in which the data were collected has already been presented in the previous section. In what follows the emphasis is therefore on the actual functions that were identified.

The following categories of functions were identified: security, networking monitoring, fault handling, broadcasting, utilization statistics, network configuration and user support. Space does not allow us to explore all the 24 or so separate subcategories of functions that were identified, so only a few examples are presented. In the category of network monitoring, for example, it was seen that the NMW should run one terminal and display data constantly; that it should condense the information from several nodes into one destination; that access to the data should be supported by appropriate storage and retrieval facilities; that individual messages (the data of the system) should preserve their individuality; and that the NMW should be flexible with respect to the addition of new devices to the network. It was further discovered that distinct system states such as functioning, down, faulty, out of service, busy and erratic were perceived by the network managers interviewed, and that the use of colour was one means of discriminating these states. Certain potential weaknesses were identified, such as failing to protect against the NMW itself crashing, causing the display to 'freeze', or not signalling a change in state to a permanent record of system behaviour. Generally, information was elicited that suggested that network managers of a large network require a model of the topography of the network. For example, when a link failed and parts of the network became inacessible as a result, it was important that only the failed link was seen as faulty, and not the entire subnetwork. Finally, it was found that a help facility, to remind the network managers about the available commands, was necessary.

As a second example, consider the category of utilization statistics. In this area, it was seen that the NMW should be able to support enquiries from general users, directed through the network manager, about how machines are coping with network trends. Summaries of such trends were generally seen to be useful in planning extensions and revisions to the network, and in reporting the efficacy of the network. Functions were also found to be mutually supporting. For example, the availability of utilization statistics such as failed log-on attempts could be used in enhancing the security of the network.

Although this is a brief selection, it is still apparent that the functions identified are diverse in nature. Some relate specifically to the system, some to the human–computer interface and some are external to the system. No attempt is made to separate HCI-related functions from the others, as (a) all are related to the perceived functionality of the system, and (b) the purpose of this stage of the method is not user interface specification. The main goal of this early stage, it is reiterated, is to present the systems analysts with a requirements specification document that will sit alongside theirs, in order to establish a common view of the system's functionality.

An outstanding problem that is not addressed in the current version of ATOM concerns the validation of the requirements that are identified. One solution to the failure of ATOM to consider this problem would be to adopt the method used by Harris and Brightman (1985). This method begins by interviewing a subsample of relevant 'knowledge workers' in order to develop a profile of task descriptors. Only a subsample is used, while the remainder are retained for use as what Harris and Brightman describe as a hold-out sample. The profile of task descriptors is validated by showing it to the sample used in the interviews, who examine it for accuracy, clarity and completeness. Finally, the hold-out sample is surveyed to identify the critical bottleneck tasks, which are tasks that inhibit or limit effectiveness and efficiency.

3.2 Conceptual modelling

In terms of the project timescale, the derivation of user requirements will occur early in the system development process. There will not have been sufficient time for the detailed analysis of the interview transcripts that is suggested by the description language. However, once the initial statement concerning desired functionality has been signed off, an opportunity for analysing the transcripts in terms of objects, actions and relations will occur.

The first step in conceptual modelling, and step 7 in ATOM involves choosing a category of interest. Each category is treated independently. A file is created with each sentence labelled with a unique identifier, for each uniquely labelled category of each labelled domain expert's transcript. This implies that we use the individual rather than the composite records (i.e. step 4). In step 8, the analyst derives object, action and relation lists. Each sentence is analysed separately for objects (nouns), actions (verbs) and relations. In step 9, sort according to object. All instances of objects are grouped into appropriate categories, based entirely on their names. All repetitions of object names, action names, and relation names are removed. The final product is a set of object categories with their associated actions and relations. No attention is paid to whether these objects fall within the domain of the proposed system (i.e. JSD's 'subject matter' concept). Instead, they are part of the 'Domain of Interest' (DI) of the proposed system.

A simple means of graphically representing the information captured by ATOM has been developed. In its present form, a prototype system has been developed that represents each object as a simple rectangle, separated into sections corresponding to object name, actions list, and messages list. Two radio buttons allow the user to specify whether an object is 'designated' and an 'actor'. Lines link the object box to two other boxes, called OtherObjs_Relations and OtherObjs_Messages. These contain lists of other objects that the specified object is related to, and that it passes or receives messages to or from respectively. An example of the specification for the object 'Team Member' is shown In Fig. 6.2.

A collection of specified objects can be stored in a Hypertext stack, and this collection is referred to as an object base. Objects are linked to the objects referred in the OtherObjs_Relations and OtherObjs_Messages boxes using a standard linking facility. The prototype interface supports certain functions at present. These are of course still in development, and futher experience with the method can only help to suggest additional and optimal functionality. Among the functions supported are (a) sorting the object base according to designated or non-designated objects, and (b) exporting the text to a specification document called the object dictionary.

These points may be clarified by reference to the case study introduced in the previous section. It is again stressed that the examples used have to do

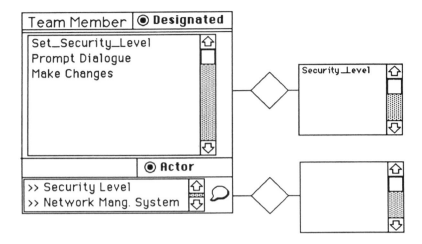

Fig. 6.2 — Graphical representation for 'Team Member'. Each representation depicts a single object, with the associated actions, related objects and message passing shown for each.

with just a few aspects of the network management task and, in particular, troubleshooting the network and gaining access to the management system itself. The examples are intended to show how objects, actions and relations were identified in the interview transcripts. This necessitates presenting the analysis in a fragmented manner. Normally, the procedure in ATOM is to capture objects, actions and relations simultaneously.

Analysis of the interview transcripts revealed that the objects that referred to troubleshooting the network included the following: fault; other person; diagnostic test; line; operator; modern; protocols; error message; and port number. Using the object classification described above, the designated objects in this list are line, other person, operator, modem and port number, and the non-designated objects are protocols, diagnostic test and error message. The subclassification of the designated objects reveals that other person and operator are actors, while line, modem and port number are not. The subclassification of the non-designated objects is difficult without further information, but it might be the case that diagnostic test is an example of an aggregate quasi-object, because it will involve a construction that depends on the aggregation of the test and the data it surveys. An error message is a simple non-designated object. There are no examples of exceptions in the actual interview transcript but, given the nature of fault finding, it might be appropriate to tag the fact that exception noting might be useful for future purposes. That is, one way of further conceptualizing this particular task would be to record the situations that are considered exceptions by the operators (i.e. whenever a fault occurs, it is an exception to normal functioning).

With respect to actions, the task that is addressed concerns access to the management system. In particular, this part of the task has to do with deciding who is an appropriate user of the actual management system (not the network itself), and how to detect and prevent inappropriate users from gaining access. In order to make the action list comprehensible, it is necessary to indicate the objects identified. These included team member and bad user , which are both actors, and security level, dialogue, management function, network, decision and error. The actions identified include decide, set security, prompt dialogue, make changes, and make error. These actions are distributed with respect to the user and the system. The action of deciding the security level is an example of a process action, because, although it must be set by the team member, it is a long-lived process. However, because once a level is set it remains in force until changed, a state action is also implied, i.e. having a security level. The other actions, concerning prompting, changing and committing errors, are all examples of action verbs. Possible message passing in the system would include the following: team member →security level; team member →NM system; bad user →NM system; NM system →all users. In addition, all these objects can message themselves.

Relations connected to objects and actions were also systematically recorded. A primary reason for gathering descriptions of relations from the interview transcripts was that they are necessary in order to ensure the clarity of object–action pairing. For example, in the portion of the transcript devoted to fault finding, some of the objects and actions identified included fault, find fault, and cause fault. Some attributes that were associated with these are noteworthy; for example, it would be useful to denote that certain objects were connected through the relations cause of, connected with, and even simply have problem. Other relations were even more essential. For example, it was important to record that, for one expert, the main attribute that connected the objects network and printer and the action record fault was that they always seemed to occur at times when the printer was unattended. Recording that bad time was a relation that held between the objects and actions was therefore useful.

In the example of access to the NM system, there are several instances where recording relations helps to bring clarity to the description. Some examples include specifying that people possess the attributes in team or not in team, or that the decisions made at the computer centres studied were considered by them to involve relatively low precision and few negative consequences.

At this point in the conceptual modelling stage, the HCI analyst should expect to possess a set of the major objects that are present in the system. These objects are represented using the graphical representation technique shown in Fig. 6.2, and therefore show the actions that are associated with the objects, plus the relations that the object has to other objects. This set of object diagrams represents a static model of the domain of interest. A static model according to Pressman (1987), presents a snapshot of a system at a point in time, e.g. data in a database between updates. A dynamic model, on the other hand, illustrates a flow of data. Every system has both dynamic and static components, but system design techniques tend to emphasize one or the other. This differential emphasis is unfortunate because user interface design is typically concerned with both static and dynamic properties of the system. A static model of the domain of interest is therefore only half of the conceptual model that is required.

The omission can be rectified because, in JSD, the emphasis is on modelling the dynamic component, that is, it examines events occurring in the real world that fall within the domain of the proposed system, and the objects that are associated with these events. JSD has been argued to be an appropriate medium for the specification of user interface behaviour (Carver, 1988). The purpose of JSD structure diagrams is to specify the behaviour of objects, including concurrent behaviour. This can be extended to the domain of task description in the Task Structure Diagrams (TSDs) can be used to specify the dynamic nature of task actions (Walsh *at al.*, 1988).

The final stage, then, in building the conceptual model is to focus on the dynamic properties of the system that is of interest, and, having done so, to reconcile the dynamic and static components. The creation of TSDs follows the same procedure as normal Jackson structure diagrams. That is, each TSD should represent the life history of a single entity as a hierarchical, tree-structured diagram which has a unique path from any node to another. The life history of an entity is concerned with the necessary time ordering among actions that are connected with an entity. The diagram will consist of nodes that represent sequence ('consists of'), selection ('either/or'), and iteration ('zero or more repetitions'). A fourth type, called backtracking, is used to indicate uncertain outcomes.

JSD, because it is concerned with specification, is principally concerned with selecting the entities that are part of the system domain of interest. Task analysis, on the other hand, should concern description as well as analysis. Therefore, there should be a TSD for all the task entities that are identified, and not just those that are envisaged for the proposed system. The identification of entities is achieved through analysis of the events in the task domain that initiate action on the part of a task participant (or actor). For each event, the relevant actions are noted for expression as a TSD. For example, in the analysis of the network manager task, an important event is detecting that a fault has occurred. This can be achieved either when a user reports a problem or when the system uncovers a fault. Some of the actions associated with the latter will include a sequence of acknowledging the warning message, checking a printout to find evidence of a fault, and determining what error category the fault is likely to be in. In addition, actions are suggested by the remedial action that the network manager carries out to resolve the problem, and these will also suggest further levels of decomposition.

The relationship of the entities modelled with the objects identified during the static model construction is important. Although it is not necessary to obtain the set of objects before entities can be modelled using

TSDs, it is important that objects are reconciled with the entities thus modelled. This will require that an entity TSD exists for every major object that has been identifed.

3.3   User interface specification

The ATOM method produces, as the product of its first and second stages respectively, a statement of user requirements and a conceptual model. The former is not used directly in user interface specification (i.e. to generate design), but it is presumed that, in what follows, the HCI analyst has access to the document and uses it to verify that the system design remains compatible with the statement of requirements. The conceptual model, on the other hand, is intended to be an object base for the task domain. If it has been successfully derived, it should represent a Generalized Task Model (GTM). The purpose of the GTM is to support the specification of the human–computer interface for the proposed system. This is accomplished by (a) transformation of the GTM into a represntation, called a Composite Task Model (CTM), that is exclusively concerned with the proposed system, and (b) through application of some or all of a set of heuristics that are developed for the purpose of human–computer interface specification. Two points are worth noting in advance. Firstly, the CTM represents a means of scoping the developing specification, and is itself an input to further transformations. Secondly, the heuristics to be described are intended to be flexible with respect to the method, that is, further developments could lead to improved heuristics, the proposal of which should not compromise the ATOM method.

Currently, a number of heuristics are available for transforming the CTM object base into a user interface specification. Three examples will be presented here. These are heuristics for (a) the design of menu hierarchies, layouts and contents, (b) the design of database or form entries, and (c) the specification of actors within the proposed system. The first two examples are chosen because they illustrate relatively low-level HCI activities, and how extant HCI is more readily expressed in the context of a specification language. The third example illustrates what is arguably a more novel application of the ATOM method.

The demonstration of these heuristics is best achieved by example. The example chosen is a simple library system. It is expedient to skip over the knowledge elicitation details, and to assume that some objects, actions and relations have already been identified. The objects identified were as follows: book, reader, and librarian. For each object, several actions were identified. Some of the actions that were identified for book, for example, included lend book, renew loan, return book, reshelve book. Objects were also related in various respects, e.g. reshelving the 'book' object was only possible if an agent, the 'librarian' object, was on hand to execute the action. The GTM for the library system was thus composed of this view of objects and actions, with relations between objects. Scoping the CTM introduced some new aspects. For example, because it is no longer a physical book that is being manipulated, it is likely that a 'file' object will be required.

The menu design heuristic suggests that the menu should always consist of an entity plus the actions that the entity can perform or suffer. In the library example, it would therefore be recommended that the top-level menu should consist of the entities, and the selection of a given entity allows access to the actions connected with that entity. In a different implementation environment, such as a graphics-based interface, the entities would be represented as items on the title bar, with the actions available as pull-down menus.

The actor specification heuristic has been developed in response to the trend to invest 'expertise' in software designs. This is exemplified by knowledge-based systems, but it is not limited to these. The problem, from a HCI perspective, is frequently one of handling user interaction with the expert system. That is, although there are times when the user wishes to 'delegate' decision making to the system, there are also times when the user will wish to 'interrogate' the system. Given that expert systems are intended to assist users by replacing some of the actions hitherto carried out by a user, it is argued that the focus on actors that is part of the conceptual model is a useful basis for handling this delegation. It helps to determine, for example, what other objects are typically interacted with. The actor object can then be used as a means of representing the expert system to the user. In the design of the network manager software, for example, it was possible to design a command dialogue in which the user (the real network manager) could delegate certain responsibility to his or her system counterpart (the network manager actor). Because the actor is available to the user, it is possible to interrogate the actor on areas that are of agreed interest, such as the status of the network, as well as altering the duties of the actor when appropriate.

Finally, the conceptual model contains a specification of the dynamic properties of the system that is of use in user interface design. It is possible, for example, to continue to refine the set of TSDs to a set that approximates the JSD structure diagrams. The HCI analyst can present a specification of the desired user–computer interaction in this form, as demonstrated in Walsh *et al.* (1988).

4.   CONCLUSIONS

The present chapter has demonstrated the current state of the ATOM method for user interface software design. However, the method is still very much in development, and treatments of the different parts of the method may not have been equal in detail. Despite this, it is argued that the ATOM method currently possesses sufficient defining factors to warrant its reporting. Among the features that define ATOM the following can be included.

ATOM differs from other TA methods in that it attempts to encompass all stages (including analysis, design and implementation) of the system development process. A model of the system development life-cycle has been proposed, and the major activities in ATOM focus on this model. Like structured methods in general, an aim of ATOM is to assist the HCI analyst in knowing what decisions are needed, the manner in which such decisions are best made, and the format in which they should be presented.

The ATOM method has been developed to assist the integration of HCI activities with systems development. This has the result that the products of ATOM are expected to be compatible with the format used by systems developers, particularly when JSD is used. There is certainly no equivalent method that enables HCI to interface with JSD, and, in general, not enough attention is paid to the problem of interfacing with other system development methods. A product of the integration of HCI with system development will be to remedy the failure of extant structured methods to pay sufficient attention to the design of the user interface.

The conceptual modelling language is based upon concepts, such as objects, actions and relations, whose utility for requirements specification is generally regarded as high, and which are familiar to their potential users. ATOM is different in the sense that, in place of a rigid, prescribed method for mapping requirements to the final design, there are instead a set of flexible heuristics whose recruitment is at the discretion of the HCI analyst. However, deriving a complete set of heuristics is the least-developed part of the ATOM method, and is the area requiring most future attention.

To summarize, the ATOM method has been proposed as an example of the manner in which it is believed that user interface design can be best integrated with the rest of the system development process. The proposal that structured methods be adopted for user interface design is the critical issue. To some extent, the issue of developing methods can be separated from other aspects of ATOM, such as the conceptual modelling language and the procedure. ATOM may be idiosyncratic to our HCI experience, and not generalizable, but this should not reduce the case for the development of user interface design methods. Indeed, it is expected that aspects of ATOM can be successfully modified without seriously compromising the method. For example, there is almost limitless scope for the development of heuristics that might be recruited for use within the method.

7

Task observation for Human–Computer Interaction

Dan Diaper
Department of Computer Science, University of Liverpool

1. INTRODUCTION

Task analysis can be thought of as a method that has two components to it. Much of this book is devoted to the second part of task analysis, the analysis of data. This chapter, in contrast, is devoted to the first data collection stage, and concentrates on the observation of task performance as the data source. While not all the task analysis examples in this book use this source of data, it is central to many task analysis methods, including those in this book, even when its use has not been explicitly described. Non-observational methods of data collection have been well described elsewhere in the published literature (e.g. Cordingley, 1989), which is the justification for this chapter's concentration on task observation.

Within the field of HCI, task analysis can be used in the system design process at many stages. Such applications are not restricted to the design of interfaces but may provide specifications for the complete functionality of a computer system. Task analysis can, for example, add quality to initial requirement specifications by providing detailed descriptions of how tasks are currently performed. Task analysis can be used to evaluate simulations and prototype systems throughout design as well as evaluating notionally completed systems. It has obvious utility in the redesign or upgrading of systems. One of its major and earliest applications was for the design of operator training (e.g. Annett *et al.*, 1971; Shepherd, Chapter 1). While not extensively covered in this book, task analysis can also provide a powerful tool for eliciting knowledge from domain experts for the encoding in knowledge-based systems such as expert systems (e.g. Diaper, 1989a; Wilson, 1987, 1988). Within the design process a considerable variety of people, not only the actual and potential users of a system, could be subjected to task analysis. However, and regrettably in the author's opinion, task analysis in HCI is usually restricted to an analysis of a system's operators.

1.1 Observation is not easy

In the following two subsections the sort of background psychology of observers that, once appreciated, should caution those unfamiliar with the difficulty of making reliable observations, is first introduced. Second, the special problems of observing a person using a computer system are introduced for expansion and explication later in this chapter.

1.1.1 Observation is not easy: a psychologist's introduction

We are all beguiled by the apparent quality of the integrated sensory world that we believe we inhabit. One of the hardest aspects of teaching psychology is to persuade students that their sensory world is a property of the enormously complicated mental processes that operate on the stunningly poor evidence provided by the senses. This is true for all the senses, though it is perhaps most pernicious in the visual modality. While the early Greek philosophers of more than two millennia ago recognized the difference between the sensory world and that of the real world, and thus preferred knowledge derived from thinking over that offered by the senses, this view is not one that is common to those outside the arcane disciplines of psychology, philosophy and the associated cognitive sciences.

To take the visual case, the eye, as an optical instrument, is of an appalling quality and this author is not the first to comment that if we were restricted to optics of equivalent quality to those of the eye then photography would never have been developed. The humours of the eye and the lens through which light must pass to reach the photosensitive retina at the back of the eye are translucent, rather than transparent, and it has often been commented on that the human retina is the wrong way around (e.g. Gregory, 1966; and many others). This claim rests on the fact that between and overlaying the light-sensitive rods and cones of the retina is a network of opaque blood vessels and nerves. The only exception to this is the fovea, the one part of the retina on which the optical image is at all reasonably well focused, and the foveal image subtends no more than about 4° of visual angle, whereas we perceive a world subtending some 120° of visual angle.

Thus the eye presents the observer with a small, poor quality image. Furthermore, the image is effectively transitory as the light-sensitive cells respond only to changes in stimulation and thus no information is signalled about unchanging images. It is thus necessary for the eye to be constantly in motion so that images are not stabilized on the retina and it is necessary for the eye to make frequent, large movements, saccades, so that different parts of the perceived visual world are allowed to project onto the fovea. During each saccade, each of which takes nearly a quarter of a second, a process called saccadic suppression occurs that prevents the information being transmitted from the eye as the image spins across the retina.

Thus, from such elementary psychophysiology, and it is possible to fill books on the limitations of the eye as an optical instrument, the stable, wide, visual world that we perceive is actually based on a series of narrow, partially focused snapshots, in a general blur. While there are numerous processes that control and determine eye and head movements, focusing and so forth, the important point for this chapter is that the perceived visual world is a mental construct and is based to a great extent, not on the bottom-up, data-driven processes operating on the visual input, but rather on top-down, concept-driven processes that take as their input a perceiver's knowledge and beliefs. It is for this reason, and with little to do with optics, that the human neonate takes such a long time to learn to see. Thus the saying that 'people only see what they wish to see' is, in fact, a very correct comment of the perceptual act based upon impeccable evidence from a number of branches of empirical, scientific psychology, psychophysics and physiology.

Similar sorts of comments can be made of the auditory modality and for the other senses, though the primacy of vision and audition in every day life, and for the purposes of this chapter, is such that because they are so sophisticated they are also the most heavily dependent on the perceiver's personal knowledge and beliefs about the world.

The constructive nature of perception thus leads observers to report events that are consistent with their beliefs and expectations and effectively to ignore or distort events that are contrary to what they expect. The literature on eye-witness testimony (e.g. Loftus and Loftus, 1980; Bekerian and Bowers, 1983; Bowers and Bekerian, 1984), for example, where people are asked to report an event that they have just witnessed, notwithstanding the enormous changes that occur over time as events are processed and consolidated in memory, leads to the conclusion that people are generally poor observers and have great difficulty reporting what they have just perceived. This is evident in the lack of agreement between observers of both real-world events, where such problems plague the courts for example, and also in the more controlled environments used by psychologists. The famous conformity experiments of Asch (1956) further point to how easily subjects can be persuaded to report untrue events, even for very simple visual stimuli.

1.1.2   Observation is not easy: particularly in HCI

While all observation is difficult, it is often particularly so in HCI applications. In many cases, the task being observed involves a direct end user, or operator, using a computer workstation consisting of a monitor, a keyboard and perhaps other input devices such as a mouse or graphics tablet. The behaviours generated by the operator are often very fast and of restricted spatial extent. The observable consequences of these actions are spatially separated in that they appear on the monitor or on other devices such as disk drives or printers. An observer, unaided by any recording equipment other than pen and paper, is thus presented in such cases with an almost impossible task. Not only is it difficult and usually impossible to observe both the operator's use of the input device and the monitor simultaneously, but it is extremely difficult to record sequences of behaviours in their correct order. The observer is often handicapped by being far less familiar with the hardware and software system than the operator and this adds an interpretational problem for the observer who is trying to relate operator behaviours to what is happening on the screen and on other devices. Even when high quality, synchronized multicamera video tapes of tasks are available as a data source, rather than live observations of a task, in many instances the same portion of video tape needs viewing many times with frequent use of frame freeze and slow-motion playback.

1.2   The myth of objectivity

It is a depressing indicator of a lack of philosophical understanding that a phrase such as 'an objective viewpoint' can be used so frequently and with so little comment or criticism. This phrase, perhaps the most offensive amongst a host of variations, is obviously contradictory. This is clear given that 'objective' has a definition which means 'external to the mind, real' or 'uncoloured by exhibitor's feelings or opinions' (*The Concise Oxford Dictionary of Current English*, sixth edition) and that all the relevant definitions of 'view' involve a psychological component (e.g. 'inspection by eye or mind'; 'what is seen'; 'manner of considering a subject, opinion, mental attitude'). Ignoring the fascinating but irrelevant philosophical issue concerning whether a real world exists or not, it is unquestionably the case that all observation can only be subjective. As the philosopher Popper (1972) points out,

> observation is a process in which we play an intensely *active* part.
> An observation is a perception, but one which is planned and prepared. We do not 'have' an observation ... but we 'make' an observation. (Popper's emphasis)

Allied to this is the problem of reporting an observation. It is self-evident that a verbal, a written, or even a drawn description of a visual observation is a poor shadow of the observer's rich percept. Such descriptions are systematically degraded and edited and Popper rightly points out 'there is no theory-free language to describe the data'. Furthermore, Adrian (1966) suggests that the very act of introspection, the mental act of attending to a percept, may itself change the percept; he calls this 'a Heisenberg effect' and, as the author (Diaper, 1987) suggests, 'this is to be expected' because the introspective act is likely to require cognitive processing resources that could be otherwise deployed.

Thus, to take up the latter part of the first quote from Popper, the observational act requires the observer to plan, in advance, what to observe, to try to make the observation and then finally to record the observation. The actual observation is likely to be constrained not only by the initial decisions concerning what to observe but also with the type of report intended. Indeed, in many cases it is the reporting constraints that principally determine the content of the observation.

The rejection of the notion of objectivity is crucial to an understanding and appreciation of both the observational and analytical components of task analysis. Both involve numerous subjective decisions and it needs to be clear to those new to task analysis that there are no correct decisions, only subjective judgements which, when made, are useful for a particular purpose (see Chapters 1, 4 and 5). In selecting what to observe it is not only essential to decide how to record the observations, but it is also necessary to have decided how to analyse the recorded observations and this in turn must be determined by a clear understanding of the purpose of the whole task analysis exercise and its required product (Chapter 4). It really is not too strong advice to say that, one should never start an observational study without knowing how the recorded observations will be analysed and why the whole exercise is being carried out.

Finally, it is perhaps worth mentioning the well-established problem of reactivity. In essence this is a Hiesenberg effect in that in most circumstances the act of observation itself changes what is observed. With the exception of methods such as computer capture (section 2.5), it is rare in HCI for a person to be unaware that they are being observed. No matter how unobtrusive the observer of her/his equipment, the very knowledge that one is being observed is likely to alter one's behaviour. There is no elegant solution to the problem of reactivity but it is an issue of which task observers should be aware as it leads to an inevitable loss of fidelity (section 2.1) between observed and unobserved performance.

1.3 Task observation alternatives

'If task observation, let alone the analysis, is so difficult', a reasonable person might ask, 'then why do it at all?' and there is no doubt that it is difficult and expensive of time (and thus money). The answer to the question lies in the alternatives to task analysis. The classic alternatives are to ask people such things as to describe how they carry out a task, what are their own, or their organization's, goals and requirements, or what are their opinions, attitudes and emotional reactions concerning, say, a new piece of software. Even these alternatives are better than computer-centric personnel, which includes many systems analysts as well as the traditional hacker of software code, relying on their own opinions of what a system should do and what its users actually need, etc. However, there are fundamental problems associated with people's verbal descriptions of what they do, what they like, what they want, and so forth.

Bainbridge (1979, 1986) has spent considerable effort outlining the problems that people who are task experts have with reporting how they carry out their tasks. In her 1986 paper, which though devoted to knowledge elicitation for expert system encoding is highly relevant to alternatives to a task observation approach, she distinguishes between 'sources of distortion' that are common to all reporting situations from those that arise because the techniques access 'the knowledge by a different route than is used during the task'. She further divides this second category of distortions into two subclasses: 'A. Reports which require translation between verbal/spatial/ movement representations'; and 'B. From reporting knowledge away from the real-task situation'.

Bainbridge identifies four sources of distortion common to all reporting situations, though it should be noted that these criticisms are only relevant if the proposed techniques are actually used. First, she suggests that concurrent protocols (i.e. where the person verbally reports what they are doing during task performance) may interfere with task performance. Second, she suggests that with some techniques the amount of knowledge elicited is constrained 'because of time or opportunity'. Third, she identifies the 'self-presentation' issue where the person providing a verbal description has personal goals concerning the image they project to their listener and she also notes that there will be an interaction between the style and content of the verbal description provided and the perceived knowledge and expertise of the listener. Fourth, she suggests that some 'techniques encourage people to develop a standard strategy for answering the questions' so that their response is biased by the context of the preceding questions and would have been different 'if each question was treated as a separate problem'. At least points 1, 2 and 4 are examples of a general problem of context sensitivity in that unless undisturbed task performance is observed then there will always be distortions caused by the verbal description task being different from the task of interest performed in its normal manner.

Bainbridge's point about translating visual representations into verbal descriptions has already been mentioned in the previous section and a similar point can be made for motor-to-verbal translations. She further suggests that 'when asked to report their methods they [task experts] may revert to using inexperienced methods, which are slower, more verbal, and less integrated, so can be reported more easily'.

Finally, Bainbridge deals with the very serious problems associated with obtaining verbal descriptions from people away from the environment where the task of interest is usually carried out. Surprisingly, her seven points are not exhaustive but the most serious issue has been previously described by the author (Diaper, 1987) as involving the 'encoding specificity principle' (Tulving, 1974). As the author stated (Diaper, 1987):

> The poorest descriptions of tasks will be obtained when the description environment is completely different from the task performance environment. In such cases, the person describing the task must rely on her/his memory alone and in an environment that provides few or no cues to facilitate recall then memory is known to be poor (Tulving and Pearlstone, 1966; Baddeley, 1976).

The author has identified a range of problems associated with verbal descriptions that are generated away from the task performance environment. First, there are 'gross omissions', as, without the appropriate environmental cues, task descriptions tend to lack temporal order information as what the describer perceives as the cultural components of the task are usually described first. This tendency is difficult to overcome even when very detailed instructions are provided. This leads to whole segments of tasks often being omitted from the verbal description. Second, there are 'fine omissions' of two types. The first type involves task components of which the task describer is generally unaware. For example, the timing and force of keystrokes. The second, and more serious, type of fine omission involves the level of description of the task provided (Diaper, 1987; Diaper and Johnson, 1989). For many reasons the task describer will often wish to hurry the description of the task and there is a powerful tendency for the task to be described at a general, high level of abstractness. The person recording the task description has little control over the level of description offered and even subsequent probing is often unsatisfactory as it is likely to disrupt the describer if she or he is interrupted and, if returned to after an initial description, there is a problem of the loss of temporal sequence. Third, such verbal reports tend to provide an idealized version of the task. Performance errors are rarely reported and where there are alternative ways of carrying out a task then only one of these is usually described, or the option is glossed over by using a higher level of description.

As the author concluded (Diaper, 1987),

> Thus the best that one can hope to obtain from the verbal descrip-
> tion of a task is a simplified, general description of how the task
> should be performed. To analyse how tasks are really performed,
> warts and all, then a method of task analysis is required that
> involves the detailed and systematic observation of task perfor-
> mance by an independent observer.

1.4 Defining a task

A classic and under-addressed problem in task analysis has been the definition of a task. Annett *et al.* (1971) contrast the notion of a job with that of a task. The former, they claim, is 'a person oriented concept; it usually has a title and contractual implications' whereas they say of tasks that 'the assignment of a set of tasks to a person defines his job'. Similarly, Wilson *et al.* (1986), for example, exemplify a task by the example of 'document production'. In contrast, Johnson and Johnson (1987), who to their considerable credit address the issue of defining a task directly, suggest that a task 'may involve only one or two activities which take less than a second to complete, for example, moving a cursor'. Clearly there is a problem as a task such as document production may take hours, days, months or years depending on the nature, size and means of production. Furthermore, document production may involve many people whereas moving a cursor is not a cooperative activity. Johnson and Johnson recognize this and they also suggest that a task may take years. However, they go no further with their attempt at definition, having only specified that 'we will describe a task as a set of activities to be carried out which will change the situation from an initial state to some specified goal state'. It has been widely lamented that no successful task taxonomies exist, even for tasks within a narrow domain (e.g. Wilson, 1987, 1989, in knowledge engineering), and it is not clear that a taxonomy of even the most general sort can precede an agreement on defining tasks. This section will outline a definition of a task which is independent of the domain of application, equipment and so forth but which focuses on tasks carried out using a computer.

It is clearly unhelpful to consider tasks, particularly for the purposes of observation and analysis, as taking very long periods of time. Given that Annett *et al.* have made a strong distinction between jobs and tasks, then large tasks, of the document production sort, might perhaps be better thought of, and called, 'projects', where projects are composed of a number of tasks. While it is obviously not possible to place an upper or a lower boundary on the duration of a task, a task would be better defined as finishing when the person stops carrying out the task's activities and leaves it in some state where it can be restarted subsequently. What is needed is some concept of the graceful termination of a task. Thus a text editing task in a document preparation project might terminate with saving the current version of the document on disk and then leaving the computer system or performing an unrelated task. However, performing an unrelated task in the middle of the task, for example taking a telephone call while editing, would not automatically signal test termination if the editing task is resumed. Focusing on task termination should also allow the beginning of the next task (i.e. project resumption) to be clearly identified.

It has been widely recognized for a long time (e.g. Annett *et al.*) that tasks involve subtasks and the suggested definition of a task above does not solve the problem of identifying subtasks. Furthermore, subtasks may confound the above definition of a task as some subtasks are quite different from what precedes or follows them. Thus, in a text editing task, saving the document and sending it to a remote printer and then collecting the printout and returning to the task might involve several subtasks, such as editing, saving, printing, walking to the printer, reading the printout and then resuming editing, that are all being part of a single task. However, where the person only resumes editing hours or days later then this would be two separate tasks in the project. While for many purposes it may not matter whether a set of activities are characterized as a task or subtask, there are likely to be critical differences at the transition points between subtasks and between tasks within a project and the identification of these will often be crucial in the task analysis. There is the possibility, for example, of failing to observe some aspects of these transitions, particularly if subtasks are treated as separate tasks, because the observer may ignore relevant activities that connect the subtasks.

Thus tasks can be seen and defined within a four-level hierarchy of project, tasks, subtasks and activities. Task observers and analysts need, at least, to be alert to the possible differences and should, perhaps, pay particular attention to the transitions between and within tasks, subtasks and also activities. Even at the micro level of activities it is frequently a problem to identify an activity from its components. Thus on a word processor, for example, the activity of deleting a character might involve locating the character on the screen, moving the cursor both vertically and horizontally using a range of different combinations of keystrokes, and then deleting the letter. However, the lower boundary of the level of detail of activities that are observed is one of the crucial decisions in task observation and is explicitly addressed in the next section.

This section has deliberately avoided discussing goals. The notion of a goal is widely used in task analysis, including all the preceding chapters in this book, with the exception of Chapter 4, and in much HCI theorizing (e.g.

Card *et al.*, 1983). However, goals are not observable entities but have to be inferred from observed behaviours, including the verbal claims made by those performing a task. Thus goals, where a relevant notion, are properly part of task analysis, rather than task observation, and invoking goals as a means of defining tasks, as Johnson and Johnson do, does not therefore aid the task observer. The next section will argue that the crucial information that allows the appropriate decisions to be made about the definition of tasks, subtasks, etc. in particular applications lies not with identifying the goals of task performers, but rather with the identification of the purpose of the task observation and subsequent analysis.

1.5   Selecting what to observe

Perhaps the most important decision facing any task observer is deciding what to observe. There are two different types of observation selection. First, there are always some behaviours which are recognized as not being relevant for a particular observation exercise. In HCI many behaviours of the user that are not directed at the computer or other tools (e.g. manuals, etc.) are treated as irrelevant, though, of course, for some purposes behaviours such as scratching, sighing, stretching, gazing into space, etc. can be highly informative.

Second, there is a level of detail about even behaviours directed toward the keyboard which is considered irrelevant for the purposes of carrying out the observation. The most obvious, common examples of this in HCI are such keyboard-directed aspects of behaviour concerned with the ballistics and force with which keys are pressed, and in some cases even which specific keys are pressed (e.g. Diaper and Johnson, 1989). Similarly, the actual movement of a cursor across a screen is often not of interest as there are numerous routes possible, though the start and end of a set of cursor movements often are of considerable interest. With no criticism intended, it can be noted that Payne and Green (Chapter 3), while analysing the function of cursor keys in detail, do not address this issue. In fact, it is probable that when editing documents, particularly late in a document's production history, that a considerable amount of the time spent in the task on the keyboard will involve cursor movement. Thus most sophisticated text editors provide a variety of methods for cursor movement that allow it to be moved at the level of characters, words, sentences, lines, paragraphs and screens. Most editors support only a subset of such movements and the more complicated ones' features are often not fully utilized all the time because they force the user into making task-irrelevant decisions (i.e. the user wants to move the cursor some considerable way in a document, has identified the current and intended location of the cursor and sometimes does not then want to make a set of selection decisions concerning cursor movement while holding in memory the important information about where and why the cursor needs moving).

However, the task observer should be aware of what decisions are made about excluding the observation of low-level behaviours and such decisions should be made explicitly, rather than implicitly. If, as in the case of the later stages of document preparation, substantial parts of the task, such as the considerable portion of the keyboard time spent on cursor movement, are ignored then quite erroneous conclusions about the task may be made, particularly if the task analyst holds a spurious belief about the objectivity of task observation and analysis (section 1.2). To make such decisions explicitly, it is clear that the task observer must, as discussed in Chapter 4, have a very clear understanding of the whole purpose of the observational and analytical exercises.

The next section of this chapter discusses observation recording technologies and while it is subdivided into sections concerned with these technologies (e.g. pen and paper, video, etc.), a more appropriate and roughly parallel classification could be based on what such technologies are likely to fail to be able to record. Thus, before deciding on how observations may be made, it is necessary for the task observer to establish just what needs to be recorded. As recording technologies are limited then their selection should be driven by this prior identification of the important task elements. Furthermore, it is generally not possible to record everything and this is not desirable. Generally, the range and detail of observations made are exponentially related to the time it takes to analyse these data. Rarely, if ever, is the task analyst unconstrained by either time or money and even the need to discard irrelevant observations can be time consuming. Thus, on the grounds of cost and efficiency the task observer should follow the rule that 'if it is not needed it should not be recorded'. The identification of such requirements is clearly the responsibility of the task observer and the decisions made obviously support the claims made earlier about objective observation being a myth.

2.   TASK OBSERVATION RECORDING TECHNOLOGIES

This section describes the major technologies that can be used for recording the behaviour of users and computer systems in HCI tasks. Apart from the comments in section 1.5 concerning the limitations of each technology, there are also usually practical limitations on what technologies can be used and these are discussed in section 2.1. Only the 'major technologies' are discussed and there are other, specialized ways of recording some aspects of tasks. For example, at the Ergonomics Unit, University College London, there was a sophisticated but 'Heath Robinson' like arrangement for recording the force of users' keystroke behaviour. The measurement of the small forces involved necessitated that the keyboard was permanently mounted on concrete blocks to reduce noise and, even though a permanent piece of equipment, it was still one of considerable fragility. Fortunately, such specialized equipment is not usually necessary for most task analyses concerned with HCI issues.

2.1   Recording environment fidelity
Section 1.3 discussed the relationship between the environment in which a person usually performs a task and the environment in which they are asked

to describe the task verbally. It was argued that, the less similar these environments are, the poorer would be the task description. It is hardly surprising that the same is true for task performance. The principle reason, of course, is that people are context sensitive and are likely to perform what is notionally the same task differently in different environments. There is almost inevitably a difference between the usual task environment and one in which recording takes place. Section 1.2 has already introduced the notion of reactivity and the influence an observer or observing device is likely to cause. An exception to this general problem is described in section 2.5. Wherever possible, reactivity should be minimized as it is difficult to evaluate the biases it causes and this issue is exemplified in the description of recording technologies in the following four sections.

Recording environments can be roughly divided into two types. The first is where the recording takes place in the usual task environment and the observer is an additional element to this environment. The second is where the task environment is substantially different and is usually an impoverished form of the the normal one. Impoverished, of course, means with respect to the target task environment and does not preclude the task analysis environment's being a rich one, but only that it fails to match the environment of interest. There is a substantial literature in the area of human–machine simulations regarding the fidelity of simulations which is basically the same notion as that being discussed above. Thus Diaper (1989c) provides a definition of fidelity from the *Oxford Concise Dictionary* (sixth edition): 'Faithfulness ... exact correspondence to the original; ... precision of reproduction'. Stammers (1989), for example, identifies nine 'dimensions of fidelity put forward in a training context (Stammers, 1983): (a) stimuli/displays; (b) Responses/controls; (c) Display–control relationships/feedback; (d) Task complexity; (e) Temporal aspects; (f) Environmental stress; (g) Situational payoffs; (h) Social environment; (i) Instructional control', and these 'dimensions' are themselves capable of being subdivided further.

Within HCI and task observation, as with simulations, it is clear that perfect fidelity is unachievable and the important issue is 'to identify the aspects that are critical from those that make little difference to the performance on the simulation and real systems' (Diaper, 1989c). The identification of these aspects currently relies on the expertise of the analyst and her/his understanding of the application domain. However, one advantage of using task analysis throughout the design process first to identify user requirements, then to evaluate design decisions and subsequently to test prototypes and delivery system implementations is that the issue of fidelity can be addressed repeatedly and many of the fidelity issues will be clarified during the later applications of task analysis. However, what is needed, and not currently available, are data from case studies that used task analysis in system development and an analysis of how task analysis' simulations of the delivery system differed importantly from the final system. A sufficiently large corpus of data would allow the identification of the critical fidelity aspects that generally affect the quality of task analyses. Furthermore, there may be cultural differences in these fidelity issues. When using video recording, for example, it has been suggested that the 'furniture effect', that those observed come quickly to ignore the equipment, is more effective in the USA than in the UK (Clare, 1989).

Another way to classify the next four sections is in terms of a dimension of increasing fidelity. However, it is not the case that in the real world one can or should always use the highest fidelity task environment possible as there is a high correlation between cost and fidelity. In general there are two issues that will determine the recording technology selected by the task observer. First, as already discussed, will be the level of observation required (section 1.5) and, second, the practical limitations. On the latter point, it is often the case that in real work environments, it is not possible to use video recording and, in noisy environments, audio recording.

2.2   Pen and paper

The utility of pen and paper methods of recording task observations should not be underestimated because they appear 'low tech.' The advantage of pen and paper is that they allow task analysis to be carried out in most real-world work environments and thus, with respect to this aspect, they are a high fidelity recording method. However, they can be very intrusive as the person observed often wants to know what is being written down about her/his performance and will often attempt to talk to the task observer, even when requested not to do so. Thus, unless carefully carried out, the task is accompanied by an unwanted concurrent verbal protocol with its attendant disadvantages (section 3.2). Pen-and-paper methods can also cause considerable stress to the observed person as they can appear to be rather like the time-and-motion studies of Taylorist origins (e.g. Holden, 1989) which are not popular with the work forces who have suffered from such methods. Other disadvantages of pen-and-paper methods are the following: (i) they require considerable skill and domain knowledge on the part of the observer; (ii) they provide only a high-level recording of the task; (iii) they are labour intensive and stressful for the task observer at the time of observation; (iv) they do not, generally, allow a post-task walkthrough to be collected.

In many circumstances, however, pen-and-paper methods are highly desirable. For example, the original development of TAKD (Chapter 4; Diaper and Johnson, 1989) for syllabus design used only pen and paper methods because a wide range of tasks were to be observed in their real-world environments and these environments were very different as they included offices, factories and training centres. This work used the most unstructured and ill-prepared version of task analysis as the observers arrived at a work place and after a series of brief interviews selected to observe tasks that were taking place. The advantage was that genuine tasks were sampled, though not necessarily typical ones in every case. The task observer generally sat behind or to the side of the person performing the task and wrote down as much of the task in as much detail as possible. Issues such as the level of observation had been generally worked out previously but because of the range of tasks, which included microelectronics as well as programming and the use of applications packages, the recording was very much 'by the seat of the pants' and required considerable skill and know-ledge on the part of the task observer. This approach was only possible because a concurrent protocol was asked of task performers which was used immediately by the task observer to structure his observations. Such protocols also tend to slow down task performance (section 3.2) and thus make written recording easier. Subjects were immediately debriefed after a task and any points on which the observer was unclear were, where possible to identify, clarified. Considerable work had to be done promptly on the scrappy, written notes of the observer to tidy them up and there was a considerable memory load on the observer. The task observation output was in the form of a high-level activity list associated with each task (section 4). Johnson *et al.* (1984) provide the following example:

> load disk into disk drive
> type in command to list file directory
> type command to LOAD appropriate file

In most cases in HCI, however, a rather more restricted range of tasks is observed. This allows more preparation on the part of the analyst and this is highly desirable. In particular, where the range or type of task is restricted then, after a small number of pilot task observations, it is usually possible for the task observer to devise a coding scheme (section 4.2) which has two advantages. First, it reduces the amount needed to be written down and so allows the observer to devote greater attention to the observation of the task. Second, it encourages the observer to establish both the level of detail and the selection of what to observe prior to undertaking the observation and thus reduces the stress, effort and likely misunderstandings which can overtake the insufficiently prepared task observer. Other advantages of coding schemes with respect to subsequent analysis also accrue. However, as with all coding schemes it is important to encourage the task observer to note behaviours which are not covered by the coding scheme.

Task observers should not shun pen-and-paper recording methods as they have considerable advantages because they are portable and can be used in a wide variety of environments. However, pen-and-paper recording is difficult for the task observer and is limited by the level of detail that can be recorded. It is impossible to establish that the observations are error free and thus 'strange' observations may be the result of observer error rather than a real peculiarity in a task's performance.

2.3 Audio recording

With the exception of purely speech-based tasks, it is rare that audio recording is used alone in task observation. However, audio recording can provide a useful additional record when using both pen-and-paper and video recording. Obviously with pen-and-paper recording there has to be some audible output and thus audio recording is suitable when a concurrent protocol is required from the task performer. In the syllabus design work of

Diaper and Johnson, described in the previous section, where such a protocol was demanded, an additional advantage of the audio record, which was taken using a cheap cassette recorder and a highly directional piezo-electric microphone, was that it provided timing information about the task. Thus, instead of having to use a stopwatch and writing down times during task performance, the audio record could be timed later and the relevant times of task elements inserted into the activity list. This very considerably reduces the load on the task observer during task performance and accuracy can be to a second or two, particularly if the microphone picks up the noise of keystrokes. Even on quiet keyboards, keystrokes are likely to be recorded as vibrations through the table on which the keyboard is placed if the microphone is stood on this surface.

It is possible to record tasks using pen and paper in a vocally silent task by later analysing the keystroke noises. However, this involves two disadvantages. First, the task observer needs to structure the written record very carefully so that there is good match between the written record and audio record of keystrokes. Such written records are very difficult to produce because of the level of detail required of them. Second, the analysis of these records is very difficult and time consuming. The major difficulty arises because inevitably not all the keystrokes are recorded on the tape and often they will blur together as keystrokes may have only a few thousandths of a second between them. Thus it is easy for the analyst to get lost in the analysis and it is essential that pauses of any duration are recorded in the written record so as to recalibrate the audio recording of the task. The more frequently such check points are available the better will be the subsequent analysis. However, this technique is rare in that it is only really appropriate in environments where video recording is precluded.

With video recording it is normal for an audio recording to be made as well as nearly all modern video cameras possess a built-in microphone and thus there are no additional costs in collecting audio information. These audio records can provide several types of useful additional information to that captured by a visual record. First, task performers will often generate spontaneous speech, particularly when errors are made in the task and these can be illuminating in themselves and are often a good source of probe questions if a post-task walkthrough is carried out. Second, the audio record can sometimes be used to inform the observer of a video recording of a task activity that was carried out off camera. Examples of this might be the sound of turning pages in a manual or other document, or the sounds accompanying the swopping of disks in a disk drive.

The principle problem associated with audio recordings is that of ambient noise. Unless very expensive recording equipment is used there is usually a large mismatch between the observer's percept of signal-to-background noise ratios and that recorded by the equipment. This can be simply caused by the difference between the frequency sensitivities of people and audio equipment. However, the human auditory system is backed up by an intelligence at all its levels of processing which is currently inimitable by even the best AI systems. The human system is able automatically and unconsciously to tune out extraneous noise (selective attention) and with speech, in particular, the top-down and known parallel processing used by the mind allows speech to be understood in environments where, according to information theory, such perception should not be possible (i.e. where d' is negative in signal detection theory terms). As Cordingley (1989) concludes, 'Heating, air-conditioning and lighting devices are much louder than might be expected, as are street noises in some settings' and these, of course, are in addition to the noises the observer may expect in factories and offices. Obviously the task observer using audio recordings needs to check the quality of the recording before starting to record in earnest as the location of the microphone is often critical. This does not prevent the record from being swamped by infrequent events such as the use of a printer elsewhere in an office or the passage of a lorry outside.

2.4   Video recording
The use of video (the term 'video recording' is taken here to include traditional filming, which is just less versatile, though potentially of a higher resolution, both spatially and temporally) is the most popular of recording technologies. However, it is important to differentiate the recording of events from their observation. Properly, the use of video merely allows the extension of observation over a longer period than the duration of the event recorded (i.e. taking a video recording of a task is not, itself, an observation).

The actual technology associated with video recording can vary considerably, although the basic issues are the same irrespective of the sophistication of the hardware. There are basically two main approaches which blur together. First, videos can be made of tasks being performed in their real environments. Second, the task can be transported into a studio or usability laboratory. The fidelity issues associated with these two approaches have been discussed in section 2.1.

A full usability laboratory will normally consist of at least two rooms. One room contains the recording and control equipment and may also be fitted with a one-way mirror into the observation room. The observation room is likely to contain the work area where a task is performed and perhaps three remotely controlled cameras whose output is sychronized so that their different views can be mixed into a single video tape. Given that the task most commonly of interest in HCI involves a user (operator) performing a task with a computer then the three views recorded by the cameras would normally be (i) a general, wide-angled shot of the user and the computer, (ii) a shot of the computer display, and (iii) a shot of the keyboard or other input devices. The reason for the use of three cameras is based around the simple problem of all optical recording equipment that their field of view is severely restricted compared with the 120° of visual angle enjoyed by human visual perception (Diaper, 1987; Cordingley, 1989). As commented on in section 1.1.1, the human percept is an artificial construction of the mind generated by the intelligent sampling of small parts of the perceived visual space, a process not likely to be available in even AI vision systems for many years to come.

   While remote-control cameras are a desirable luxury, if affordable, they do not overcome the basic angle-of-vision problem. Remote control may involve the repositioning of a camera (panning) or the change in the visual angle (zooming). These operations, however, need to be controlled by a person and it is a skilled and difficult job to pan and zoom during unscripted task performance. Part of the problem is that the camera operator usually has the same restricted view as provided by the camera(s), which makes it difficult for the operator to know what is happening outside the camera image that should be recorded. Furthermore, there is a considerable lag in these systems, whether the camera is remotely controlled or not. This lag is caused by the human decision and execution times and the inertia of the camera. Motor driven, remotely controlled cameras are frustratingly slow for the speed at which tasks may change and there is considerable distortion in the image recorded during camera movement. Even the simple operation of zooming with automatic cameras causes distortions in image brightness: as one zooms in (i.e. reducing the visual angle while enlarging the objects still in view) there is a tendency for the recorded image brightness first to darken and then to lighten as the camera automatically adjusts. In many cases it is desirable to turn off such automatic camera features, which tend to operate slowly, and to make adjustments manually or at a later stage when mixing the video recordings.

   Thus expensive, sophisticated usability laboratories are not without their problems. Furthermore, rather too much time can be spent playing with the equipment at the expense of making the important decisions about what needs to be observed in a task (sections 1.1 and 1.5). The limited angle of view of cameras means that the human task observer must decide on such issues before recording begins and also recognize that zooming and panning cameras are really only suitable for fine tuning of the recording while the task is in progress. Furthermore, the frequent use of remotely controlled motors for either panning or zooming can distract the subject and reduce the beneficial furniture effect (section 2.1).

   With modern cameras lighting tends not to be a problem and ambient noise is usually minimal in a usability laboratory. A feature of most modern cameras is a capability to print a time stamp onto the video tape at the time of recording. With multiple camera systems this can be done at a later point when images from different cameras are mixed. The other main problem with video is that the image resolution is very poor. In general it is usually just about possible to read text on a standard VDU if the VDU is the only object within a camera's field of view. However, if during analysis the image is frozen then there is a considerable loss of resolution because each frame of video image is composed of two interdigitated raster scans. The more expensive video recorders allow one of these raster scans to be frozen on the screen, which prevents the jumping that is noticeable on recorders that do not provide this facility, but also entails reducing the quality of the recorded image. There are sophisticated video analysis devices on the market that allow points on a recorded image to be given coordinates and these can be useful if details at the level of finger trajectories on keyboards, for example, are of interest. In most HCI work, however, this level of detail is not of interest.

For researchers with fewer resources, a great deal can be achieved with the use of a single video camera and there are major advantages in terms of task fidelity in having a portable system that can allow recording to take place in the normal task environment. While there are many variations, the system of recording described below has been successfully used by the ɦor in a number of studies and describes a typical scenario where the task performer is first recorded and then undertakes a post-task walkthrough immediately after task completion (section 3.3). The equipment required consists of a small, tripod-mounted, automatic video camera and video recorder or a camcorder (where the camera incorporates a recorder within its body and takes a standard VHS tape), a second video recorder, and a TV monitor. The two stages of recording the task and undertaking the post-task walkthrough are described below.

When recording a task that involves the user operating a computer, the commonly required field of view of the camera involves just the keyboard and the VDU. These should be placed as closely together as possible with the keyboard directly below the VDU because of the poor quality resolution of video. The field of view is usually most easily achieved by mounting the camera high on the tripod and shooting over the shoulder of the user. An alternative is sometimes to shoot flat from the side of the user. In general the VDU will occupy most of the video image and, because nearly all user inputs to a computer have an immediate consequence on the VDU, it is often appropriate to dispense with recording the input devices completely and just to record the VDU. Where it is deemed important to record user perfor-mance, such as keystroke behaviour, with a single camera then the quality of the recording can be improved by placing reflective decals, or even liquid correction fluid, on the user's fingernails (although the latter can make one unpopular with those who wear nail varnish). Another trick worth consider-ing if it is essential to record both keyboard and screen and where these cannot be closely juxtaposed is to mount a mirror on top of the VDU which reflects an image of the keyboard. The disadvantage of this is that in analysis the keyboard image is inverted, although the left–right reversal is not usually problematic.

It is highly desirable to time stamp the video recording at the time of task performance as this aids the post-task walkthrough. However, this means that the time counter needs to be placed on a part of the image which is not used in the task. This can be problematic and the author has on several occasions had to move the counter frantically around the image so as not to obscure a screen area in which an interesting activity takes place. If it is possible with the equipment it is desirable for the task observer to monitor the recording on the TV monitor, although this is not its primary role. The camera should be fixed for a recording session and the task observer needs to consider the fact that people change their positions considerably during any extended task. Without careful monitoring it is easy to discover that what has been recorded for a part of a task is not the VDU and keyboard but the user's shoulder. It is often easier to ask the subject to move a litte rather than attempting to adjust the camera position, but wherever possible this should be avoided by being conservative in camera location and not over-zooming so that there is less chance of the user obscuring the camera's view.

Many users are uncomfortable about being recorded and can usually be reassured by being shown how little, if anything, of themselves will be recorded before a recording session starts. An ideal position for the TV is thus in front of, or to the side of, the user. Before starting, however, the TV should either be moved or be turned away from the user, but still viewable by the task observer, or it should be turned off, otherwise the user will be tempted to look at themselves on the TV during the task.

Once a task has been completed the task performer may be debriefed and it is often easiest to leave the camera running during this period and to rely on the audio record plus written notes of comments or replies to questions. The task performer generally gets a brief break while the camera is moved before taking part in the post-task walkthrough. In the walk-through the newly recorded video tape is placed in the second video recorder and the camera is now directed at the TV which can be seen by both the user and the task observer. The video recorder should have a remote control unit which can be operated by either the user or the task observer, depending on the proficiency of the user with such equipment. The user views the recording of the task and makes comments, sometimes prompted by the observer. During a comment the original recording is halted and the camera records the user's verbal comments and also any pointing at the TV, which should be encouraged, preferably with a short pointer so that the user's arm or body does not obscure the camera's view of the TV. The presence of the time stamp on the original recording is, of course, re-recorded onto the walkthrough recording which greatly helps subsequent analysis.

There are a number of minor problems with this particular method; however, its great advantage is that it is simple and reasonably free of potential observer errors with the equipment. Not surprisingly, the image of a VDU display redisplayed on a TV monitor is of much poorer resolution than even the original. However, this is not normally a major problem in the subsequent analyses which will principally use the original recording (section 3.3). In addition, if the user has made any verbal comments or other noises during the original task performance then, even with the TV's volume turned up quite high, these are often poorly picked up during the re-recording. An alternative to pointing the camera at the TV is simply to copy the original recording onto the second video tape while simultaneously displaying it on the TV. This has the advantage of not losing much in the way of video image quality but is not possible with all types of equipment. The important auditory aspect of the walkthrough can be dubbed onto the walkthrough version of the tape by taking advantage of a stereo audio channel, if available (i.e. the original recording is made with audio on one stereo channel and the walkthrough dubbed onto the other — at playback both can be heard simultaneously if necessary). However, this alternative does not allow the recording of non-auditory behaviours, such as pointing at the TV screen, during the walkthrough. Some expertise is needed with the video equipment to ensure that errors are not made in configuring the various leads and so forth. Obviously, it is important that the remote control device only operates the playback video recorder and not the recording recorder, which may sound trivial but leadless remote controls often cannot be disabled on many video recorders short of physically blocking the recorder's sensor (this is harder with sonic than infrared remote control devices).

The end-product of a recording session is thus two video tapes, one containing a recording of the original task performed by the user and the second a copy of the first on which the walkthrough has been recorded. In planning a recording session it is worth remembering that the walkthrough will take longer to carry out than the original task and can quite easily be twice as long. Thus, to avoid fatigue, tasks lasting longer than about 20 minutes, should, whenever possible, be avoided.

There are numerous constraints on carrying out video recordings in many normal task environments. These range from the physical problems associated with space, noise, lighting (although modern cameras are now very robust with respect to illumination levels) and access to electrical power points, to the social problems which are often far harder to deal with. Even in a single-occupancy office there are likely to be intrusions, if not by people arriving at the door then by telephones ringing and so forth, although these may be of interest in some applications. In more open-plan environments in offices and factories there can be major social problems with colleagues unconnected with the task observation which can make the user feel self-conscious, particularly during a post-task walkthrough. The task observer should consider these problems before beginning a recording session.

2.5   Computer capture

All the techniques discussed so far have involved the external observation of tasks either directly by an observer or indirectly by making a record suitable for subsequent observation. In contrast, computer capture involves recording the task from inside the computer. The simplest means of doing this is either by spooling VDU screen output into a file or by storing every keystroke. The latter is often easier to program but requires that the computer's responses to keystrokes are subsequently added to the file which may be trivial or difficult depending on the application software. In some cases an immediate post-task walkthrough can be carried out by redisplaying the screen, although this often necessitates the use of video equipment so as to coordinate user's comments with screen events, but an audio recording can be used provided that there are sufficient comments so as to be able to match the commentary to the screen events. Windows and graphics can make such immediate playback very difficult to program on many systems.

It is usually essential that the recording does not interfere with the application software by calling on resources that would usually be used by the application. Thus, even in a multitasking environment such as UNIX, the application software can become unacceptably slow by the recording program's performing frequent disk writing operations. Rather helpfully in this context, operating systems that have a history command automatically store user inputs and can thus provide a very simple means of recording keystrokes (but not the use of delete operations). When recording keystrokes it is often desirable also to record their time of execution, or at least the time the return/input key is pressed. This time information is also not usually available if just a user input history is recorded.

The major advantages of computer capture of observational data are that it is automatic, error free and very large volumes of data can be collected very quickly. Draper (1984), for example, was able to use computer capture as a technique to investigate the usage of UNIX commands by 94 users over a period of 8 months by taking advantage of 'the Unix system accounting facility which records every process run and who ran it'. In addition, the data collected by computer capture is often in a format that is readily analysable statistically.

The main disadvantage of computer capture, if used as the only observational method, is that, while often voluminous, the data are impoverished because all the other user behaviours that do not involve actually using the computer's input device(s) are not recorded. Thus, for the purposes of task analysis, computer capture is often best used in addition to other recording methods. In particular, computer capture can remove much of the burden of using pen-and-paper recording methods as it allows the observer to concentrate on only the user behaviours not captured by the computer.

Computer capture is not used that commonly in HCI because most commercial microcomputer-based software is difficult, if not impossible, to modify by those who are not its developers. Furthermore, it is often the case with smaller microcomputers that there are insufficient free resources as the software is shoehorned into small machines.

3.   VERBAL BEHAVIOUR

This section briefly looks at three methods that are used in task analysis for gathering verbal data from people. The section concentrates on those methods that are used in conjunction with task observation, although it will be apparent to the reader from several of the other chapters in this book (e.g. Walsh, Chapter 6) that interviews without the observation of task performance may serve as an appropriate input to some task analysis methods in some cases.

3.1   Interviews and other methods

Cordingley (1989) provides an extensive review of interview techniques and other methods of collecting non-observational data in the context of knowledge elicitation for expert systems, although they are equally appropriate to most HCI applications, and this section merely summarizes her main points. First, she distinguishes three properties of these methods: focus; structure; and systematicity. Following Killin (1987), focus refers to the degree of detail associated with questions. Structure is characterized as 'the extent to

which the elicitation (interview) is designed to fit a preplanned format'
(Cordingley, 1989), whereas systematic refers to the exhaustiveness with
which a topic is covered, perhaps by mixing different methods or interview
styles in a systematic, predetermined way.

In interviews there are many different styles of question that may be
asked. For example, LaFrance (1987) identifies six question types: grand
tour questions; cataloguing the categories; ascertaining the attributes;
determining the interconnections; seeking advice; and cross-checking.
There are other classifications of question type (e.g. open versus closed —
Labaw, 1980) and LaFrance's list is by no means exhaustive. Cordingley
identifies three styles of interviews: structured; semistructured; and unstructured. These interview styles reflect the amount of preparation of questions
and their order. Structured interviews include written questionnaires where
the questions and order are entirely fixed, although there are often optional
sets of questions that are determined by previous answers. In semistruc-
trured interviews there tends to be a fixed list of questions but the interviewer retains some flexibility in their order of presentation so as to be
sensitive to an interviewee's responses. Unstructured interviews are without
a doubt the most difficult to carry out successfully because 'They provide
"capacity for surprise" for interviewers' (Cordingley, 1989) and generally
the interviewer needs to be knowledgeable about the interview topic.
Unstructured interviews require careful preparation if they are not to
become bogged down in irrelevancies and if they are not to be the same as
simply having a conversation with a person.

There also exists a range of non-observational methods other than
interviews or discussions with people. Cordingley describes the following
methods: teachback; construct elicitation; sorting; laddering; 20 questions;
matrix generation; critiquing; and role play. This list is not exhaustive (e.g.
choice dilemma) and she lists a number of other methods such as simulations, object tracing, collection of artefacts, etc. which are partly observational and partly based on the verbal responses of people.

Section 1.3 briefly addresses the psychological issues surrounding the
collection and utility of verbal behaviour and those who use interviews and
other such techniques must realize that they are a difficult and complicated
method of gathering information. All these techniques have their strengths
and weaknesses and all need considerable expertise and preparation by
those who employ them.

3.2   Concurrent verbal protocols

The term 'protocol' has been widely and ambiguously used; its dictionary
definition of relevance (*Concise Oxford*, seventh edition) is 'record of
experimental observations'. A concurrent verbal protocol in the context of
task observation in theory involves the task performers' explaining what
they are doing in a task while doing it; in practice, however, they are rather
different from this. Johnson (Chapter 5) provides an example of the use of
protocols. The major advantages of concurrent verbal protocols lie in the
immediacy of a task performer's verbal comments and the binding of the

protocol to task performance. Furthermore, because the task performer does not know the outcome of activities in the task, such protocols are particularly good at identifying task performers' expectations of the consequences of their actions. Thus there are circumstances where concurrent verbal protocols are an ideal means of acquiring relevant data, for example, where a task performer's plans and goals are a major concern. However, people vary considerably in their ability to generate useful concurrent protocols and in extreme cases the occasional prompts sometimes necessary from the task observer can degenerate into what Cordingley (1989) identifies as a 'focused discussion' where the focus is the task.

There are, however, very major disadvantages to concurrent verbal protocols (Bainbridge, 1979, 1986; Diaper, 1987, 1989a). The heart of the problem with them can be explained by the vast literature in experimental psychology on selective attention. While people can perform more than one task simultaneously (divided attention), there are some tasks that require so much of a person's cognitive resources that any concurrent task is likely to suffer performance decrements. Talking is one of these tasks and, with only very special exceptions (e.g. Allport *et al.*, 1972), all tasks that are performed with a speech task are likely to be performed less well than if carried out alone. Of course, this does not mean that people cannot, for example, drive a car and hold a conversation, but it is noticeable that when the primary driving task becomes more difficult then the conversation is temporarily halted. What is likely to happen with concurrent verbal protocols is that the task performer tends to switch between the task and the protocol task, either performing a part of the task and then describing it, or vice versa. This means that the primary task is considerably slowed in its execution. Such slowing may be advantageous to the task observer in cases where the recording technique involves pen and paper, but there are also qualitative differences as well as this quantitative difference that can be caused by demanding a concurrent verbal protocol.

Even with highly expert task performers, the disruption to their normal behaviour by the imposition of a verbal task can cause them to perform a task differently. Bainbridge (1986) suggests that people can regress to using less expert methods because these are more accessible to verbal description than the sort of proceduralization that accompanies the acquisition of high levels of skill in a task (section 1.3). Furthermore, the act of describing what is being done can itself lead to discovery on the part of the expert and thus to changes from how the task is normally carried out. With less expert task performers the additional cognitive demands made by concurrent verbal protocols can lead to a complete disruption of task performance.

Also, it is not the case that the concurrent verbal description of a task is error free and compatible with actual performance. Diaper (1989a) offers the following example: 'in a video-tape of Peter Johnson (Queen Mary College, London) performing a word-processing task while producing a concurrent verbal protocol, he can be seen placing the cursor, correctly for what he wishes to do, at the beginning of the word while saying "I have now placed the cursor at the end of the word" '. Particularly in cases where there is not a strong tie between description and performance, for example, where goals or plans are being described, it is often difficult to determine subsequently whether the verbal description or the task performance is to be believed and such inconsistencies are sometimes very difficult to detect during the task observation.

Furthermore, and even under the expert prompting of the task observer, it is likely that the type of information in a concurrent verbal protocol will be varied. Cordingley (1989) identifies four different types of pure protocol. She says 'In practice, however, elicitors (task observers) are likely to get a mixture of kinds of material. It is difficult for knowledge providers (task performers) to stick to one kind of report. It is even difficult for them to understand the difference between them'. She exemplifies the four types of pure protocol in the context of a word-processing task where the task performer notices that the letters e and n are transposed in the word 'department' (i.e. 'departmnet') several lines removed from the current cursor position:

> *Talk aloud*: Damn, I've made a typo. I must be getting tired. I keep switching the e and the n. Mnet looks stupid there like that.

> *Think aloud*: Will it be quicker to get rid of the n move past the e and type n there; or shall I cut out the n and paste it after the e; or should I just type en over ne.

> *Eidetic reduction*: This use of the package is not as good as it might be. There is less thought involved in retyping whole sections, but when you are tired that just gives more opportunity for typing mistakes, so I should probably be trying to make better use of the cut and paste facility.

> *Behavioural description*: Notice the mistake, reach for the mouse with the right hand, place the cursor to the right of the offending letter and click the mouse button, while holding it down drag the cursor to the left over the letters that have to be replaced, release the mouse button, put the right hand back on the keyboard and type in the correct letters.

Thus there are issues concerning the validity and reliability of both the primary task and the verbal protocol when a concurrent verbal protocol is demanded. Ericson and Simon (1985) devote a considerable part of their book to a discussion of these issues. They conclude, as does this chapter, that protocols are not without value. However, requiring concurrent verbal protocols has considerable overheads of which the task observer needs to be aware before choosing to use the method. In most instances a post-task walkthrough protocol, described in the next section, is a preferred method because this does not interfere with task performance. Where concurrent task protocols are used it is usually necessary also to observe the task without the protocol demand so that the effect of the protocol on normal task performance can at least be estimated.

3.3 Post-task walkthroughs

A post-talk walkthrough involves the task performer's generating a protocol after completing a task. To carry this out successfully she or he needs as a basis some record of the task. While this can be the written notes of the task observer, an audio record or the replay of the task on a VDU if the computer capture method is used, most commonly the basis is a video recording. The basic equipment and procedure have already been described in section 2.4. The major advantage of the method is that, unlike concurrent verbal protocols, the walkthrough does not interfere with the primary task performance. Furthermore, some of the other problems, such as the mixture of pure protocol types described in the previous section, may be ameliorated as more time is available to both the task performer and the task observer who may be prompting or questioning the task performer. The video recording of the task can be halted and if necessary sections of the recording can be replayed several times at normal speed, in slow motion or frame by frame. For obvious reasons it is highly desirable that the walkthrough immediately follows the completion of the task, although returning to it after some analysis for further comments by the task performer is not excluded.

While the author has a very strong preference for post-task walkthroughs rather than concurrent ones, the method is not without its disadvantages, the primary one being that the verbal description produced is made with the benefit of hindsight. There is at least one major school of thought in psychology (e.g. Bem, 1972; Nisbett and Wilson, 1977; Diaper, 1982, 1987, 1989a) which claims that most, if not all, explanations produced by people are of a *post hoc* nature because people do not have privileged access to their own cognitive processes and thus they attribute reasons for their behaviour after observing themselves performing the behaviour. Where the outcome of an act is known it is likely that this bias will be overwhelming. This bias is also present when concurrent verbal protocols are used unless the task observer successfully enforces a requirement that the task performer describes what they intend to do before they do it. This requirement is difficult to enforce, however, and is generally very disruptive of task performance.

Another disadvantage associated with the post-task walkthrough technique is the time it takes, often twice the duration of the task itself. This often leads to fatigue and boredom. Furthermore, following the comments made in section 1 of this chapter, it will come as no surprise to point out that for the technique to be maximally productive it is necessary for the task observer to be very well prepared and to have identified exactly what sort of description is required from the task performer.

Given that there are disadvantages to all verbal reports and that these disadvantages need to be understood by the task observer, the author has a strong preference for using post-task walkthroughs as a method to disambiguate and understand the behaviour of task performers. The technique is used in the study described in Chapter 4 of this book for this purpose but the main emphasis of this work was on the behaviours carried out during the task, rather then their subsequent explanation. Other researchers are no doubt differently biased as to the quality, reliability and validity of verbal data but all should be aware of the psychologists' Pandora's box one opens if too much reliance is placed on this source of information.

4.   TASK OBSERVATION RECORDING TECHNIQUES

The end-product of task observation and the input to task analysis is generally an 'activity list'. An activity list is a prose description of the sequence of events that takes place in a task. An example is offered in Chapter 4 along with a description of how it may be analysed within the TAKD methodology. The following two sections describe two approaches to how such activity lists are generated from the observation of a task.

4.1   Transcripts

The terms 'transcript' and 'protocol' are very similar in meaning. The difference within the context of this chapter's topic is that whereas a protocol provides a record of a task and is often also used to describe the process of obtaining the protocol, what is meant by a transcript is a written record of a task and it is often produced after the task by a transcribing process, except, perhaps, where the only task observation technology used is pen and paper. There is an implication that a transcript is a complete, written record of a task and it is sometimes produced by a secretary who is not knowledgeable about either the task or the task's domain. In fact, even with audio records, transcribing is not an easy task and as Clare (1989) says of it, 'This is a tedious business and it helps to have experienced transcribers. The Arthur D. Little team used agencies for this work and were able to find one that was very good in that the typists typed what was said, rather than trying to interpret coherent sentences. The "ugh" is a useful pointer to an individual grasping for a concept or idea that is difficult to express'. Clare's justification for using audio typists for transcription lies in the waste of commercially expensive expertise by people whose 'time is too valuable to spend large portions of it in transcript production'. In contrast, Bell and Hardiman (1989) strongly recommend that the task observer (the naturalistic know-ledge engineer (NKE) in their context of knowledge elicitation for expert systems) transcribes audio records herself/himself. They state that 'there are two main reasons here. One is to ensure that the transcription is indeed verbatim (we have experienced many transcriptions done by typists where the transcription turns out to be a paraphrase of what was said, rather than what was actually said). The other reason is to do with NKEs own understanding of the material. . . . We find that our understanding of what was said in an interview is greatly enhanced having done the verbatim transcription ourselves'.

While it may be possible to find audio typists whose office skills can be perverted such that they do produce a faithful transcription, there is no equivalent set of experts to transcribe video recordings and these almost have to be done by the task observer. This is hardly surprising given the comment made in section 2.4 that a video recording is not iteslf an observation but rather allows the extension of observation over a longer period than that actually taken by the task. Cordingley (1989) suggests that when merely transcribing an audio tape 'one should budget at least eight times the length of the tape for simply transcribing the verbal data if this is going to be done at all'. To transcribe a video tape can take appreciably longer, depending on the level of description that is chosen. Cordingley's final phrase, however, is important, as with video tapes and particularly with post-task walkthroughs, as opposed to concurrent protocols, it may not be necessary to transcribe the audio record fully at all. The whole point of transcription is to convert a clumsy, serial, real-time record into a paper- or computer-based representation that can then be analysed. The post-task walkthrough described in Chapter 4 was not transcribed. It was used in the early stages of video recording analysis to aid in the comprehension of the task and after a couple of showings was only then used very occasionally to aid understanding of a particular point from the original task recording. Clearly, in these circumstances, transcribing the walkthrough protocol would not have been a cost-effective procedure. While transcribing a video recording is possible, it is generally not desirable because it takes considerable time and effort and once a transcript is produced this usually has to be processed further to produce a product such as an activity list. The next section briefly describes a short cut to transcription which can greatly speed up the conversion of video recordings into a useful form.

The analysis of transcripts is a part of task analysis, rather than of task observation, and is thus outside the boundaries of this chapter. Walsh (Chapter 6) provides a manual illustration of analysing transcript data and there are a number of software tools such as KEATS (Motta *et al.*, 1986), FACTFINDER, and ETHNOGRAPH, and the OXFORD CONCORDANCE PACKAGE (Cordingley, 1989) available that can facilitate such analyses.

4.2　Coding schemes

Coding schemes are a means of recording task observations in a coherent, consistent short-hand. While they are discussed in this section in the context of observing video recordings, they are also suitable for directly observing tasks when a pen-and-paper recording technology is used. For example, over several generations psychologists have developed coding schemes for observing rats in environments richer than the T-maze, most commonly in 'open field boxes' (these consist of a large, by rat standards, enclosure and often have a grid marked on the floor). Psychologists observing the behaviour of rats in this environment have almost completely standardized the recording of behaviours. Apart from noting transitions across the floor's grid, they tend to count a small number of behaviours such as rearing, defecation, whisker twitching and so forth that occur within each time sample. The observational recording is thus quite simple as on a single sheet of paper there is a matrix with time on one axis and the small set of behaviours on the other and each occurrence of the behaviour is simply checked off in the appropriate cell of the recording matrix. The technique, with a more variable set of behaviours, has also been used 'in the fields of applied behaviour analysis, developmental and educational psychology, (Harrop *et al.*, 1989). However, Harrop *et al.*'s analysis of the reliability of two observer's agreeing on the occurrence or non-occurrence of three simple behaviours during the same task (writing notes, reading from a book, and turning pages) and sampled every 10 seconds indicates that even in such a simple observational task there is a subjective element as agreement is by no means complete. This reinforces the comments made about the difficulty of making observations in section 1.

What is critical to the development of a coding scheme is the prior identification of what events are to be recorded and which events and what level of detail will be ignored. In complex tasks such as those often of interest in HCI, it is generally not possible to identify all the behaviours of interest prior to observing the video recording of the task or tasks. One approach to this complexity is first to sample parts of the video recording and to produce partial transcripts. These can then be used to develop a coding scheme which can then be used for the complete set of video recordings. It is crucial that such coding schemes are open ended and that new categories of behaviour can be added to the scheme during the full observational exercise.

The advantage of such coding schemes is that they can substantially reduce the time it takes to observe video recordings of tasks. Furthermore, the coding scheme should provide data in a form suitable for subsequent analyses. The disadvantage of such schemes is that the observer can become blind to events that do not fit the scheme and thus data of interest are lost. Data may be lost for two reasons: (i) as a result of erroneously interpreting events to fit the coding scheme; and (ii) by lumping events together inappropriately. Inevitably, when using a coding scheme on a complex, behaviourally rich task, there will be a small set of behaviours that do not neatly fit into one of the scheme's categories. It is vital that notes are kept of these, and, if necessary, the complete coding scheme can be redesigned after the initial observations. Such a redesign often does not require the observer to return to the video recording. Ideally, once a video recording is coded or transcribed then the task analyst should never have to return to it because it is very costly to have to work with real-time records.

5.   IN CONCLUSION

This chapter has attempted to introduce the main issues associated with observing tasks in HCI. The techniques and technologies are not themselves conceptually difficult. However, task observation is a skilled enterprise and requires considerable effort before, during and after a task if the resulting data are to be of much value. Clearly there is little point in expending a great deal of effort on the anlysis of observational data if the data are inadequate. At one HCI conference a few years ago in the UK there appeared to be developing a stock answer from those involved in the system development side of HCI when asked to justify why they had made particular design decisions. They replied 'Oh, we did a task analysis'. The suspicion must exist that what they meant by this was that they rather casually observed a user or two as task analysis was rarely mentioned in the papers published in the conference proceedings. Task observation is not easy and, as the other chapters in this book demonstrate, task analysis is probably even harder. However, task analysis is potentially the most powerful method available to those working in HCI and has applications at all stages of system development, from early requirements specification through to final system evaluation. Furthermore, 'the quality of task descriptions in all but the most degraded forms of task analysis are still of enormous potential ... simply because they cause those involved in such observations to treat real tasks ... in a detailed, rich and more comprehensive manner than any other method' (Diaper, 1989c).

References

Adrian, E. (1966) Consciousness, in Eccles, J. (ed.) *Brain and conscious experience,* Berlin: Springer.

Agha, G. (1986) An overview of Actor languages, *SIGPLAN Notices* **21**, 58–67.

Allport, D., Antonis, B. & Reynolds, P. (1972) On the division of attention: a disproof of the single channel hypothesis, *Quarterly Journal of Experimental Psychology* **24**, 225–235.

Anderson, J. R. (1982) Acquisition of cognitive skill, *Psychological Review* **89**, 369–406.

Anderson, J. R. (1983) *The architecture of cognition,* Cambridge, MA: Harvard University Press.

Annett, J. & Duncan, K. D. (1967) Task analysis and training design, *Occupational Psychology* **41**, 211–221.

Annett, J., Duncan, K. D., Stammers, R. B. & Gray, M. J. (1971) Task analysis, *Training Information Paper No. 6,* London: HMSO (Republished (1980) Task analysis, *Training Information Paper Series,* London: Manpower Services Commission, 36 pp).

Ariav, G. (1986) A temporally oriented data model, *ACM Transactions on Database Systems* **11**, 499–527.

Armstrong, S. L. Gleitman, L. R. & Gleitman, H. (1983) What some concepts might not be, *Cognition* **13**, 263–308.

Asch, S. (1956) Studies of independence and conformity. A minority of one against a unanimous majoirty, *Psychological Monographs* **70**, 416, 9.

Astley, J. A. & Stammers, R. B. (1987) Adapting hierarchical task analysis for user–system interface design, in Wilson, J. R., Corlett, E. N. and Manenica, I. (eds) *New methods in applied ergonomics,* London: Taylor & Francis, pp. 174–184.

Baddeley, A. (1976) *The psychology of memory,* London: Harper & Row.

Bainbridge, L. (1979) Verbal reports as evidence of the process operators knowledge, *International Journal of Man–Machine Studies* **11**, 411–436.

Bainbridge, L. (1986) Asking questions and accessing knowledge, *Future Computing Systems* **1**, 143–150.

Balzer, R. & Goldman, N. (1979) Principles of good software specification,

Proceedings, Conference on Specifications of Reliable Software, New York: IEEE, pp. 58–67.

Banks, M. H., Jackson, P. R., Stafford, E. M. & Warr, P. B. (1983) The job components inventory and the analysis of jobs requiring limited skill, *Personnel Psychology* **36**, 57–66.

Bannerjee, J., Chou, H. T., Garza, J. F., Kim, W., Woelk, D., Ballou, N. & Kim, H. J. (1987) Data model issues for object-oriented applications, *ACM Transactions on Office Information Systems* **5**, 3–26.

Barlow, J., Rada, R. & Diaper, D. (1989) Interacting WITH computers, *Interacting with Computers* **1** (1), 39–42.

Barnard, P. (1987) Cognitive resources and the learning of human–computer dialogues, in Carroll, J. M. (ed.) *Interfacing thought: cognitive aspects of human–computer interaction,* Cambridge, MA: MIT Press.

Barnard, P. J., Hammond, N. V., Morton, J., Long, J. & Clark, I. A. (1981) Consistency and compatibility in human–computer dialogue, *International Journal of Man–Machine Studies* **5**, 87–134.

Becker, J. D. (1975) Reflections on the formal description of behaviour, in Bobrow, D. G. and Collins, A. (eds), *Representation and understanding* New York: Academic Press, pp. 83–102.

Bekerian, D. & Bowers, J. (1983) Eyewitness testimony: were we misled?, *Journal of Experimental Psychology, Learning Memory and Cognition* **9**, 139–145.

Bell, J. & Hardiman, R. (1989) The third role — the naturalistic knowledge engineer, in Diaper, D. (ed.) *Knowledge elicitation: principles, techniques and applications,* Chichester: Ellis Horwood, pp. 49–85.

Bellotti, V. (1988) Implications of current design practice for the use of HCI techniques, in Jones, D. M. and Winder, R. (eds) *People and computers IV,* Cambridge: Cambridge University Press.

Bem, D. (1972) Self perception theory, in Berkowitz, L. (ed.) *Advances in experimental social psychology 6,* New York: Academic Press.

Black, J. B. & Moran, T. P. (1982) Learning and remembering command names, *Proceedings of the CHI'82 Conference on Human Factors in Computer Systems,* New York: ACM, pp. 8–11.

Bliss, J., Monk, M. & Ogborn, J. (1983) *Qualitative data analysis: a guide to the use of systemic networks,* London: Croom Helm.

Borgida, A. (1985) Language features for flexible handling of exceptions in information systems, *ACM Transactions on Database Systems* **10**, 565–603.

Bowers, J. & Bekerian, D. (1984) When will post-event information distort eyewitness testimony?, *Journal of Applied Psychology* **69** (3), 466–472.

Bresnan, J. & Kaplan, R. M. (1983) Introduction: grammars as mental representations of languages, in Bresnan, J. (ed.) *The mental representation of grammatical relations,* Cambridge, MA: MIT Press, pp. xvii–lii.

Brown, P. (1987) Turning ideas into products: the Guide system, in *Proceedings of the Conference Hypertext '87,* pp. 33–40.

Bruner, J. S., Goodnow, J. & Austin, G. (1956) *A study of thinking,* New York: Wiley.

Bubenko, J. A. (1986) Information system methodologies — a research view, in Olle, T. W., Sol, H. G. and Verrijn-Stuart, A. A. (eds) *Information systems design methodologies: improving the practice,* Elsevier: North-Holland.

Burton, R. R. (1976) Semantic grammar: an engineering technique for constructing natural language understanding systems, *BBN Report No. 3453,* Bolt Beranek & Newman, Cambridge, MA.

Byrne, R. (1977) Planning meals: problem solving on a real data-base *Cognition* (5), 287–332.

Cameron, J. (1983) *JSP & JSD: the Jackson approach to software development,* New York: IEE Computer Society.

Canfield Smith, D., Irby, C., Kimball, R. & Verplank, W. (1982) Designing the Star user interface, *Byte* (April), 242–282.

Card, S. K., Moran, T. P. & Newell, A. (1983) *The psychology of human computer interaction,* Hillsdale, NJ: Lawrence Erlbaum.

Carey, M. S. (1985) The selection of computer input devices for process control, *CR 2773 (CON),* Warren Spring Laboratory, Stevenage, Herts.

Carroll, J. M. (1982) Learning, using and designing command paradigms, *Human Learning* 1, 31–62.

Carroll, J. M. (1989) Evaluation, description and invention: paradigms for human–computer interaction, in Yovits, M. C. (ed.) *Advances in computers,* Vol. 28, New York: Academic Press.

Carroll, J. M. & Campbell, R. L. (1988) Artifacts as psychological theories: the case of human–computer interation, *IBM Research Report RC 13454,* IBM, Yorktown Heights, NY.

Carroll, J. M. & Currithers, C. (1984) Training wheels in a user interface, *Communications of the ACM* 27, 800–806.

Carroll, J. M. & Mack, R. L. (1985) Metaphor, computing systems and active learning, *International Journal of Man–Machine Studies* 22, 39–57.

Carver, M. (1988) Practical experience of specifying the human–computer interface using JSD, in McGaw, E. (ed.) *Contemporary ergonomics,* London: Taylor and Francis.

Chase, W. G. & Simon, H. A. (1973) Perception in chess, *Cognitive Psychology* 4, 55–81.

Chen, P. P. S. (1976) The entity–relationship model — toward a unified view of data, *ACM Transactions on Database Systems* 1, 9–3.

Chomsky, N. (1965) *Aspects of the theory of syntax,* Cambridge, MA: MIT Press.

Clare, J. (1989) Knowledge elicitation for financial dealers, in Diaper, D. (ed.) *Knowledge elictation: principles, techniques and applications,* Chichester: Ellis Horwood, pp. 235–246.

Cordingley, E. (1989) Knowledge elicitation techniques for knowledge based systems, in Diaper, D. (ed.) *Knowledge elicitation: principles, techniques and applications,* Chichester: Ellis Horwood, pp. 89–172.

Crawley, R. C., Spurgeon, P. & Whitfield, D. (1980) Air traffic controller reaction to computer assistance, Vols 1–3, *AP Rep. No. 94,* Department of Applied Psychology, Aston University, Birmingham.

Crossman, E. R. F. W. (1960) *Automation and skill,* London: HMSO.

Davies, S. (1988) The application of Task related Knowledge Structures to the design of human computer interfaces. Undergraduate dissertation, Department of Computer Science, Queen Mary College, London.

DeMarco, T. (1979) *Structured analysis and system specification,* Englewood Cliffs, NJ: Prentice-Hall.

Diaper, D. (1982) Central backward masking and the two task paradigm. Unpublished Ph.d. Thesis, University of Cambridge, UK.

Diaper, D. (1984) An approach to IKBS development based on a review of 'Conceptual structures: information processing in mind and machine.' by J. F. Sowa. *Behaviour and Information Technology* 3, 249–255.

Diaper, D. (1986) Will expert systems be safe?, in *Proceedings of the Second International Expert Systems Conference,* Oxford: Learned Information, pp. 561–572.

Diaper, D. (1987) Designing systems for people: beyond user centred design, in *Software Engineering: Proceedings of the SHARE European Association Anniversary Meeting 1987,* Vol. 1, pp. 283–302.

Diaper, D. (1988a) Task analysis for knowledge descriptions: building a task descriptive hierarchy, in Megaw, E. D. (ed.) *Contemporary Ergonomics 1988: Proceedings of the Ergonomics Society's 1988 Annual Conference, April 11–15, 1988, Manchester,* London: Taylor and Francis, pp. 118–124.

Diaper, D. (1988b) The promise of POMESS, in Berry, D. and Hart, A. (eds) *Proceedings of Conference on Human and Organisational Issues of Expert Systems,* Ergonomics Society.

Diaper, D. (1989a) Designing expert systems: from Dan to Beersheba, in Diaper, D. (ed.) *Knowledge elicitation: principles, techniques and applications,* Chichester: Ellis Horwood, pp. 1–46.

Diaper, D. (1989b) The discipline of human–computer interaction, *Interacting with Computers* 1 (1), 3–5.

Diaper, D. (1989c) Bridging the gulf between requirements and design. Proceeding of the Ergonomics Society conference on 'Simulation in the Development of User Interfaces', 129–145.

Diaper, D. & Johnson, P. (1989) Task analysis for knowledge descriptions: theory and application in training, in Long, J. B. and Whitefield, A. (eds) *Cognitive ergonomics,* Cambridge: Cambridge University Press.

Douglas, S. (1983) *Learning to text edit: semantics in procedural skill acquisition,* Doctoral Dissertation, Stanford University, Palo Alto, CA, unpublished.

Dowell, J. & Long, J. B. (1988) Human/computer interaction engineering (HCIE), in Heaton, N. and Sinclair, M. (eds) *Designing end-user interfaces,* Oxford: Pergamon Infotech.

Downs, E., Clare, P. & Cole, I. *Structured Systems Analysis and Design Method: Application and Context*. London: Prentice Hall.

Draper, S. (1984) The nature of expertise in UNIX, in *Proceedings of Interact '84, the First IFIP Conference on Human–Computer Interaction*, Vol. 2, pp. 182–186.

Drury, C. G. (1983) Task analysis methods in industry, *Applied Ergonomics* **14**(1), 19–28.

D'Souza, N. F. (1988) *Development of a computer software manual*, M.Sc. Dissertation, Loughborough University of Technology.

Duncan, K. D. (1972) Strategies for the analysis of the task, in Hartley, J. (ed.) *Strategies for programmed instruction: an educational technology*, London: Butterworths, pp. 19–81.

Duncan, K. D. (1974) Analytical techniques in training design, in Edwards, E. and Lees, F. P. (eds) *The human operator in process control*, London: Taylor and Francis, pp. 283–319.

Duncan, K. D., Praetorius, N. & Milne, A. B. (1989) Flow displays of complex plant processes for fault diagnosis, in Megaw, E. D. (ed.) *Contemporary Ergonomics 1989: Proceedings of the Ergonomic Society's 1989 Annual Conference, April 3–7, 1989, Reading*, London: Taylor and Francis, pp. 199–206.

Edmondson, D. & Johnson, P. (1989) Detail: an approach to task analysis, in *Proceedings of Conference on Simulation in the Development of User Interfaces*, pp. 146–157.

Ehrenreich, S. L. & Porcu, T. (1982) Abbreviations for automated systems: teaching operators the rules, in Badre, A. and Shneiderman, B. (eds) *Directions in human computer–interaction*, Norwood, NJ: Ablex, pp. 111–135.

Ericsson, K. & Simon, H. (1985) *Protocol analysis: verbal reports as data*, London: MIT Press.

Finkelstein, A. & Potts, C. (1985) Evaluation of existing requirements extraction strategies, *Alvey Forest Report R1*, Imperial College, Department of Computing.

Furnas, G. W., Landauer, T. K., Gomez, L. M. & Dumais, S. T. (1987) The vocabulary problem in human–system interaction, *Communications of the ACM* **30**, 964–971.

Galambos, J. A. (1986) Knowledge structures for common activities in Galambos, J. A., Abelsohn, R. P. and Black, J. B. (eds) *Knowledge structures*, Hillsdale, NJ: Lawrence Erlbaum.

Gardner, A. & McKenzie, J. (1988) *Human factors guidelines for the design of computer-based systems*, Issue 1, Vols 1–6, London: Ministry of Defence (PE) and Department of Trade and Industry.

Garner, W. R. (1974) *The processing of information and structure*, New York: Wiley.

Gibbs, C., Kim, W. C. & Foley, J. (1986) Case studies in the use of IDL: interface definition language, *Report GWU-IIST-86-30*, Department of Electrical Engineering and Computer Science, George Washington University, Washington, DC 20052.

Gilbreth, F. (1911) *Motion study,* New York: Van Nostrand.

Graesser, A. C. & Clark, L. F. (1985) *Structures and procedures of implicit knowledge,* Norwood, NJ: Ablex.

Green, T. R. G. (1987) Limited theories as a framework for human–computer interaction, *Austrian Computer Society's 6th Interdisciplinary Workshop on Mental Models and Human–Computer Interaction, June 9–12, 1987, Scharding, Austria,* invited address.

Green, T. R. G. (1988) Chopper: an executor for task–action grammars, Applied Psychology Unit, Cambridge, unpublished.

Green, T. R. G. & Payne, S. J. (1984) Organisation and learnability in computer languages, *International Journal of Man–Machine Studies* **21**, 7–18.

Green, T. R. G. & Schiele, F. (in press) HCI formalisms and cognitive psychology: the case of task–action grammar, in Thimbleby, H. and Harrison, M. (eds) *Formal methods in human–computer interaction,* Cambridge: Cambridge University Press, to be published.

Green, T. R. G., Bellamy, R. K. E. & Parker, J. M. (1987) Parsing and gnisrap: a model of device use, in H. J. Bullinger, and B. Shackel, (eds) *INTERACT 87 Proceedings of the Second IFIP Conference on Human–Computer Interaction, September, 1–4, 1987,* Elsevier: North-Holland.

Green, T. R. G., Schiele, F. & Payne, S. J. (1988) Formalisable models of user knowledge in human–computer interaction, in van der Veer, G. C., Green, T. R. G., Hoc, J.-M. and Murray, D. M. (eds) *Working with computers: theory versus outcome,* London: Academic Press.

Gregory, R. (1966) *Eye and brain,* London: World University Library.

Halasz, F. & Moran, T. P. (1982) Analogy considered harmful, in *Proceedings of the Human Factors in Computer Systems Conference, March 15–17, 1982, Gaithersburg, MD,* New York: ACM.

Halasz, F. & Moran, T. P. (1983) Mental models and problem solving using a calculator, *Proc CHI'83 Conference on Human Factors in Computing Systems,* New York: ACM.

Hallam, J. & Stammers, R. B. (1985) Man–computer dialogues within future systems, *Final Report to APU, ARE,* Division of Applied Psychology, Aston University.

Halliday, M. (1978) *Language as a social semiotic,* London: Edward Arnold.

Harris, S. E. & Brightman, H. J. (1985) Design implications of a task-driven approach to unstructured cognitive tasks in office work, *ACM Transactions on Office Information Systems,* **3**, 292–306.

Harrop, A., Foulkes, C. & Daniels, M. (1989) Observer agreement calculations: the role of primary data in reducing obfuscation, *British Journal of Psychology* **80** (2), 181–190.

Hayes-Roth, F. (1983) Using proofs and refutations to learn from experience, in Michaelski, R. S., Carbonell, J. G. and Mitchell, T. M. (eds) *Machine learning,* Palo Alto, CA: Tioga Press, pp. 221–240.

Hayes-Roth, F., Waterman, D. & Lenat, D. (1983) *Building expert systems,* Reading, MA: Addison-Wesley.

Hesse, M. (1964) Francis Bacon, in O'Connor, D. (ed.) *A critical history of western philosophy,* London: Macmillan pp. 141–152.

Hirsh-Pasek, K., Nudelman, S. & Schneider, M. (1982) An experimental evaluation of abbreviation schemes in limited lexicons, *Behaviour and Information Technology* **1**, 359–369.

Hodgkinson, G. P. & Crawshaw, C. M. (1985) Hierarchical task analysis for ergonomics research, *Applied Ergonomics* **16**(4), 289–299.

Holden, P. (1989) 'Working to rules': a case study of tailor-made expert systems, *Interacting with Computers* **1**(2), 197–219.

Hollnagel, E. (1984) A conceptual framework for the description and analysis of man-machine system interaction, in *Institution of Chemical Engineers, Ergonomics Problems in Process Operations, July 11–13, 1984, University of Aston in Birmingham, Brimingham,* Institution of Chemical Engineers Symposium Series 90, Oxford: Pergamon Press.

Hoppe, H. U. (1988) Task-oriented parsing — a diagnostic method to be used by adaptive systems, in Soloway, E., Frye, D. and Sheppard, S. B. (eds) *CHI'88 Conference Proceedings, Human Factors in Computing Systems,* New York: ACM.

Hoppe, H. U. (in press) A grammar based approach to unifying task-oriented and system-oriented interface descriptions, in Ackermann, D. and Tauber, M. (eds) *Mental models and human–computer interaction,* Amsterdam: North-Holland, to be published.

Howes, A. & Payne, S. J. (1989) Display-based competence: towards user models for menu-based systems, Department of Computing, University of Lancaster, unpublished.

Jackendoff, R. (1983) *Semantics and cognition,* Cambridge, MA: MIT Press.

Jackson, M. A. (1983) *System development,* Englewood Cliffs, NJ: Prentice-Hall.

Johnson, H. & Johnson, P. (1987) The development of task analysis as a design tool: a method for carrying out task analysis, *ICL Report,* March 1987, unpublished.

Johnson, N. (1987) Mediating representations in knowledge elication, in Addis, T., Boose, J. and Gines, B. (eds) *Proceedings of the First European Workshop on Knowledge Acquisition for Knowledge-Based Systems,* Reading University and IEE.

Johnson, N. (1989) Mediating representations in knowledge elication, in Diaper, D. (ed.) *Knowledge elicitation: principles techniques and applications,* Chichester: Ellis Horwood, pp. 177–194.

Johnson, P. (1985) Towards a task model of messaging: an example of the application of TAKD to user interface design, in Johnson, P. and Cook, S. (eds) *People and computers: designing the interface,* Cambridge: Cambridge University Press, pp. 46–62.

Johnson, P., Diaper, D. & Long, J. B. (1984) Tasks, skills and knowledge: task analysis for knowledge based descriptions, in Shackel, B. (ed.)

INTERACT'84 — Proceedings of the First IFIP Conference on Human–Computer Interaction, Amsterdam: North-Holland, pp. 23–27.

Johnson, P., Johnson, H., Waddington, R. & Shouls, A. (1988) Task-related knowledge structures: analysis, modelling and application, in Jones, D. M. and Winder, R. (eds) *People and computers: from research to implementation,* Cambridge: Cambridge University Press, pp. 35–62.

Johnson, P. & Johnson, H. (1989 in press) 'Knowledge Analysis of Tasks: Task analysis and specification for human–computer systems' in Downton, A. (ed.) *Engineering the human computer interface.* New York: McGraw Hill.

Kaehler, T. & Patterson, D. (1986) A small taste of Smalltalk, *Byte,* (August).

Katz, J. J. (1972) *Semantic theory,* New York: Harper & Row.

Keane, M. & Johnson, P. (1987) Preliminary analysis for design, in Diaper, D. and Winder, R. (eds) *People and computers,* Cambridge: Cambridge University Press.

Kellogg, W. A. (1987) Conceptual consistency in the user interface: effects on user performance, in Bullinger, H. J. and Shackel, B. (eds) *Human–computer interaction, Interact 87,* Amsterdam: North-Holland.

Kieras, D. E. & Bovair, S. (1984) The role of a mental model in learning to use a device, *Cognitive Science* **8**, 255–272.

Kieras, D. E. & Polson, P. G. (1985) An approach to the formal analysis of user complexity, *International Journal of Man–Machine Studies* **22**, 365–394.

Killin, J. (1987) Interview techniques, a knowledge acquisition module for the course 'Pragmatic Knowledge Engineering', Knowledge-Based Systems Centre, South Bank Polytechnic, London, unpublished.

Knowles, C. (1988) Can cognitive complexity theory (CCT) produce an adequate measure of system usability?, in Jones, D. M. and Winder, R. (eds) *People and computers IV,* Cambridge: Cambridge University Press.

Knuth, D. E. (1968) Semantics of context-free languages, *Mathematical Systems Theory* **2**, 127–145.

Kramer, J., Ng, K., Potts, C. & Whitehead, K. (1988) Tool support for requirements analysis, *Software Engineering Journal* (May), 86–96.

Labaw, P. (1980) Advanced questionnaire design. Abt: Mass.

LaFrance, M. (1987) The knowledge acquisition grid: a method for training knowledge engineers, *International Journal of Man–Machine Studies* **26**, 245–255.

Laird, J. & Newell, A. (1983) A universal weak method, *Tech. Rep. CMU-CS-83-141,* Computer Science Department, Carnegie–Mellon University, Pittsburgh.

Landauer, T. K. (1987) Psychology as a mother of invention, in Carroll, J. M. and Tanner, P. P. (eds) *Proceedings of CHI+GI'87: Human Factors in Computing Systems and Graphics Interface,* New York: ACM.

Leddo, J. & Abelson, R. P. (1986) The nature of explanations, in Galambos, J. A., Abelson, R. P. and Black, J. B. (eds) *Knowledge structures,* Hillsdale, NJ: Lawrence Erlbaum.

Lee, J. (1972) *Computer semantics,* New York: Van Nostrand Reinholt.

Loftus, E. & Loftus, G. (1980) On the permanence of stored information in the human brain, *American Psychologist,* **35**, 409–420.

Long, J. (1986) People and computers: designing for usability, in Harrisson, M. and Monk, A. (eds) *People and computers: designing for usability,* Cambridge: Cambridge University Press, pp. 2–23.

Long, J. (1989) Cognitive ergonomics and human–computer interaction: an introduction, in Long, J. and Whitefield, A. (eds) *Cognitive ergonomics and human–computer interaction,* Cambridge: Cambridge University Press, pp. 3–34.

Lundberg, B. G. (1987) CONST — a constructive approach to information modelling, *Information Systems* **12**, 157–165.

Lyons, J. (1977) *Semantics,* Vols 1 and 2, Cambridge: Cambridge University Press.

Marr, D. (1972) *Vision: A computational investigation into the human representation and processing of visual information.* San Francisco: Freeman.

Martin, R. M. (1987) *Events, reference and logical form.* Washington D.C.: Catholic University of America Press.

McCracken, D. D. & Jackson, M. A. (1982) Life cycle concept considered harmful, *Software Engineering Notes* **7**, 29–32.

McDonald, J. E., Molander, M. E. & Noel, R. W. (1988) Color-coding categories in menus, in Soloway, E., Frye, D. and Sheppard, S. B. (eds) *Proceedings, Conference on Human Factors in Computing (CHI88),* pp. 101–105.

Maibaum, T. S. E. (1987) A logic for the formal requirements specification of real-time embedded systems, *Alvey Forest Report R3,* Imperial College, Department of Computing.

Martin, R. M. (1978) *Events, reference & logical form,* Washington, DC: Catholic University of America Press.

Mayes, J. T., Draper, S. W., McGregor, A. M. & Oatley, K. (1988) Information flow in a user interface: the effect of experience and context on the recall of MacWrite screens, in Jones, D. M. and Winder, R. (eds) *People and computers IV,* Cambridge: Cambridge University Press.

Medin, D. L. & Schaffer, M. M. (1978) A context theory of classification learning, *Psychological Review* **85**, 207–238.

Meister, D. (1971) *Human factors: theory and practice,* New York: Wiley.

Miller, G. A. & Johnson-Laird, P. N. (1976) *Language and perception,* Cambridge: Cambridge University Press.

Miller, G. A., Galanter, E. & Pribram, K. H. (1960) *Plans and the structure of behavior,* New York: Holt, Rinehart and Winston.

Miller, R. B. (1962) Task description and analysis, in Gage, R. M. (ed.) *Psychological principles in system development,* New York: Holt, Reinhart and Winston.

Miller, R. B. (1967) Task taxonomy: science or technology?, in Singleton, W. T., Easterby, R. and Whitfield, D. J. (eds) *The human operator in complex systems,* London: Taylor and Francis, pp. 54–60; *Ergonomics* **10**, 167–176.

Moran, T. P. (1981) The command language grammar: a representation for the user interface of interactive computer systems, *International Journal of Man–Machine Studies* **15**, 3–50.

Moran, T. P. (1983) Getting into a system: external–internal task mapping analysis, in *Proceedings of CHI'83 Human Factors in Computing Systems, December 12–15, 1983, Boston, MA,* New York: ACM, pp. 45–49.

Motta, E., Eisenstadt, M., West, M., Pitman, K. & Everstz, R. (1986) KEATS: the knowledge engineer's assistant, final project report, *Technical Report No. 20,* Human Cognition Research Laboratory, Open University, Milton Keynes.

Newell, A. (1981) Reasoning, problem solving and decision processes: the problem space as a fundamental category, in Nickerson, R. J. (ed.) *Attention and performance,* Vol. 8, Hillsdale, NJ: Lawrence Erlbaum.

Newell, A. & Simon, H. A. (1972) *Human problem solving,* Englewood Cliffs, NJ: Prentice-Hall.

Nisbett, R. & Wilson, T. (1977) Telling more than we can know: verbal reports on mental processes, *Psychological Review* **84**, 231–259.

Norman, D. A. (1983) Design rules based on analyses of human error, *Communications of the ACM* **4**, 254–258.

Open Systems Group (1972) *Systems behaviour,* London: Harper & Row.

Pagan, F. G. (1981) *Formal specification of programming languages: a panoramic primer,* Englewood Cliffs, NJ: Prenctice-Hall.

Patrick, J. (1980) Job analysis, training and transferability, in Duncan, K. D., Gruneberg, M. M. and Wallis, D. (eds) *Changes in the nature and quality of working life,* Chichester: Wiley.

Patrick, J., Spurgeon, P. & Shepherd, A. (1985) *A guide to task analysis: applications of hierarchical methods,* Aston Science Park, Birmingham: Occupational Services Ltd.

Payne, S. J. (1984) Task Action Grammars. In proceedings of *Interact '84* the first IFIP conference on Human–Computer Interaction, **1**, 139–144.

Payne, S. J. (1985) *Task–action grammars: the mental representation of task languages in human–computer interaction,* Doctoral Dissertation, University of Sheffield, unpublished.

Payne, S. J. (1987) Complex problem spaces: modelling the knowledge needed to use interactive devices, in Bullinger, H. J. and Schackel, B. (eds) *Human–computer interaction, Interact 87,* Amsterdam: North-Holland.

Payne, S. J. (1989a) Metaphorical instruction and the early learning of an abbreviated-command computer system, *Acta Psychologica.* (in press).

Payne, S. J. (1989b) A notation for reasoning about learning, in Long, J. and Whitefield, A. (eds) *Cognitive ergonomics and human–computer interaction,* Cambridge: Cambridge University Press.

Payne, S. J. & Green, T. R. G. (1983) The user's perception of the interaction language: a two-level model, *Proceedings of the CHI'83 Conference on Human Factors in Computer Systems,* New York: ACM, pp. 202–206.

Payne, S. J. & Green, T. R. G. (1986) Task–action grammars: a model of the mental representation of task languages, *Human–Computer Interaction* **2**, 93–133.

Payne, S. J. & Green, T. R. G. (1989) The structure of command languages: an experiment on Task-Action Grammar. *International Journal of Man–Machine Studies,* **30**, 213–234.

Payne, S. J., Squibb, H. & Howes, A. (1989) The nature of device models: the yoked state space hypothesis and some experiments with text editors, Department of Computing, University of Lancaster, unpublished.

Phillips, M. D. & Tischer, K. (1984) Operations concept formulation for next generation air traffic control systems, in *INTERACT'84: Proceedings of the First IFIP Conference on Human–Computer Interaction, September 4–7, 1984, Imperial College of Science and Technology, London,* Vol. 2, Amsterdam: Elsevier Science Publishers, pp. 242–247.

Piso, E. (1981) Task analysis for process control tasks: the method of Annett *et al.* applied, *Journal of Occupational Psychology,* **54**(4), 247–254.

Pollock, C. (1988) Training for optimising transfer between word processors, in Jones, D. M. and Winder, R. (eds) *People and computers IV,* Cambridge: Cambridge University Press.

Popper, K. (1972) *Objective knowledge: an evolutionary approach,* Oxford: Oxford University Press.

Potts, C., Finkelstein, A., Aslett, M. & Booth, J. (1986) "Structured common sense": a requirements elicitation and formalization method for modal action logic, *FOREST Deliverable Report 2,* GEC Research Laboratories, Marconi Research Centre.

Pressman, R. S. (1987) *Software engineering — A practitioner's approach.* New York: McGraw Hill.

Pylyshyn, Z. W. (1980) Computation and cognition: issues in the foundations of cognitive science. *Behavioural and Brain Sciences* **3**, 111–169.

Pylyshyn, Z. W. (1984) *Computation and cognition: issues in the foundations of cognitive science,* Cambridge, MA: Bradford Books.

Rasmussen, J. (1988) Information technology: a challenge to the human factors society? *HFS Bulletin* **31**, 1–3.

Regoczei, S. & Platinga, E. P. O. (1987) Creating the domain of discourse: ontology and inventory. *International Journal of Man–Machine Studies* **27**, 235–250.

Reisner, P. (1977) Use of psychological experimentation as an aid to development of a query language, *IEEE Transactions on Software Engineering* **3**, 218–229.

Reisner, P. (1981) Formal grammar and design of an interactive system, *IEEE Transactions on Software Engineering* **5**, 229–240.

Reisner, P. (1982) Further developments toward using formal grammar as a design tool, in *Proceedings of the Human Factors in Computer Systems Conference, March 15–17, 1982, Gaithersburg, MD*, New York: ACM, pp. 304–308.

Robertson, S. P. & Black, J. B. (1983) Planning units in text editing behavior, in *Proceedings of CHI'83, Human Factors in Computing Systems, December 12–15, 1983, Boston, MA*, New York: ACM, pp. 217–221.

Rogers, D. (1989) *Undergraduate Dissertation*, Liverpool Polytechnic, unpublished.

Rosch, E. (1985) Prototype classification and logical classification: the two systems, in Scholnick, E. K. (ed.) *New trends in conceptual representation: challenges to Piaget's theory?*, Hillsdale, NJ: Lawrence Erlbaum.

Rosch, E. & Mervis, C. B. (1975) Family resemblance studies in the internal structure of categories, *Cognitive Psychology* 7, 573–605.

Rosch, E., Mervis, C., Gray, W., Johnson, D. & Boyes-Braem, P. (1976) Basic objects in natural categories, *Cognitive Psychology* 8, 382–439.

Rosenberg, J. K. (1982) Evaluating the suggestiveness of command names, *Behaviour and Information Technology* 1, 118–128.

Rossen, M. B., Maass, S. & Kellogg, W. A. (1988) The designer as user; building requirements for design tools from design practice, *Communications of the ACM* 31(11), 1288–1298.

Rumbaugh, J. (1987) Relations as semantic constructs in an object-oriented language, *OOPSLA'87 Proceedings*, pp. 466–481.

Rumelhart, D. E. & Norman, D. A. (1978) Accretion, tuning and restructuring: three modes of learning, in Cotton, J. W. and Klatzky, R. (eds) *Semantic factors in cognition*, Hillsdale, NJ: Lawrence Erlbaum, pp. 37–53.

Scapin, D. L. (1982) Generation effect, structuring and computer commands, *Behaviour and Information Technology* 1, 401–410.

Schank, R. C. (1975) *Conceptual information processing*, Amsterdam: North-Holland.

Schank, R. C. (1982) *Dynamic memory: a theory of reminding and learning in computers and people*, New York: Cambridge University Press.

Schank, R & Abelson, R. (1977) *Scripts, plans, goals and understanding*, Hillsdale, NJ: Lawrence Erlbaum.

Schmucker, K. (1987) Using objects to package user interface functionality, *ACM SIGGRAPH Workshop on Software Tools for User Interface Development*.

Sharratt, B. D. (1987) Top-down interactive systems design: some lessons learnt from using command language grammar, in Bullinger, H. J. and Shackel, B. (eds) *Human–Computer Interaction — INTERACT'87: Proceedings of the Second IFIP Conference on Human–Computer Interaction, September 1–4, 1987, Stuttgart*, Amsterdam: North-Holland, pp. 395–399.

Shepherd, A. (1976) An improved tabular format for task analysis, *Journal of Occupational Psychology* 49, 93–104.

Shepherd, A. (1985) Hierarchical task analysis and training decisions, *Programmed Learning and Educational Technology* **22**, 162–176.

Shepherd, A. (1986) Issues in the training of process operators, *International Journal of Industrial Ergonomics* **1**, 49–64.

Shepherd, A. (1989) Training issues in information technology tasks, in Ruiz-Quintanilla, A. and Bainbridge, L. (eds) *Information technology and training*, Chichester: Wiley.

Shepherd, A. and Duncan, K. D. (1980) Analysing a complex planning task, in Duncan, K. D., Gruneberg, M. M. and Wallis, D. (eds) *Changes in the nature and quality of working life*, Chichester: Wiley.

Smith, D., Irby, C., Kimball, R., Verplank, W. & Harslem, E. (1982) Designing the Star user interface, *Byte* **7** (4), 242–282 (Reprinted in Baecker, R. & Buxton, W. (eds) (1989) *Readings in human–computer interaction: a multidisciplinary approach*, San Francisco, CA: Morgan Kaufmann, pp. Morgan Kaufmann, pp. 653–661.

Smith, E. E. & Medin, D. L. (1981) *Categories and concepts*, Cambridge, MA: Harvard University Press.

Smolensky, P., Monty, M. L. & Conway, E. (1984) Formalizing task descriptions for command specification and documentation, in *INTER-ACT'84: Proceedings of the First IFIP Conference on Human–Computer Interaction, September 4–7, 1984, Imperial College of Science and Technology, London*, Vol. 1, Amsterdam: Elsevier Science Publishers, pp. 16–22.

Stammers, R. (1983) Simulators for training, in Kvalset, T. (ed.) *Ergonomics of work station design*, London: Butterworths, pp. 229–242.

Stammers, R. (1989) Simulation in training and in user interface design, in *Simulation in the development of user interfaces*, Ergonomics Society, pp. 1–4.

Stammers, R. B. & Morrisroe, G. C. (1985) Operator training in future on-board naval command systems, *Final Report to APU, ARE*, Division of Applied Psychology, Aston University, Birmingham.

Stefik, M., Bobrow, D., Mittal, S. & Conway, L. (1983) Knowledge programming in loops, *AI Magazine* **4** (3), 3–14.

Sutcliffe, A. (1988a) *Human–computer interface design*, Houndsmills: Macmillan.

Sutcliffe, A. (1988b) Some experiences in integrating specification of Human computer interaction within a structured system development method, in Jones, D. M. and Winder, R. (eds) *People and computers IV*, Cambridge: Cambridge University Press.

Tauber, M. (1988) On mental models and the user interface, in van der Veer, G. C., Green, T. R. G., Hoc, J.-M. and Murray, D. M. (eds) *Working with computers: theory versus outcome*, London: Academic Press.

Tesler, L. (1981) The Smalltalk environment, *Byte* (August).

Tulving, E. & Pearlstone, Z. (1966) Availability versus accessibility of information in memory for words, *Journal of Verbal Learning and Verbal Behaviour* **5**, 381–391.

Tversky, A. (1977) Features of similarity, *Psychological Review* **69**, 344–354.

Umbers, I. G. & Jenkinson, J. (1989) Operator aids within a complex operator interface, in Megaw, E. D. *Contemporary Ergonomics 1989: Proceedings of the Ergonomic Society's 1989 Annual Conference, April 3–7 1989, Reading,* London: Taylor and Francis, pp. 227–233.

Waddington, R. & Johnson, P. (1989) Designing and evaluating interfaces using task models, *11th World Computer Congress, August 28–September 1, 1989, San Francisco.*

Walsh, P. A., Lim, K. Y., Long, J. B. & Carver, M. K. (1988) Integrating human factors with system development, in Heaton, N. and Sinclair, M. (eds) *Designing end-user interfaces,* Oxford: Pergamon Infotech.

Walsh, P. A., Lim, K. Y., Long, J. B. & Carver, M. K. (in press) JSD and the design of user interface software, *Ergonomics,* to be published.

Wilson, M. (1987) Task analysis for knowledge acquisition, in Pavelin, C. and Wilson, M. (eds) *Proceedings of an SERC Workshop on Knowledge Acquisition for Engineering Applications,* Rutherford Appleton Laboratory, RAL-87-055, pp. 68–83.

Wilson, M. (1989) Task models for knowledge elicitation, in Diaper, D. (ed.) *Knowledge elicitation: principles, techniques and applications,* Chichester: Ellis Horwood, pp. 197–218.

Wilson, M., Barnard, P. & MacLean, A. (1986) Task analysis in human computer interaction, *Report HF122,* IBM Hursley Human Factors.

Wilson, M. D., Barnard, P. J., Green, T. R. G. & Maclean, A. (1988) Knowledge-based task analysis for human–computer systems, in Van Der Veer, G. C., Green, T. R. G., Hoc, J. and Murray, D. M. (eds), *Working with computers: theory versus outcome,* London: Academic Press, pp. 47–87.

Wright, P. (1977) Presenting technical information: a survey of research findings, *Instructional Science* **6**, 93–134.

Yasdi, R. & Ziarko, W. (1988) An expert system for conceptual schema design: a machine learning approach, *International Journal of Man-–Machine Studies* **29**, 351–376.

Yourdon, E. & Constantine, L. (1978) *Structured design,* New York: Yourdon Press.

Zave, P. (1982) The operational versus the conventional approach to software development, *Communications of the ACM,* **27**, 104–118.

Author index

Subject index